The *SAINT MARY'S PRESS Essential Bible Dictionary* is a great resource for the high school Scripture teacher and student. A feature I really appreciate is the expanded information provided for certain entries, such as parables, Ten Commandments, and Old Testament feasts and festivals.

For example, following the parable entry is a chart listing all the parables and where they are located in each Gospel. This provides easy access to key information without the need for another resource. I also found the additional material provided for a number of entries very helpful. Many listings contain a detailed description of the character or the geographical site, and some entries provided a mini–history lesson. I think high school students will appreciate the format, the cross-referencing, and the examples of where the word(s) is found in the Bible.

—Patricia Gorman, religious studies department chairperson,
Saint Mary's Academy, Portland, OR

Opening the pages of the *SAINT MARY'S PRESS Essential Bible Dictionary* creates a sudden longing to learn more about the stories and fascinating people of the Bible. This concise, beautifully written dictionary has multifaceted appeal. It will support teachers as they seek to bring sparkle and life to classroom encounters with Bible heroes and themes. It will help students deliver top-notch assignments and glean timeless truths that are so relevant to teen life today. It will inspire homeschooling parents, pastors, RCIA directors, educators, Catholic writers, and lifelong students of our faith heritage. Every parish, school, home, and library will be richer for having this jewel of a resource.

—Therese Vorndran Nichols, coauthor (with Dr. Sheila O'Connell-Roussell) of
Lectionary-Based Gospel Dramas for Advent, Christmas, and Epiphany and
Lectionary-Based Gospel Dramas for Lent and the Easter Triduum,
both published by Saint Mary's Press

The *SAINT MARY'S PRESS Essential Bible Dictionary* acts as a bridge between Sunday school simplicity and full-fledged scholarship. It provides an approachable introduction to the Bible and acts as a launch point for further research. Dr. Sheila has embraced Pope Pius XII's call to scholarship, but she has done more. She has created a path for curious students to enter the biblical world as well.

—Madeline Wyse, sophomore in Dr. Sheila's high school religion class

Though geared for Catholic teens and their teachers, the *SAINT MARY'S PRESS Essential Bible Dictionary* provides wonderful foundational material for any Christians seeking to grow in their faith knowledge through the Scriptures. We know that a house will last only as long as its foundation, and this book offers an eternal foundation in God. Dr. Sheila O'Connell-Roussell has given us a valuable resource to delve into the understanding of the Bible and its ultimate author. May all who read this work be changed and saved by God's love forever.

—Fr. John Amsberry, pastor and national youth speaker, Archdiocese of Portland, OR

The *SAINT MARY'S PRESS Essential Bible Dictionary* is an accessible, readable, narrative-type tool for young people, making their Bible study both fascinating and critically accurate. Teens will appreciate the charts that allow them to see data and relationships at a glance, the color with which the characters are portrayed, the cross-references to each word to orient them to interrelated material, the relevance of the definitions to their contemporary experiences, and the ways the material is related to their Catholic Christian Tradition.

Adults who have had little opportunity for Bible study, alone or in groups, will welcome the *SAINT MARY'S PRESS Essential Bible Dictionary* as a handbook that provides a degree of personal assurance and sophistication for their interfaith dialogue experiences. In a sense, reading this book will give the Bible student of any age an accurate and interesting review of salvation history.

—Cecilia A. Ranger, SNJM, PhD; former chair/dean of religion, Marylhurst University; currently adjunct professor, Scripture and theology, Marylhurst University and San Francisco Theological Seminary

SAINT MARY'S PRESS

ESSENTIAL
BIBLE
DICTIONARY

Saint Mary's Press
Essential
Bible
Dictionary

Sheila O'Connell-Roussell

Contributing Author
Brian Singer-Towns

Saint Mary's Press®

The publishing team included Brian Singer-Towns, development editor; Lorraine Kilmartin, reviewer; Mary Koehler, permissions editor; The Crosiers/Gene Plaisted, OSC, cover image; prepress and manufacturing coordinated by the prepublication and production services departments of Saint Mary's Press.

The illustration on page 27 is by Paul Casper; all other illustrations are by Vicki Shuck The photos in the color insert are by Dennis Kurtz

Printed in the United States of America

4319

ISBN 978-0-88489-872-6

Library of Congress Cataloging-in-Publication Data

O'Connell-Roussell, Sheila.
    Saint Mary's Press essential Bible dictionary / Sheila O'Connell-Roussell ; contributing author, Brian Singer-Towns.
        p. cm.
Includes bibliographical references and index.
    ISBN-13: 978-0-88489-872-6 (pbk. : alk. paper) 1. Bible. English—Versions—New Revised Standard—Dictionaries. I. Title: Essential Bible dictionary. II. Singer-Towns, Brian. III. Saint Mary's Press. IV. Title.
BS191.5.O36 2006
220.3—dc22
                                                                    2005012952

TABLE OF CONTENTS

Author Acknowledgments	6
Introduction	7
Bible Book Abbreviations	8
Pronunciation Guide	8
Dictionary Entries, A to Z	9
Photographs and Maps	following page 94

List of Charts

The Books of the Bible	27
Biblical Exegesis	57
Old Testament Feasts and Festivals	60
Gospel Comparison	70
The Titles of Jesus	87
The Judges of Israel	95
The Hebrew Kings	97
The Parables of Jesus	130
The Ten Plagues of Egypt	137
The Ten Commandments	166

I dedicate this work to my granddaughter, Stella Noelle Richman, who is five years old today. I want her to know that she is part of God's great love story for humanity and that one person living her truth can change the world forever.

Dr. Sheila O'Connell-Roussell, grandmom
February 23, 2005

AUTHOR ACKNOWLEDGMENTS

Let me begin by offering thanksgiving to His Holiness Pope Pius XII, who, on September 30, 1943, issued his now-noteworthy encyclical *Divino Afflante Spiritu*. This document directed Catholic scholars to explore the historical world of the inspired authors of the Scriptures, thereby opening modern Scripture research to the Catholic world. Much of what is contained in this dictionary would not be known today if not for Pius XII's vision.

Thank you, Vicki! I so appreciate the beautiful drawings by artist Vicki Shuck of Bend, Oregon. They offer a rich variety of images for contemplation. The same Spirit who guided the authors of the sacred Scriptures also inspires religious artists like Vicki.

I have profound appreciation for my editor, Brian Singer-Towns, and his vision, direction, counsel, craft, and faith. Brian is far more than editor. He has spent many hours encouraging and directing me and rewriting this text. Although gifted with holy humility, he is truly my coauthor and partner in this work; its clarity reveals his skillful hand. I'm also grateful for the dedication to detail and the beautiful work of editor Ginny Halbur and her commitment to this project.

I proclaim my love and gratitude to my husband, Dr. Jerry O'Neil Roussell Jr., for his patience, love of the Scriptures, teaching, counsel, and prayer. Finally, I wish to thank my high school students at St. Mary's Academy in Portland and my adult students at Marylhurst University of Oregon, who have encouraged me and touched my heart with their longing.

I pray that the *SAINT MARY'S PRESS Essential Bible Dictionary* helps young people to love the sacred Scriptures. Within the pages of the Bible, we hear God's voice, meet Jesus, Mary, and our ancestors in faith, and find a treasure for our study, worship, and prayer. Blessings.

INTRODUCTION

It has been said that the Bible is God's love letter to humans. The Scriptures are a collection of inspired ancient texts written by our ancestors in faith so all generations would remember and celebrate the sacred story of salvation.

The *SAINT MARY'S PRESS Essential Bible Dictionary* offers concise definitions for the essential people, places, events, and themes of the Holy Scriptures. This resource is designed to help young people and others deepen their understanding of the words and themes found in the word of God. We have sought to strike a balance between children's Bible dictionaries, with too little information, and scholarly dictionaries that overwhelm with too much information. We used the words and spellings found in the New American Bible (NAB) and the New Revised Standard Version (NRSV): Catholic Edition translations. These are the most commonly used translations for Catholic Bibles in the United States.

We did not include definitions for words commonly used outside the Bible with no special biblical meaning attached to them. You may consult a regular dictionary to find pronunciations and definitions for those words. Nor did we include entries giving background for each book of the Bible. You can find this information in the book introductions of *The Catholic Youth Bible (CYB)* and other similar resources.

We faced a challenge in determining which terminology to use for the Jewish people at different times throughout their history. At various times, they have been called Semites, Habiru, Hebrews, Israelites, Judeans, and Jews. Modern scholarship tells us that the religious terminology *Jew* and *Jewish* did not truly develop until centuries after the New Testament period. What has been translated in English bibles as *Jews* should probably be translated as *Judeans*. This dictionary attempts to strike a balance between common usage and this modern scriptural scholarship. We have identified those loyal to Yahweh after the Exile (sixth century BC) occasionally as the *Judean* people. More often, we have used the more commonly understood terms *Jew* or *Jewish* to refer to them, especially in New Testament times. Our prayerful hope is that the Jewish people feel honored and treasured by our efforts.

Finally, while the definitions contain many scriptural citations, please understand that these citations are not exhaustive. This would have been too distracting. Rather, we offer a sampling of references for each entry that will support users in their search to locate the crucial biblical passages associated with a particular word or phrase. You can locate additional related Bible passages by following the cross-references included in many Bibles or by using a concordance like the *SAINT MARY'S PRESS Essential Bible Concordance*.

Bible Book Abbreviations

Abbr.	Book
Acts	Acts
Am	Amos
Bar	Baruch
1 Chr	1 Chronicles
2 Chr	2 Chronicles
Col	Colossians
1 Cor	1 Corinthians
2 Cor	2 Corinthians
Dan	Daniel
Deut	Deuteronomy
Eccl	Ecclesiastes
Eph	Ephesians
Esth	Esther
Ex	Exodus
Ezek	Ezekiel
Ezra	Ezra
Gal	Galatians
Gen	Genesis
Hab	Habakkuk
Hag	Haggai
Heb	Hebrews
Hos	Hosea
Isa	Isaiah
Jas	James
Jdt	Judith
Jer	Jeremiah
Jn	John
1 Jn	1 John
2 Jn	2 John
3 Jn	3 John
Job	Job
Joel	Joel
Jon	Jonah
Josh	Joshua
Jude	Jude
Judg	Judges
1 Kings	1 Kings
2 Kings	2 Kings
Lam	Lamentations
Lev	Leviticus
Lk	Luke
1 Macc	1 Maccabees
2 Macc	2 Maccabees
Mal	Malachi
Mic	Micah
Mk	Mark
Mt	Matthew
Nah	Nahum
Neh	Nehemiah
Num	Numbers
Ob	Obadiah
1 Pet	1 Peter
2 Pet	2 Peter
Phil	Philippians
Philem	Philemon
Prov	Proverbs
Ps	Psalms
Rev	Revelation
Rom	Romans
Ruth	Ruth
1 Sam	1 Samuel
2 Sam	2 Samuel
Sir	Sirach
Song	Song of Solomon
1 Thess	1 Thessalonians
2 Thess	2 Thessalonians
1 Tim	1 Timothy
2 Tim	2 Timothy
Titus	Titus
Tob	Tobit
Wis	Wisdom of Solomon
Zech	Zechariah
Zeph	Zephaniah

Pronunciation Guide

a	cat	j	joke	r	run
ah	father	k	king	s	so
ahr	lard	kh	ch as in German *Buch*	sh	sure
air	care			t	toe
aw	jaw	ks	vex	th	thin
ay	pay	kw	quill	*th*	then
b	bug	l	love	ts	tsetse
ch	chew	m	mat	tw	twin
d	do	n	not	uh	ago
e, eh	pet	ng	sing	uhr	her
ee	seem	o	hot	v	vow
er	error	oh	go	w	weather
f	fun	oi	boy	y	young
g	good	oo	foot	z	zone
h	hot	*oo*	boot	zh	vision
hw	whether	oor	poor		
i	it	or	for		
i	sky	ou	how		
ihr	ear	p	pat		

Stress accents are printed after stressed syllables:

ˈ   primary stress

ˌ   secondary stress

A

AARON (air´uhn): The first high priest of the old Law and a member of the tribe of Levi, Aaron was born into slavery in Egypt. With his sister, Miriam, Aaron supported their brother, Moses, during the Exodus. Aaron spoke for Moses (Ex 4:13–16), demanding Pharaoh free the Israelite slaves. Aaron witnessed the first Passover (Ex 12:27), the plagues and wonders (Ex 5—10), the escape across the sea, and forty years in the desert (Ex 12—15).

Aaron's story took a negative turn when he lost faith, fell into peer pressure, and led the people back to idolatry by worshipping a golden calf (Ex 32). Aaron and the people repented, and Leviticus 8—9 tells how he and his sons were ordained for priesthood.

The priests and historians who were the final editors of the Pentateuch lived centuries after Aaron. Most likely they were captives in the Babylonian Captivity, who, once freed, worked to unify and rebuild the people of Israel. (See **Ezra**.) Their stories of Aaron helped reclaim the religious identity and the centrality of the priestly role within the Israelite people.

From Aaron's story, we learn about the importance of God's Covenant, the devastations of sin and idolatry, the pain of betrayal, the need for forgiveness, and the strength of reconciliation and faith. See also **Exodus; Levi, Levite; Miriam; Moses; Priest.**

ABBA (ah´buh): A personal title used by Jesus to identify his—and our—intimate relationship with God. Abba means "my Father" or "our Father" in Aramaic. Even though the New Testament was written in Greek, this Aramaic word is specifically used in Mk 14:36, Rom 8:15, and Gal 4:6. This usage indicates that the early Christians recalled that Jesus regularly addressed God as Abba. When Jesus taught his disciples to pray the Our Father, he invited them to understand that their relationship with the God of Creation was that of a precious child and loving parent (Mt 6:9). Like the Father in the parable of the prodigal son, God longs for us to know the love and protection of home, which also becomes an image of the Church (Lk 15:11–32).

ABEDNEGO (uh-bed´ni-goh): A friend of the folk hero Daniel who, along with Shadrach and Meshach, refused to worship the golden idols of King Nebuchadnezzar of Babylon. Because of their faith, these three were spared death in the fiery furnace in Babylon (Dan 3). See also **Babylonian Captivity; Meshach; Shadrach.**

ABEL: See **Cain and Abel.**

ABIMELECH (uh-bim´uh-lek): A title used to designate the kings of Syria and Palestine (Gen 20:2, 26:26), as well as a personal name (Judg 8—9; 1 Chr 18:16).

ABOMINATION: A defilement caused by a major offense against God's Law. Sacrificing unclean animals in worship or committing idolatry, blasphemy, or sinful behaviors caused religious impurities (Deut 7:25, 17:1, 25:16, 27:15). Other abominations included eating with nonbelievers (Gen 43:32; Acts 10:28) or inappropriate interaction with lower classes such as socializing with shepherds (Gen 46:34).

ABOMINATION OF DESOLATION: Phrase used in the Bible to describe the worst offenses against the Jewish or Christian faith. The title was first used in the Old Testament Book of Daniel to condemn the Syrian Warlord Antiochus Epiphanes, who persecuted the people, forbade the Torah, and murdered thousands of Jewish people (167 BC). His dedication of an altar to Zeus in the holy Temple of Jerusalem was called an abomination of desolation (Dan 9:27, 11:31; 1 Macc 1:54, 6:7).

In New Testament times, a number of Roman Emperors (Caligula [AD 41], Nero [65], Domitian [90–95]) demanded by law that the people revere them as divine. Jesus used the phrase "desolating abomination" or "desolating sacrilege" as a condemnation of this blasphemy (Mk 13:14; Lk 21:20).

ABORTION: The killing of a baby within the womb. Abortion ends the life and the earthly potential of one of God's little ones. From ancient times, the prophets condemned as evil those who had "no mercy on the fruit of the womb" and no pity on children (Isa 13:18).

From within the sacred safety of the womb, God has called us to life and named and formed us from the moment of conception (Jer 1:5; Job 31:15; Ps 22:9). Scripture reveals the heart of God, who loves so infinitely that even if a mother were to "show no compassion for the child of her womb" (Isa 49:15), God would never forget the little one.

ABRAHAM (ay´bruh-ham)**:** The father of monotheism. His original name was Abram, the eldest son of Terah (Gen 11:27) of Ur of the Chaldeans of Mesopotamia. Abram was husband to Sarai—to whom he was related, maybe even as a half brother—and kept her Egyptian slave Hagar as concubine. The biblical account says the family went north to the village of Haran (Gen 11:31). There, Abram encountered God and accepted the call to enter his legendary journey of faith, to leave everything he knew, and to go to the land of Canaan (Gen 12:1–6). God promised old Abram and barren Sarai that they would become the ancestors of a multitude, a great nation, would receive the land of Canaan, and become a blessing to the whole earth (Gen 12:2, 17:1–22).

This first patriarch of the Old Testament responded to God's call and entered into a covenant relationship with God. God changed Abram's name to Abraham and Sarai's name to Sarah. Because of his faith in God, Abraham changed the world forever (Rom 4; Gal 3:9; Heb 11:8–22).

Abraham and Sarah were the parents of Isaac, a patriarch of the Twelve Tribes of Israel. Isaac's son Jacob fathered the tribes who were the ancestors of the Jewish people. Abraham and Hagar are the parents of Ishmael and the ancestors of the Arab peoples who embraced the Islamic religion. Christians consider themselves adopted children of Abraham and Sarah because Jesus Christ was a Jew. Thus, Abraham is the spiritual parent of three great world religions: Judaism, Islam, and Christianity. See also **Covenant; Isaac; Lot; Patriarch; Sarah.**

ABSALOM (ab´suh-luhm): The adored son of David and Maacah, the daughter of King Talmai of Geshur (2 Sam 3:3). Absalom was handsome and popular with the people. His story turned to grief when his sister Tamar was raped by her half brother Amnon, the eldest son of David by Ahinoam of Jezreel. Absalom took the shamed Tamar into his home and plotted revenge. After ordering the execution of Amnon, Absalom feared for his life. He ran away and hid for three years in Geshur with his grandfather.

David's counsel from the wise woman of Tekoa resulted in reconciliation; but upon his return, Absalom proclaimed himself king and took the throne. In the battle that followed, Absalom was killed. David was inconsolable. His heart was broken at the death of Absalom (2 Sam 13—18).

ADAM, ADAMAH (ad´uhm, ad´uh-muh): *Adam* is a Hebrew word that means "human." It comes from the Hebrew word *adamah,* which means "fertile land" or "soil." In the second Creation story in Genesis 2, the first human being is called Adam because God made him from the *adamah* (Gen 2:7). Later, God created Eve to be a companion for Adam. They were created in the divine

image, male and female. Humans were made from soil—the watery clay into which the Creator breathed the breath of life. Created in holiness, God asked the man and woman to be stewards of creation and to care for one another, the animals of the planet, and Eden (Gen 1:28).

The story of the garden of Eden is mythic—meaning it was not written as history or science. It paints a picture of creation as God intended it to be. Eden represents the ideal state of perfect harmony between God, human beings, and all creation. The Creator's intent for us is happiness and covenant love, but human sin has bruised this bliss and turned it into the condition of woundedness. Jesus has healed the pain and loss of sin and taught us how to reconcile this alienation, so we can accept ourselves as new creatures. This is why the New Testament contrasted Adam's sin with Jesus' obedience (Rom 5:18; 1 Cor 15:21–22). See also **Earth; Eden; Eve; Original Sin.**

ADONAI (ad´oh-ni´): A Hebrew word meaning "Lord" and used as a title for God. *Adonai* is not a personal name but rather a respectful substitution for the divine name Yahweh. The word LORD (in small capitals) is substituted for *Adonai* in English translations of the Bible. See also **God; Lord; Yahweh.**

ADULTERY: The name for a sin against the sixth commandment, when a married man or woman has sexual intercourse with someone who is not his or her spouse (Ex 20:14; Deut 5:18). Adultery is a sexual, emotional, and spiritual fracture of the marriage covenant. Adultery is also compared in the Scriptures to idolatry, the breaking of the bond of covenant relationship between God and humanity (Jer 3:9, 7:9; Ezek 23:37).

ADVOCATE: A name for the Holy Spirit that means protector, a divine defense attorney of sorts who functions as a helper and guardian, also translated as Paraclete (Jn 14:16–17, 26). Jesus is also called our advocate (1 Jn 2:1). See also **Paraclete.**

AHAB (ay´hab): The seventh king of Israel, son of Omri (869–850 BC). The infamous Jezebel of Sidon was his queen. Together, they served foreign gods in idolatry and injustice. They erected sacred poles, built temples for Baal, and dedicated the royal gates of Jericho with the sacrifice of their firstborn children Abiram and Segub. When famine struck the land, Ahab supported Jezebel's slaughter of the prophets of God.

Elijah condemned Ahab for his idolatry and murders. Ahab ignored the prophet, sat in rich robes in his ivory house, and died without repentance (Kings 16:29—22:40). See also **Elijah; Idolatry; Jezebel; Samaria.**

AHASUERUS (uh-has´yoo-er´uhs): This king was known in the Bible as Ahasuerus and to history as Xerxes I (486–465 BC). He married the Jewish heroine Esther after he banished his queen Vashti (Esth 2:7). He was remembered as the ruler of vast lands from India to Ethiopia (Esth 1:1). Ahasuerus, along with Esther, is a hero to the Jews and is celebrated in the feast of Purim (Esth 11).

Ahasuerus was connected to Cyrus the Great and was honored with the title king of kings under his Persian name, Artaxerxes (Ezra 7:12; 2 Macc 13:4). The Book of Daniel identified him as Ahasuerus, the father of Darius the Mede (Dan 9:1). See also **Esther; Xerxes, Artaxerxes.**

ALEXANDRIA (al´ig-zan´dree-uh): A large shipping center on the coast of the Mediterranean founded and named after Alexander the Great. Alexandria was renowned in the Hellenistic world as the capital of Egypt (Acts 27:6; 28:11). By the first century AD, Alexandria had the largest Jewish population outside of Jerusalem. In Alexandria, the Septuagint, or Greek-language version of the Old Testament, was translated (285–246 BC).

The city had early Christian roots. According to tradition, the Evangelist Mark founded Alexandria's Christian community. Apollos, who ministered with Saint Paul to spread the faith, was an Alexandrian (Acts 18:24).

ALIEN: See **Foreigner.**

ALLEGORY: A literary form in which something is said to be like something else. Allegories are often used to communicate a hidden or symbolic meaning commonly understood by the people it is addressed to. The Bible often used allegories to explain spiritual reality. For example, Jesus was called the Lamb of God (Jn 1:29), an allegory symbolizing that Jesus was the sacrifice for our sins. See also **Hosea.**

ALLELUIA: See **Hallelujah.**

ALPHA AND OMEGA (al´fuh) (oh-meg´uh): The first and last letters of the Greek alphabet, the alpha and the omega were often used as symbols that referred to the beginning and the end of all things. The prophet Isaiah taught that God was the source, the first and last of all things (Isa 41:4). In Revelation, the Lord God says, "I am the Alpha and Omega" (Rev 1:8) and at the end of the book, Christ calls himself by the same title (Rev 22:13).

Across the centuries, Christians have proclaimed that Jesus Christ is "the Alpha and the Omega" of all history; he is yesterday, today, and tomorrow. Christians have used the Greek letters for alpha and omega to represent Christ in monuments, paintings, and sacred vestments. See also **John of Patmos.**

ALTAR: From a Hebrew word meaning "place of sacrifice." Altars are elevated platforms where rituals that are intended to honor the holiness of God are performed. The Bible contains more than 400 mentions of altars. Altars were signs of people's faith, the focal point that drew humanity close to the presence of the Lord (Gen 26:23–25; Josh 22:26–29).

Altars were made of stone, brick, metal, and earth and were enclosed within temples, at shrines, in courtyards, and within sacred sites in nature. On Hebrew altars, gifts of grain, oil, animals, salt, wine, and incense were sanctified and offered to the Creator. See also **Sacrifice.**

ALTAR OF BURNT OFFERINGS: This altar was the site of burnt offerings of animal sacrifice and grain holocausts. It was made of acacia wood overlaid with bronze; its hooks and poles were covered with silver. It was a horned altar suspended by poles for transport and resting within the tabernacle courtyard (Ex 27:1–8). A courtyard altar of this fashion was included in the Temple of David (2 Chr 4:1).

ALTAR OF CHRIST: Like the altars of old, the altar on which the Eucharist is celebrated draws the faithful to God. The sacrifice of the Lamb of God is Christ offered as a testimony to faith in Jesus (Jn 1:29, 36). On the altar of Christ, offerings of bread and wine are made holy and consecrated by the action of the priest into the body and blood of the Lord (Mt 26:26–30; Heb 13:10). Jesus was the sacrifice and sacrament of the altar, offered to God for the reconciliation of humanity. See also **Eucharist.**

ALTAR OF INCENSE: In the time of the desert wanderings, a moveable altar made of acacia wood covered in gold was suspended by horns, carried on poles, and placed before the curtain that covered the ark of the Covenant (Ex 30:1–10). The Altar of Incense was surrounded by cherubim of God's glory, who protected the mercy seat that was the lid of the ark of the Covenant.

Every morning and night, the high priest Aaron offered a sacrifice of anointing oil and incense on the Altar of Incense (Ex 30:1–10). Once a year, the altar honored the rites of atonement offered on the feast Yom Kippur, or the Day of Atonement (Ex 30:10). The

Altar of Incense became a part of the Temple in Jerusalem (1 Kings 7:20–25). The New Testament recalls that the Angel Gabriel appeared to Zechariah beside the Altar of Incense to announce the birth of John the Baptist (Lk 1:11). See also **Ark of the Covenant.**

AMOS (ay´ muhs): The wisdom of this ancient prophet from Tekoa in Judah has stood the test of time. Amos lived in the eighth century BC and described himself as a shepherd and "a dresser of sycamore trees" called by God to proclaim justice (Am 7:14–15). He critiqued political systems, condemned unjust treatment of workers, and demanded that profits be shared. He taught that the suppression of human rights turned "justice into poison" and "righteousness into wormwood" (Am 6:12).

Amos taught that only by living justly with God would a nation live. Repentance, restitution, and justice were necessary to avert the devastations of war and exile (Am 5:14–15). God hated false spiritual practice and felt no delight in sacrifice, liturgies, or the noise of music. God's will for humanity was to "let justice roll down like waters, / and righteousness like an ever-flowing stream" (Am 5:21–24). See also **Justice; Prophet.**

ANDREW: A fisherman from Bethsaida in Galilee and one of the twelve Apostles. Andrew was a disciple of John the Baptist. When he heard John proclaim Jesus as the Lamb of God, he joined the Apostles (Mt 4:18–19; Jn 1:40). Andrew brought his brother, Simon Peter, to the Lord (Jn 1:41). Andrew presented Jesus with the little boy who had loaves and fishes, and then Andrew witnessed the miracle of the feeding of thousands (Jn 6:9).

We know little of the life of Andrew in the early Church. There is a tradition that he preached the Gospel in what is today central Asia and was martyred. See also **Apostle.**

ANGEL: Spiritual creature that serves as God's messenger, helps God's people, and fights evil. The Bible and Catholic Tradition teach that angels are immortal beings, created with intelligence and free will. They appeared frequently in the Bible to speak for God, to warn and protect, and to give God worship and praise. Some examples of the work of angels in the Bible are:

- protected Hagar and Ishmael (Gen 21:17–19)
- prevented Abraham from sacrificing Isaac (Gen 22:9–12)
- appeared to Moses (Ex 3:2)
- spoke to Gideon (Judg 6:11–23)
- healed Tobias and Sarah and protected Tobit (Tob 3:16–17)
- announced to Mary that she would be the Mother of the Messiah (Lk 1:26)
- warned Joseph of Herod's slaughter of the Holy Innocents (Mt 2:13)
- announced Christ's Resurrection to Mary Magdalene and the holy women (Lk 24:4–7)
- freed Peter (Acts 12:6–11)
- praised God in heaven (Rev 5:11–14)

See also **Archangel; Cherub, Cherubim; Seraphim.**

ANGER: As a feeling, anger is not a sin, but when it is nurtured and allowed to lead to vengeance and violence, then it can become sinful. Strong emotions can motivate us to change, and in that sense they are a gift. Recall that Jesus took a whip in righteous anger to drive the money changers from the Temple (Jn 2:13–17). In the society in which Jesus lived, it was considered a failure or cowardice not to defend the honor of God by condemning the violation of God's law.

The Proverbs offer great wisdom in avoiding sinful violence by de-escalating anger. When a situation heats up, we can choose to speak kindly (Prov 15:1–2), stay calm and not jump to conclusions (Prov 16:32), or overlook an offense (Prov 19:11). Jesus' response to anger that threatened violence was to forgive and love the enemy (Mt 5:43–45).

ANNA (an´uh): A prophet who recognized the infant Jesus as the Messiah. This barren widow was eighty-four years old when the Holy Family came to offer rites of purification in the Temple. Anna witnessed Simeon's prophecy (Lk 2:28–32), and she proclaimed that the child was the "redemption of Jerusalem" (Lk 2:38). A non-Scriptural tradition relates that Anna was the Blessed Mother's childhood teacher who taught young Mary the Scripture. The prophet Anna remains a model of faith for all who long to see Jesus. See also **Presentation of Christ; Simeon.**

ANNAS AND CAIAPHAS (an´uhs) (kay´uh-fuhs)**:** During the reign of Caesar Tiberius (AD 14–37), the Sadducee Caiaphas and his father-in-law, Annas, both held the office of high priest in the Temple of Jerusalem (Lk 3:2). Caiaphas was chief priest during Pontius Pilate's administration, and Annas was his alternate high counsel. Together with members of the Sanhedrin and the Roman rulers, these were the authorities who crucified Jesus (Jn 18:13–14). See also **High Priest.**

ANNUNCIATION (uh-nuhn´see-ay´shuhn)**:** The event in which the archangel Gabriel came to Mary and announced that she had found favor with

God and would become mother of the Messiah (Lk 1:26–38). Gabriel's annunciation revealed that the child would be conceived by the Holy Spirit and that nothing was "impossible with God." Mary said "Yes," and the world was never the same. See also **Archangel; Gabriel; Mary of Nazareth.**

ANOINTING: In the ancient world, anointings with perfumed oil were offered as gestures of hospitality, cleansing, perfuming, and happiness (Ruth 3:3; 2 Sam 14:2; Ps 45:7). Anointing was also used as a gesture of reverence and to prepare a dead person's body for burial (Mk 14:8; Lk 23:56).

Formal anointings were sacred consecrations used to appoint priests, prophets, and kings. The rite involved a ceremonial pouring of sacred oil onto the head of the person. The anointed person was called *messiah,* which is a Hebrew word for "anointed one" (Ex 30:30–32; 1 Sam 16:13; Ps 132:10). See also **Messiah; Oil.**

ANOINTING OF THE SICK: Jesus healed the sick and empowered his Apostles to do the same (Mk 6:13). The first Apostles healed the sick and offered forgiveness of sin through an anointing with oil (Jas 5:14). This ministry became one of the seven sacraments, the sacrament of the Anointing of the Sick.

Through the Anointing of the Sick, Jesus' healing presence continues to be made present in the world. During the sacrament, the priest anoints a sick or dying person with the oil of the sick and asks for Christ's healing presence to be with the person. See also **Sacrament.**

ANTICHRIST (an´tee-krist´): Title given to any spirit, person, or government that stands in conflict with the teachings of Jesus Christ or that denies the reality of Jesus as Lord (1 Jn 2:18; 2 Jn 1:7).

ANTIOCH (an´tee-ok): An important city of the Roman Empire and a significant founding community for early Christianity. After the Romans destroyed Jerusalem (AD 70), many people fled to Antioch in Syria, and the city became the home of one of the earliest Christian communities (Gal 2:11; Acts 11:19). Scripture attests that Paul, Silas, Barnabas, and Luke all ministered in the city (Acts 13:1, 15:22–35). In Antioch, the followers of Jesus were first called Christians (Acts 11:26).

ANTIOCHUS EPIPHANES (an-ti´uh-kuhs) (i-pif´uh-neez): A Syrian warlord, a politically cunning, evil, and cruel ruler of Palestine who tortured and persecuted the Jewish people. The Book of Daniel records some of the perversions of his reign. Mattathias Hasmon and his sons—the Maccabees—organized a resistance that defeated him (167 BC). Their victory is celebrated during Hanukkah. The ancient city of Antioch in Turkey is named after Antiochus. See also **Maccabees; Mattathias Hasmon.**

APOCALYPTIC LITERATURE (uh-pok´uh-lip´tik): Literary form that speaks about the end times, prophesies

catastrophic upheavals on earth, and promises a new creation. Common in apocalyptic literature are angelic messengers; dreams; judgments; oracles that show human destiny; visions of death, heaven, purgatory, and hell; the resurrection of the just; the promise of a heavenly hope; and the construction of a new world order.

The purpose of apocalyptic literature is to offer hope during a time of persecution. Its images of divine judgment, God's vengeance on those who do evil, and God's reward for the faithful are intended to comfort faithful people who are being persecuted. The Book of Daniel, parts of Matthew's Gospel (Mt 24:29–30), and the Book of Revelation represent this literary form.

APOCRYPHAL BOOKS (uh-pok´ruh-fuhl): In the first centuries of Christianity, a great number of books and letters written by Christians did not become part of the Bible. These writings were not included in the New Testament because they were not in complete agreement theologically with the Apostolic Tradition. They are called apocryphal writings, and they include such works as the gospels of Thomas, Peter, and Mary Magdalene, the Epistle of Barnabas, the Acts of John and Paul, and the Shepherd of Hermas.

Some of the images in apocryphal writings are quite beautiful, some are Gnostic (an early Christian heresy), and some are just strange. With the exception of Thomas, most were written in the second through the fourth centuries AD. Apocryphal writings provide a resource that helps scholars reconstruct and understand the diversity of the early Christian period, but they are not inspired Scripture, and they are theologically in error. See also **Canon; Deuterocanonical Books.**

APOSTLE: One sent to carry the Gospel and to serve in the mission of Christ. The Lord called twelve Apostles as representatives of the Twelve Tribes of Israel, to be his chosen leaders. Simon Peter, James the son of Zebedee, John, Andrew, Bartholomew, Simon the Zealot, Thomas, Jude Thaddaeus, Matthew, Philip, James the son of Alphaeus, and the betrayer Judas Iscariot are listed as the Twelve (Mt 10:1–4; Mk 3:13–19; Lk 6:12–16). After Jesus ascended into heaven, Judas was replaced by Matthias (Acts 1:21). Later, Paul of Tarsus was called by Christ to be an Apostle and to proclaim Jesus to the Gentiles (Acts 9—26).

The Apostles' experience of Jesus as the risen Christ became the basis of their preaching and the foundation of the Church. Jesus gave the Apostles his authority to teach, heal, and forgive sins (Mt 10:5–8; 28:18–20; Jn 20:22–23), and he left them the Holy Spirit to guide them into all truth (Jn 16:13).

Today the bishops—under the authority of the Pope, who is the successor of Saint Peter—serve as the Apostles of this age and hold the same ministries, rights, authority, and responsibility as the original Apostles. See also entries for individual Apostles.

APOSTOLIC TRADITION: This phrase refers to the process of "handing down" the Gospel (the word tradition comes from Latin, and means "to hand on"). Apostolic Tradition—sometimes just called Tradition—began with the oral communication of the Gospel by the Apostles, was written down in the Scriptures, and is handed down and lived out in the life of the Church. It is interpreted by the Magisterium (the bishops of the Church in union with the Pope) under the guidance of the Holy Spirit. See also **Inerrancy; Revelation.**

AQUILA: See **Priscilla and Aquila.**

ARAMAIC (air-uh-may´ik): A language that developed from Semitic roots blending Hebrew, Assyrian, and Babylonian dialects to create a new tongue. After the captivity in Babylon, the Hebrew people who returned to Jerusalem could no longer speak Hebrew. Thus, Hebrew remained the sacred language of the Temple and synagogue, but Aramaic was the language of the street and home. It became the common language spoken by the Jewish people at the time of Christ. Some Aramaic phrases are recorded in the Gospels (Mk 5:41; Mt 27:46).

ARARAT (air´uh-rat): A mountainous region in present-day southeast Turkey and the location where Noah's ark came to rest after the Flood (Gen 8:4). See also **Ararat, Mount; Flood; Noah.**

ARARAT, MOUNT (air´uh-rat): After the great Flood, the Bible says Noah's ark rested on the mountains of Ararat (Gen 8:4). Assyrian records identify Ararat as the land of Urartu, an area that spans present-day northwestern Iran into southeastern Turkey. It has become part of popular language to talk about Ararat as a single mountain rather than a mountain range. See also **Ararat.**

ARCHAEOLOGY: The study of antiquities, ancient sites, objects, and cultures. This science is essential for understanding the culture, places, and history of ancient peoples, as well as how they used and understood language and literature. Archaeology has reconstructed the ancient world that birthed the Scriptures, providing us with a better understanding of that world.

ARCHANGEL: A chief of the choir of angels. Scripture identifies a number of archangels by name: Michael, the patron of Israel (Dan 10:13; Jude 1:9); Gabriel, the messenger of God (Dan 9:21; Lk 1:19, 26); and Raphael, protector and healer (Tobit 3:17). See also **Angel; Gabriel; Michael, the Archangel.**

ARK OF THE COVENANT: In the Old Testament, this sacred chest housed the holy presence of God. The Book of Exodus contains the details of its construction (Ex 25:10–22; 37:1–9; 39:16–21). In the time of Moses, the ark was carried during the desert wanderings (1250 BC) and kept in the Tent of Meeting. In the period of the kings (about 1000 BC), it was placed in the holy of holies in the Temple (1 Kings 8:6–8). It held the tablets of the Law of Moses, manna from heaven, and the rod of Aaron. It was also called the ark of God (1 Sam 3:3).

Legend holds that the ark of the Covenant was lost in the Babylonian Captivity, but 2 Maccabees notes that the prophet Jeremiah hid the ark in a cave on the mountain where Moses

died. There it would stay until the day of the Lord (2 Macc 2:5–7). In the apocalyptic writings of Revelation, the ark is seen as blessed with eternal veneration in the Temple in the New Jerusalem (Rev 11:19). See also **Altar of Incense.**

ARMAGEDDON (ahr´muh-ged´uhn): See **Megiddo.**

ARTAXERXES (ahr´tuh-zuhrk´seez): See **Ahasuerus; Xerxes, Artaxerxes.**

ASCENSION: Forty days after Easter, as the Apostles gathered on Mount Olivet outside Jerusalem, they listened to what were the last earthly teachings of the Lord. As they gazed in awe, Jesus, the glorious Son of Man, was taken up into heaven within a cloud of glory and honored at the "right hand of God" (Mk 16:19).

This Ascension of Christ is a sign that Jesus is truly the Son of God, that he is Lord over all creation, and that through the Holy Spirit he is present to all people throughout the ages (Eph 4:8–10). "Without any doubt, the mystery of our religion is great: / He was revealed in flesh, / vindicated in spirit, / seen by angels, / proclaimed among Gentiles, / believed in throughout the world, / taken up in glory" (1 Tim 3:16). See also **Resurrection of Christ.**

ASHER (ash´uhr): Son of Jacob and Zilpah, who was a slave of Leah. Also the name of one of the Twelve Tribes of Israel that claims Asher as its patriarch. See also **Zilpah.**

ASHERAH (uh-shihr´uh): A Canaanite goddess. Her name meant "increase" or "progeny." The gods of Canaan were thought of as the children of Asherah and El. Asherah was the Canaanite female companion of Baal, a mother deity symbolized as a sacred tree or a serpent who was honored in groves (Ex 34:13; 2 Kings 21:7; Judg 3:7, 13). Throughout Canaan, she was revered as the Asherah of the Sea, a goddess of fertility and sexual love and a divine courtesan.

Asherah was called Elat, Anat, Astarte, Tanit of the Serpent, Ishtar of Babylon, Queen of Heaven, the Shameful, the Holy, the goddess of eroticism and warfare (1 Sam 31:10; 2 Kings 23:13–14). Her cult was outlawed and condemned, along with that of the Baals. Jeremiah condemned her under the title of Queen of Heaven (Jer 7:18, 44:17–19). See also **Grove; Idolatry; Queen of Heaven.**

ASTROLOGY: An ancient system of divination based on reading the horoscope to interpret the influence of celestial bodies on human nature and earthly events. Astrologers believed they could foretell the future by the movements of the heavens. Scripture criticized this practice, because it stole the gift of free will and placed worship on the creation rather than on the Creator (Job 38:33; Isa 47:13–14).

ATHENS: The capital of the Greek province of Attica. Since 4000 BC, people have lived on this peninsula on the southeastern coast of Greece. Attica is surrounded by mountains on its eastern and northern borders and by water to the southwest. Between 454 and 414 BC, Athens was a center of world civilization and home to the legendary Parthenon, the Acropolis, the Theater of Dionysius (which seated 14,000–17,000 people), and the Temple of Zeus. During the time of the New Testament, Greece was a Roman province of Macedonia (Acts 20:2), its glory days long past. However, Greece was still considered a great center of art, learning, and spirituality. Saint Paul traveled to Athens on his way to Corinth and spoke there, making several converts (Acts 17:16–33).

ATONEMENT: A healing rite intended to restore holiness and reconcile the people with God. The Old Testament taught that any kind of abomination, impurity, or infraction of the Law wounded the relationship between the individual, the community, and God. Atonement was the way to cleanse oneself from the guilt caused by such sins. This was accomplished through a sacrificial offering (Lev 22).

In an annual ritual called the Day of Atonement, the high priest made a special sacrifice as an offering for the forgiveness of the people's sins. A young bull and a goat were sacrificed. A second goat—the scapegoat—upon which symbolically all the sins of the people were placed, was led into the desert and abandoned so as to purge the community's guilt by the goat's death (Ex 16).

In Christianity, the life and death of Jesus is understood as the ultimate atonement for the sins of all humankind. Jesus offered his life as a sacrifice to heal the relationship between God and humanity (Heb 10). See also **Azazel; Redemption; Salvation; Scapegoat; Yom Kippur.**

AZAZEL (uh-zay´zuhl): The name for the angry spirit, the scapegoat that was sent into the desert on the Day of Atonement (Lev 16:8–10). See also **Atonement; Demon; Scapegoat.**

B

BAAL (bay´uhl): A generic Semitic word meaning "master," "owner," "husband," or "lord." The word could be used to refer to Yahweh or to the master of a slave (Hos 2:16). However, in Scripture, the word *Baal* most often referred to the practices of idolatry or the worship of gods other than Yahweh. Baal was both the name of a specific god and a generic title that could refer to any number of gods such as Baal Peor or Baal of Hermon. Knowing which foreign god the Bible is talking about is sometimes difficult.

The Baal religions required the devotion of a priestly class. The Baals spoke only through the king and priests. Often, the religion included the use of temple prostitutes and even demanded human sacrifice, especially of infants. The worshippers of Baal were generally seen as the enemies of the Israelites (1 Kings 18:20–40). See also **Idolatry.**

BABEL, TOWER OF (bay´buhl): The word *babel* meant "confusion," specifically the misunderstanding of the ways of God. In its Semitic form, it meant the "gate of the gods." In Bath, the city and land of Babel were known as "Babylon."

The story of the tower of Babel is set in a mythic time when people lived in unity with God and spoke one language. They migrated east to the plain of Shinar (or Babylon), built a city with a tower that reached heaven, and planned to make a name for themselves. Yahweh saw their idolatrous plans and confused their language, which stopped the construction (Gen 11:1–9).

The Hebrew people suffered a devastating exile to the land of Babylon. This Babylonian Captivity lasted an entire generation (586–539 BC) and remained a memory of devastation, the lost covenant, and national grief. While in captivity, the Israelites would have been forced into building tall buildings devoted to the gods of Babylon. No doubt the story of the tower of Babel was meant to make the Israelites think of the pride and idolatrous behavior of the Babylonians. The story is a warning against human pride and the temptation for humans to act like God. See also **Babylon; Babylonian Captivity; Exile; Ziggurat.**

BABYLON (bab´uh-luhn): The name of an ancient kingdom and its capital city. The city was called the "gate of the gods" and was located on the west bank of the Euphrates River where it meets with the Tigris River, about fifty miles south of today's Baghdad. In the time when the Babylonians conquered ancient Israel, Babylon was well known for its huge brick quarries, libraries, rich palaces, and the beautiful hanging gardens—a wonder of the ancient world. Isaiah called the city "the glory of kingdoms" (Isa 13:19).

In future centuries, the memory of Babylon's idolatries and injustice came to symbolize the ultimate evil empire, called the Great Whore in the Book of Revelation (Rev 14:8, 17:5). See also **Babel, Tower of; Babylonian Captivity; Whore.**

BABYLONIAN CAPTIVITY (bab´-uh-loh´nee-uhn): Babylon pillaged Judah three different times, eventually causing the ultimate demise of the holy city, Jerusalem. In 587 BC, King Nebuchadnezzar murdered thousands of Israelites, destroyed the Temple, stole anything of value, burned Jerusalem to the ground, and enslaved a large portion of the population, sending them into exile in Babylon.

The captivity resulted in the death of multitudes, the destruction of the land, the devastation of the nation, and the loss of national identity, and the infliction of hopelessness. The captivity lasted an entire generation (586–539 BC), but it, too, ended. Cyrus the Persian, the king of Elam, conquered the Babylonians and let the Israelite people return home to Jerusalem (Ezra 1). A remnant returned, but the majority of the Israelites chose to stay in Babylon. They became known as part of the Diaspora—Jewish peoples living outside the Holy Land. See also **Cyrus of Persia; Daniel; Diaspora; Exile; Ezra; Nebuchadnezzar; Zerubbabel.**

BALAAM (bay´luhm): His name meant "foreign glutton." Balaam was a favorite folk character of the storytellers of Israel. His tale taught the power of God and the dangers of trusting foreigners. Balaam was a prophet for hire. He would bless one or curse one's enemies, whatever one paid him to do. King Balak of Moab hired Balaam to curse Israel, but God prevented the attack. Balaam tried to enter the Israelite camp, but his donkey refused to walk. After Balaam beat the animal, the donkey spoke back, revealing the angel of the Lord that prevented their passage (Num 22:23–35). The storyteller's point was that an ass had clearer vision then Mesopotamia's most famous prophet.

BALM: A perfumed spice harvested from the sap of certain trees. The balm of the tree grown in Gilead was highly prized as a restorative medicinal salve (Jer 8:22, 46:11). An ancient tradition says Solomon first received a balm tree as a gift from the Queen of Sheba and had it planted in his gardens around the Dead Sea (1 Kings 10:1–2).

BAPTISM, SACRAMENT OF: The sacrament of Baptism has deep roots in the Bible. We see Baptism prefigured, or hinted at, in the story of Noah being saved from the flood and in the story of the Israelites saved by passing through the Red Sea. The baptism of John the Baptist sets the precedent of being immersed in water for the forgiveness of sins.

Jesus elevated Baptism to a sacrament. As he told Nicodemus, Christian Baptism means being born again "of water and the spirit" (Jn 3:1–6). Just before his Ascension into heaven, Jesus told the Apostles to "make disciples of all nations, baptizing them in the name of the Father, and of the Son, and of the Holy Spirit" (Mt 28:19).

Baptism is the first of the seven sacraments of the Catholic Church. Baptism, Confirmation, and Eucharist are the three sacraments of Initiation. Baptism offers purification and strength, a blessing with the waters of life, a cleansing of original and personal sin, and a marking of a person as a child of God, a member of the Church. See also **Sacrament.**

BAPTISM OF REPENTANCE: A cleansing rite for the sake of repentance. This was the baptism performed by John the Baptist. John led people into the Jordan River as a sign of the forgiveness of their sins and to prepare for the Reign of God (Mk 1:4–8; Lk 3:1–18). Some thought John was the long-awaited Messiah, but he insisted that one would come whose sandals he wasn't "worthy to fasten," one who would baptize with the "the Holy Spirit and fire" (Mt 3:11). See also **John the Baptist.**

BAPTISM OF THE LORD: The day Jesus approached the Jordan River and asked his cousin John for the Baptism of

Repentance, there was a union of heaven and earth. As John poured the water, the heavens opened and the Spirit of God hovered over the head of Jesus in the form of a dove. A voice from heaven proclaimed, "This is my Son, the Beloved, with whom I am well pleased" (Mt 3:5–17; Jn 1:29–36). John proclaimed Jesus as the long-awaited Lamb of God, who would take away the sins of the world (Jn 1:29–36). The Church celebrates the Baptism of the Lord as the last liturgy of the Christmas season, making the bridge to Christ's public life.

BAR: A Hebrew word identifying a parent-child relationship. Jesus bar Joseph means "Jesus, son of Joseph." See also **Ben.**

BARABBAS (buh-rab´uhs): The incarcerated bandit released by Pontius Pilate instead of Jesus of Nazareth (Mt 27:15–26). Barabbas was guilty of insurrection and murder. In honor of the holidays, it was a Roman custom to release one prisoner who was condemned to death. The mob chose Barabbas, and Jesus was sentenced to die.

Barabbas is a symbol of rebellious humanity imprisoned by sin. Jesus' Passion is the ultimate atonement; his Crucifixion releases us from every form of bondage and sin that binds the soul and alienates us from our eternal destiny with God. Just as Barabbas was saved from death because Jesus was put to death in his place, so we are saved by Jesus, who accepted death for our sake.

BARAK (bair´ak): His name meant "lightning." Barak was the leader of the Israelite warriors who served under the direction of Deborah, the fourth judge of Israel. As the powerful Canaanites attacked the fearful Israelites, Deborah assured Barak that God would be with the humble Israelite troops in the battle. At Barak's plea, Deborah joined the standoff on Mount Tabor. She entered the battle, and Barak claimed the victory against Sisera's infamous 900 Canaanite chariots by the waters of Megiddo (Judg 4—5). See also **Deborah; Judge.**

BARNABAS (bahr´nuh-buhs): An early Christian leader and missionary, baptized by the original Apostles. His name in Hebrew meant "son of encouragement." He was a Jew of the Diaspora, a landowner from Cyprus, the cousin of John Mark (Col 4:10), and the nephew of Mary of Jerusalem, in whose home the Church gathered.

The Acts of the Apostles calls Barnabas "a good man, full of the Holy Spirit and of faith" (Acts 11:24). Barnabas helped the Apostles forgive Paul's early persecution of Christians and to trust his witness and mission (Acts 9:27). Later, he searched for Paul, took Paul under his wing in Antioch (Acts 11:25–26), and then traveled with Paul on Paul's first missionary journey. He and Paul fought for the acceptance of Gentile Christians at the Council of Jerusalem (Acts 15:12). Throughout his life, Barnabas lived up to the meaning of his name. See also **Paul.**

BARREN: Childless. In the Bible, to be barren and denied children was a great sadness and shame. It was thought to be a curse and punishment from God (Gen 16:2; 1 Sam 1:6; Lk 1:25). See also **Elizabeth; Hannah; Sarah.**

BARTHOLOMEW (bahr-thol´uh-my*oo*)**:** One of the twelve Apostles, he is called Nathanael in the Gospel of John (Jn 1:45–51) and Bartholomew in Matthew, Mark, and Luke (Mt 10:3; Mk 3:18; Lk 6:14). Little is known about Bartholomew except that his friend, the Apostle Philip, with whom he is always mentioned, brought him to Jesus. A non-Scriptural tradition says Bartholomew traveled from India to the shores of the Black Sea, spreading the faith, being martyred in Armenia. See also **Apostle.**

BARTIMAEUS (bahr´tuh-mee´uhs)**:** As Jesus walked past, a blind man shouted, "Jesus, Son of David, have mercy on me!" (Mk 10:47). Jesus touched the man, Bartimaeus, son of Timaeus of Jericho, and the blind man's sight was immediately restored (Mt 20:29–34; Mk 10:46–52; Lk 18:35–43). The story of Bartimaeus taught that illness was not evidence of sin or fault from a past life and that Jesus was a man of compassion and power who offered faith as a path to redemption and freedom (Mt 11:5).

The story of Bartimaeus teaches that faith in Christ heals blindness in all its forms. Disciples of Christ across the ages have embraced this story as inspiration for personal healing and enlightenment and as a means to understand Jesus' na-

ture and mission. During Lent, the story of Bartimaeus's healing is part of the Scrutinies, the rituals that prepare adults to receive the sacraments of Initiation during the Easter Vigil.

BARUCH (bair´uhk)**:** A friend and scribe of the prophet Jeremiah, a member of the tribe of Judah, and a royal clerk of King Zedekiah (Jer 36). Baruch recorded the prophet Jeremiah's words that proclaimed God's demand for justice. Jeremiah's words angered King Jehoiakim, who burned the first scroll recorded by Baruch. After the fall of Jerusalem in 587 BC, Some Israelite survivors accused Baruch of being a Babylonian sympathizer, and he was taken prisoner along with Jeremiah into Egypt (Jer 43:1–7). See also **Jeremiah.**

BATHSHEBA (bath-shee´buh)**:** Her name meant "daughter of abundance." Bathsheba's story, recorded in 2 Samuel 11 is a sad tale of lust, betrayal, murder, and the tragic consequences of sinful actions. Bathsheba was married to a warrior named Uriah the Hittite, who fought with Joab against the Ammonites. Bathsheba was a beautiful woman, and when King David saw her on her rooftop as she bathed, he sent his messengers to bring her into his quarters, where he seduced and impregnated her.

When David couldn't arrange for Uriah to think the child was his own, he arranged for Uriah to be killed on the battlefield. After permitting Bathsheba time to grieve the death of her husband, David called her to his house and married her, making her a queen of Israel. However, the child conceived in adultery sickened, and although David fasted, prayed, and begged the Lord for its survival, the child died in infancy. Bathsheba had another son, Solomon, who succeeded David on the throne

(1 Kings 1). She is referred to in the genealogy of Jesus (Mt 1:6). See also **David; Nathan; Queen; Solomon; Uriah.**

BEAST: Grazing animal, alone or in flocks or herds. Beasts are animals that are property and food and are used for transportation or farming. Beasts are also animals used in sacrifice or religious rites.

Beast also had another symbolic meaning in the Bible. People who let sinful appetites control them were called beasts or irrational animals (2 Pet 2:12). Evil governments or kingdoms who ruled by unjust, ferocious, violent, and inhumane power were referred to as beasts in apocalyptic literature. The Book of Daniel identified four kingdoms as beasts (Dan 7). In the Book of Revelation, the beast was the Roman Empire and the false prophets who served it (Rev 13). See also **Nero.**

BEATITUDES (bee-at´uh-tyoodz): The wisdom teachings of Jesus summarized in the form of blessings. Recorded in the Sermon on the Mount (Mt 5:3–11) and the Teachings on the Plain (Luke 6:20–26), the Beatitudes presented Jesus' vision for the Kingdom of God. The versions in the two Gospels differ slightly. Matthew's version focused more on spiritual reality ("Blessed are the poor in spirit"), Luke's more on material reality ("Blessed are the poor"). The blessings promised by the Beatitudes reversed the world's value system. They were the basis for a new moral vision, one that demanded a complete conversion of the heart.

BEELZEBUB: (bee-el´zi-buhb). The biblical name for the Philistine god, Baal-zebub, who was worshipped at Ekron (2 Kings 1:2–6). The Hebrews called him "Lord of the Flies" or "Dung god." His name came to represent the personification of evil, and it became used as another name for the devil. Some people in the Bible said Jesus' power came from Beelzebub, a charge Jesus strongly denied (Mt 12:24–27). See also **Devil; Satan.**

BEL: See **Marduk.**

BEN: Hebrew for "son." See also **Bar.**

BENJAMIN (ben´juh-muhn): The younger son of Rachel and Jacob; Joseph was his older brother. Rachel died giving birth to Benjamin, breaking Jacob's heart. Rachel named him Ben-oni, meaning "son of my suffering," but Jacob renamed him Benjamin, meaning "son of the right hand" (Gen 35:18). Benjamin had ten brothers besides Joseph, and one of the Twelve Tribes of Israel is named after him. Saul, the first king of the Hebrews, was of the tribe of Benjamin (2 Sam 9:1–2), as was the Apostle Paul (Rom 11:1). See also **Twelve Tribes.**

BETHANY (beth´uh-nee): The hometown of the disciples Martha, Mary, and Lazarus. Bethany, which means "house of figs," got its name from the fig trees that grew about the area. The village was located on the southeastern slope on the

Mount of Olives, east of the Jordan River about two miles from Jerusalem on the road to Jericho.

Jesus retired to Bethany after cleansing the Temple with a bullwhip (Mt 21:17). In Bethany, at the home of Simon the leper, an unnamed woman with an alabaster jar filled with perfumed oil anointed Jesus as Messiah and prepared him for the cross (Mt 26:6; Mk 14:3). In Bethany, Jesus raised Lazarus from the dead and Mary anointed his feet (Jn 11:1, 12:1). And in Bethany, the Lord gave the disciples their final blessings and ascended into the heavens (Lk 24:50). See also **Lazarus; Martha of Bethany; Mary of Bethany.**

BETHEL (beth´uhl): A Canaanite town ten miles north of Jerusalem. It had Hebrew origins from Abraham's time (Gen 12:8). In Bethel, God first spoke with Jacob, who also had visions of angels traveling a ladder that reached heaven (Gen 28:10–19). In Bethel, God affirmed the promises of the Covenant and gave Jacob a new name: Israel. Jacob built a shrine, poured libation, erected a pillar, and called the place Bethel, or "house of God" (Gen 35:1–15).

In the time of the Judges (1200 BC), the Hebrews took Bethel through stealth (Judg 1:22–25). After the civil war that divided Israel and Judah (922 BC), King Jeroboam committed idolatry by enshrining golden calves in Bethel and worshipping them as the god who freed Israel in the Exodus (1 Kings 12:28–33). The reforms of King Josiah reclaimed Bethel for Yahweh (2 Kings 23:15–18).

BETHLEHEM (beth´li-hem): A city five miles south of Jerusalem. In Hebrew, Bethlehem means "house of bread." Bethlehem was the site where Rachel died giving birth to Benjamin (Gen 35:19). Bethlehem was the birthplace of David and the place where the prophet Samuel anointed him king (1 Sam 16:4–13). Bethlehem is remembered as the traditional birthplace of the infant Jesus (Mt 2:1). On the site today stands the ancient Church of the Nativity, built by order of Emperor Constantine around AD 330.

BETHSAIDA (beth-say´uh-duh): Galilean town west of the Sea of Tiberias at the mouth of the Jordan River. Bethsaida was home to the Apostles Peter, Andrew, and Philip (Jn 1:44). Bethsaida was the site where Jesus miraculously fed more than 5,000 people with just a few fish and loaves of bread (Lk 9:10) and where he healed the blind man (Mk 8:22). It was renamed Bethsaida-Julias by the tetrarch Philip in honor of the daughter of Julius Caesar.

BETH SHAN, BETH SHEAN (beth-shan´) (beth-shee´uhn): This sacred site in the ancient Near East was considered holy for more than 400 years. It is where the temples of many peoples—Canaanite, Egyptian, and Philistine—were built across the centuries (Judg 1:27). In Beth Shan, the Philistines built a temple to Asherah, where the bodies of King Saul and his sons were nailed to the wall (1 Sam 31:12).

BETROTHAL: The engagement of a man and a woman as the first step in the marriage ritual. The betrothal was a contract agreed upon by the two fathers-in-law the year before the marriage feast. At the betrothal, the girl—often as young as fourteen or fifteen years old—was legally the property of the future husband. If the bonds of betrothal were broken, the man had to seek a legal divorce. The Virgin Mary was betrothed to Joseph when the archangel Gabriel asked her to mother the Messiah (Mt 1:18). See also **Husband; Wife.**

BIBLE: A word that literally means "books." The Bible is also called the Scriptures. It is an ancient collection of sacred writings that contain the Revelation of God. The Bible is the word of God, written by human authors under the inspiration of the Holy Spirit. It is without error regarding the things human beings need to know for their salvation. The Bible is a treasure of faith, wisdom, history, theology, and spiritual insight that provides an account of the story of salvation beginning with God's original Creation and ending with a new creation in the heavenly Jerusalem.

The Bible is proclaimed in the Church's liturgies (public prayer) and is used for private prayer, study, and inspiration. The canon of the Catholic Bible contains both the forty-six books of the Old Testament and the twenty-seven books of the New Testament. Protestant Bibles have seven fewer books in the Old Testament. See chart **The Books of the Bible.** See also **Canon; Deuterocanonical Books; Word of God.**

BILHAH (bil´huh)**:** Her name meant "bashful" or "faltering." Bilhah was Rachel's maidservant. When Rachel was barren for the first years of her marriage with Jacob, she gave Bilhah as a concubine (mistress) to Jacob. Bilhah gave birth to two sons, who were raised as Rachel and Jacob's children. Rachel named them Dan and Naphtali (Gen 30:1–8). See also **Concubine; Jacob; Rachel.**

BIRTHRIGHT: The special blessings intended for the firstborn male of a free woman. The firstborn son received a double portion of the family's inheritance (Deut 21:15–17). The birthright also gave to this chosen son the father's authority over the clan.

One could lose his birthright because of immorality (1 Chr 5:1) or by foolishly trading it (Gen 25:29–34). When the early Christians called Jesus the "first-born," they were making the connection that he was worthy of the authority of his heavenly Father (Col 1:18). See also **Esau; Jacob.**

BISHOP: A Greek word meaning "overseer" or "guardian." As the early Church grew, leaders were needed to teach the Gospel and lead the communities in the Eucharist. These early leaders were called bishops; their qualities were described in some of the New Testament letters (1 Tim 3:1–7; Titus 1:5–9). Bishops came to be understood as Church leaders who had been ordained as successors to the Apostles and entrusted as the shepherds of particular diocesan churches. See also **Holy Orders.**

BLASPHEMY (blas´fuh-mee)**:** Speech or action that is inherently evil or disrespectful to God or God's law. In the Law of Moses, blasphemy was an offense punishable by death (Lev 24:10–16). The religious leaders who wished Jesus'

The Books of the Bible

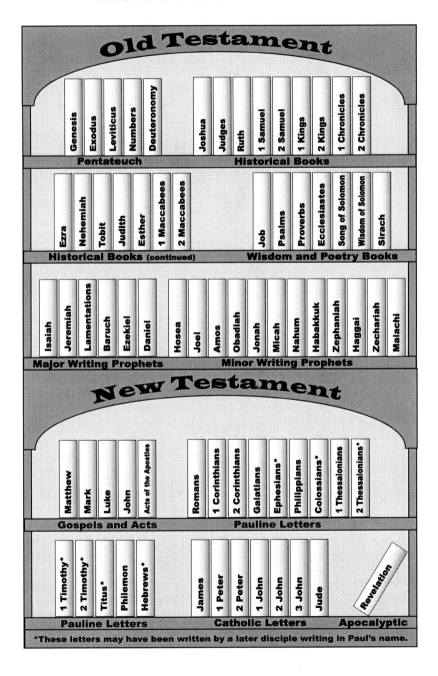

Old Testament

Genesis, Exodus, Leviticus, Numbers, Deuteronomy
Pentateuch

Joshua, Judges, Ruth, 1 Samuel, 2 Samuel, 1 Kings, 2 Kings, 1 Chronicles, 2 Chronicles
Historical Books

Ezra, Nehemiah, Tobit, Judith, Esther, 1 Maccabees, 2 Maccabees
Historical Books (continued)

Job, Psalms, Proverbs, Ecclesiastes, Song of Solomon, Wisdom of Solomon, Sirach
Wisdom and Poetry Books

Isaiah, Jeremiah, Lamentations, Baruch, Ezekiel, Daniel
Major Writing Prophets

Hosea, Joel, Amos, Obadiah, Jonah, Micah, Nahum, Habakkuk, Zephaniah, Haggai, Zechariah, Malachi
Minor Writing Prophets

New Testament

Matthew, Mark, Luke, John, Acts of the Apostles
Gospels and Acts

Romans, 1 Corinthians, 2 Corinthians, Galatians, Ephesians*, Philippians, Colossians*, 1 Thessalonians, 2 Thessalonians*
Pauline Letters

1 Timothy*, 2 Timothy*, Titus*, Philemon, Hebrews*
Pauline Letters

James, 1 Peter, 2 Peter, 1 John, 2 John, 3 John, Jude
Catholic Letters

Revelation
Apocalyptic

*These letters may have been written by a later disciple writing in Paul's name.

27

death falsely accused him of blasphemy (Mt 26:16).

BLESSING: A prayer of intention that calls on the power and compassion of God to bestow a grace or empower a healing, or a plea to affect an event through God's intervention. The Bible is filled with blessing prayers.

Blessings can be given to a community when their leader offers God's blessing upon the members of the community (Num 6:22–27; 2 Cor 13:14). Blessings can be given to individuals, especially during important life events (Gen 24:60; 1 Sam 2:20). Jesus taught that we should even bless our enemies (Lk 6:28). Blessings can be as simple as grace before meals, or as life changing as the sacramental blessings of ordination or marriage or the consecration to the vowed religious life. See also **Prayer.**

BLOOD: To ancient peoples, blood was considered the essence and source of the power of life. Because of this, blood was used for ritual atonement and cleansing from sin through animal sacrifices (Lev 4:6–7). As part of the sacrifice, a priest sprinkled blood on and around an altar (Lev 8:15). Blood was used to anoint the person of the priest and his vestments at his ordination (Lev 8:20).

The word *blood* also described human flesh or relationships. The blood of the covenant symbolized the love of God and the requirement for justice (Ex 24:6–8). The blood of the circumcision brought people of various cultures into the family of Israel and functioned as a symbol of the initiation into the tribe (Ex 4:25–26).

The Law of Moses mandated proper respect in the handling of blood. There were laws against improper butchering of animals, against drinking or eating blood, and against bloodshed (Lev 17). See also **Kinship; Sacrifice.**

BLOOD OF CHRIST: The blood of Christ had great spiritual meaning in the New Testament. Jesus described the shedding of his blood as "the [New Covenant], which is poured out for many for the forgiveness of sins" (Mt 26:28). In many places, the Bible called Jesus the Lamb of God, whose blood was sacrificed for salvation (1 Pet 1:19). The Letter to the Hebrews described Christ as the great high priest who gained our redemption not by the blood of animal sacrifice, but by the sacrifice of his own blood (Heb 9:11–14).

At the Last Supper, Jesus invited his disciples into a profoundly intimate relationship marked by his body and blood. Jesus said that "those who eat my flesh and drink my blood abide in me, and I in them" (Jn 6:56). During the meal, he offered the wine of blessing, saying, "This cup that is poured out for you is the new covenant in my blood" (Lk 22:20). In the Eucharist, the priest consecrates the bread and wine into the body and blood of Christ (1 Cor 10:16). See also **Eucharist; Redemption; Salvation.**

BOAZ (boh´az): An ancestor of David who married the widow Ruth, his relative. Boaz cared for Ruth and her abandoned mother-in law, Naomi (Ruth 4:1–13). See also **Ruth.**

BOOTHS, FEAST OF: See **Tabernacles, Feast of.**

BREAD: One of the basic foods in biblical times. Bread was made from available grains, mainly wheat or barley. It was relatively easy to make, and hard breads could be taken on long journeys.

A human being could live on basic bread and water.

Because it was so basic to sustaining life, bread took on several symbolic meanings in the Bible. Unleavened bread (bread without yeast) was connected to the escape from Egyptian slavery and was used in the Passover celebration (Ex 13:3–10). The bread made from the manna that appeared in the desert (Ex 16:14–30) symbolized God's providence. See also **Eucharist; Manna; Passover; Wheat.**

BREAD OF LIFE: Jesus is the Bread of Life (1 Cor 11:23–26). From the beginning of Christianity, early disciples connected the sacrament of the Eucharist (Mk 14:22–25; Lk 22:14–23) with the ancient Bread of Presence reserved at the ark of the Covenant. It was also closely associated with the bread used in the celebration of the Passover meal.

Jesus is the sacrifice and sacrament of the altar, offered to God for the reconciliation of humanity (Mt 5:23, 23:19, 26:26–29; 1 Cor 5:7; 1 Pet 1:19). Jesus is known in the breaking of the bread (Lk 24:35; Acts: 42, 46, 20:7, 20:11). On the altar of the Lord, the action of the priest consecrates offerings of bread and wine into the body and blood of the Lord (Heb 13:10; Rev 6:9). See also **Blood of Christ; Eucharist.**

BREAD OF PRESENCE: Special bread offering to God, reserved on a golden table with the tabernacle in the Tent of Meeting near the sacred ark of the Covenant. This bread was changed every Sabbath, and only priests ate it (Ex 25:23–30; 40:1–33; Lev 24:5–9). On one occasion, David and his men were given the Bread of Presence when it was the only food available (1 Sam 21:1–6). Jesus used that story to make the point that religious rituals were not more important than people themselves (Lk 6:1–4)

One of the sad memories in salvation history is when in 167 BC, the Syrian warlord Antiochus stole the sacred utensils and the Bread of the Presence reserved in the Temple of Jerusalem (1 Macc 1:22). When the Maccabees defeated Antiochus, they reestablished the Temple rites and respectfully reserved the Bread of Presence in the Temple (2 Macc 10:3).

BURNING BUSH: A crucial event in salvation history, Moses was in the Sinai Desert when God called to him from within a burning bush. All God's sacredness, all God's mystery, and all God's holiness were present in that moment. Yet the fires of this God were compassionate; not even a leaf of the bush was consumed (Ex 3:1–6).

From the bush, the LORD told Moses, "I AM WHO I AM" (Ex 3:14). That name has been translated as Yahweh. Yahweh heard the cry of the poor and responded by sending Moses to lead the slaves out of "the misery of Egypt" and offered the people a Law and "a land flowing with milk and honey" (Ex 3:17). See also **Exodus; Moses.**

C

CAESAR (see´zuhr): Name given to the emperors of Rome. After the reign of Gaius Julius Caesar (100–44 BC), "Caesar" became the title for all Roman emperors. All Jews paid taxes to Caesar (Mt 22:17), but only Roman citizens like Saint Paul had the right to appeal a law case to the emperor (Acts 25:11).

The New Testament period knew a number of Caesars (Lk 2:1, 3:1, 20:22; Acts 11:28, 25:8; Phil 4:22). Numerous Caesars of Rome ruled during the writing of the Christian Scriptures. Some of the most famous Caesars were Augustus (31 BC–AD 14), Tiberius (AD 14–37), Caligula (37–41), Claudius (41–54), Nero (54–68), Titus (79–81), and Domitian (81–96). Claudius, Nero, and Domitian were particularly noted for promoting the persecution of Christians. The numeric value of Nero's name equaled 666, the number of the beast in Revelation (Rev 13:18). See also **Deification; Nero; Roman Religion.**

CAESAREA (ses´uh-ree´uh): A coastal town once known as "Strato's Tower," located seventy miles north of Jerusalem on the shore of the Mediterranean Sea. In its heyday, Caesarea was the beach resort of kings. Herod the Great rebuilt the city and named it after Caesar Augustus (31 BC–AD 14). Caesarea Maritima was graced with palaces, public buildings, a hippodrome for chariot races (which held 20,000 spectators), a theater, an impressive aqueduct, and a temple dedicated to the "divine" Caesar Augustus—which was blasphemy to the Jews.

Caesarea was the headquarters of the Roman governors of Judea, including Pontius Pilate. Caesarea was the home of the evangelist Philip, his wife, and four daughters (Acts 21:8–9). Saint Peter baptized the first Gentile Christian, the Roman centurion Cornelius, in Caesarea (Acts 10). Saint Paul was imprisoned there for two years (Acts 24:7), and from its harbor, he sailed to Rome to stand before Nero.

In the second and third centuries AD, Caesarea was a Christian center, the see of bishops, and the home of the early Scripture scholar Origen. Caesarea was renowned for its great library and memorable scholarship.

CAIAPHAS: See **Annas and Caiaphas.**

CAIN AND ABEL (kayn) (ay´buhl): The story of Cain and Abel is set in prehistory after Adam and Eve were expelled from the garden of Eden. The Cain and Abel story is an allegory offering timeless wisdom based on Israelite history. The backdrop of this story was the ongoing historic conflict between the farmers (represented by Cain) and the shepherds (represented by Abel). Cain symbolized the rich and powerful who had betrayed the laws of the Covenant and had taken land for their farms from nomads and shepherds. As so often happens to those who suffer injustice, Abel had no voice in the story.

Both brothers offered sacrifice to God. Abel offered the best of his flock and was deemed honorable. Cain did not offer God his best. God shamed Cain by rejecting his sacrifice. In jealousy, Cain plotted Abel's murder. God told Cain to resist evil. Cain ignored God's counsel and killed Abel anyway. The cycle of violence began with the children of Adam and Eve.

God told Cain that Abel's innocent blood "cried out from the soil" (Gen 4:10). The teaching is clear. God hears the cry for the poor, and only justice will create peace on earth. The Scriptures teach that we must resist the temptation to see violence as an answer to our problems. Even Cain is spared capital punishment (Gen 4:12–15). In the New Testament, Jesus called Abel righteous (Mt 23:35), and his innocent blood was remembered as a foreshadowing of the sacrifice of Jesus (Heb 12:24). See also **Murder.**

CALEB (kay´luhb): He was called by Moses to assist Joshua in entering the Holy Land (Num 13:1–17). Caleb and Joshua were the only ones who had faith that the Canaanites could be conquered (Num 14:5–10), and they were rewarded by being the only two people of their generation to enter the Promised Land. See also **Joshua.**

CALVARY: See **Golgotha.**

CANA (kay´nuh): A town in Galilee, near Capernaum. In Cana, Jesus performed his first public miracle, turning water into wine (Jn 2:1–11).

CANAAN, CANAANITE (kay´nuhn) (kay´nuh-nit): The name of the land to which God directed Abraham to make his home, the Promised Land, also called Palestine. It occupied the territory that is modern-day Israel. The people who occupied the land were Canaanites. In the Bible, they were called idolaters because of their worship of Baal and Asherah. Through a series of occupations and wars, the Israelites eventually took over most of Canaan. See also **Palestine.**

CANON: From a Greek word meaning "rule" or "standard." The word *canon* has come to mean an approved collection or list. The canon of Scripture refers to the list of books that the Church recognizes as the inspired Word of God. The Catholic Church has a slightly larger canon for the Old Testament than most other Christian churches.

When the Church fathers evaluated the writings that were presented for the New Testament canon, they used the following criteria to evaluate whether writings were worthy to be included in the New Testament. If the manuscripts agreed with all three criteria, it was considered inspired text.

- Was the manuscript written by an Apostle or a student of an Apostle?
- Did the image of Christ and the theology within the manuscript agree with the Apostolic Tradition?
- Was this text well known and accepted by the community?

See also **Apocryphal Books; Bible; Deuterocanonical Books; Inspiration; Old Testament.**

CAPERNAUM (kuh-puhr´nay-uhm): A town on the western shore of the Sea of Galilee in Palestine. This well-known city was on the highway from Damascus to Tyre. Jesus knew Capernaum well (Mt 4:13–16; Lk 4:31), and it was a focus of his ministry.

CAPTIVITY: See **Babylonian Captivity; Exile.**

CARMEL (kahr´muhl): Hebrew word meaning "garden." Carmel was well loved in biblical history. It was a beautiful, fifteen-mile stretch of Palestine, bordered on the west by the Mediterranean Sea, on the east by the hills of Samaria, and on the south by Mount Carmel. In Carmel, King Saul erected a monument to his reign (1 Sam 15:12). Carmel was remembered as the site where Elijah's prayers to God defeated Jezebel's "four hundred fifty prophets of Baal and the four hundred prophets of Asherah" (1 Kings 18:19).

CENTURION: A Roman commander responsible for the discipline and safety of 100 soldiers. Scripture mentions centurions several times, often in favorable ways.

A centurion from Capernaum loved the Galilean people, built a synagogue, and was a man of faith. His servant had become deathly ill, and he asked Jesus to heal the servant, which Jesus did because of the centurion's great faith (Mt 8:5–13; Lk 7:1—8:3). We repeat his words at Mass, "Lord . . . I am not worthy . . . Speak the word, and let my servant be healed" (Lk 7:6–7). A centurion stood at Calvary and recognized Jesus as the Son of God (Mt 27:54; Lk 23:47). Cornelius, the first Gentile to convert to Christianity, was a centurion (Acts 10:1).

CHALDEES, CHALDEANS (kal-deez´) (kal-dee´uhnz): The homeland of the tribe of Abraham (Gen 11:28). Ur of the Chaldees was the ancient name for Babylon (2 Kings 25; Isa 13:19). The people were known as Chaldeans. The name became synonymous with divination, mysticism, and a class of magi that practiced the arts of astrology and magic.

CHARIOT: A horse-drawn cart, invented for use in warfare by the Hyksos-Semitic shepherd kings (1700–1500 BC). Only the powerful and wealthy

possessed a chariot, a vehicle of honor and prestige used by kings and officers in the army. Several Bible stories involved chariots. Pharaoh's chariots and chariot drivers were lost when God closed the Red Sea after the Israelites had passed through (Ex 14:28). Elijah was taken to heaven in a "chariot of fire" (2 Kings 2:11). The evangelist Philip baptized an Ethiopian, who was traveling by chariot (Acts 8:28).

CHARITY: Another word for love. See also **Faith, Hope, and Charity.**

CHERUB, CHERUBIM (cher´uhb) (cher´uh-bim): A type of angel in the Bible having both human and animal characteristics. Cherubim guarded the way back to the tree of life (Gen 3:24). Ezekiel had visions of them with human and animal faces (Ezek 1, 10). The ark of the Covenant and the tabernacle of God from where Yahweh spoke to Moses were decorated with cherubim (Ex 37:1–10). They also decorated Solomon's Temple (1 Kings 6:23–35). See also **Angel; Archangel; Seraphim.**

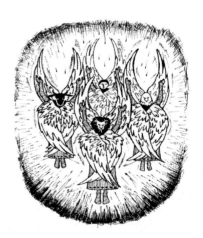

CHILD: At birth, a child was cleansed with water and a salt rub (Ezek 16:4), wrapped in swaddling clothes (Lk 2:7), and nourished by the mother or wet nurse. The mother remained in seclusion until after she had submitted to rites of purification. A male child was considered unclean for seven days. A girl was considered unclean for two weeks and was fully purified in sixty-six days (Lev 12:1–8). On the eighth day, a boy was circumcised and the firstborn son consecrated to God (Gen 17:10–12).

At age three, a child was weaned from its mother's breast. The event was honored with a day of celebration (Gen 21:8; 1 Sam 1:22–24). Schooling began at age five. Children were considered adults at around thirteen and could be committed to marriage.

CHOSEN: Being called by God for some special purpose. The Bible is essentially a collection of stories about people who were chosen by God to bring about God's divine will in human history.

God chose Abraham and Sarah as the parents of the people of Israel (Gen 12:1–9). God chose Moses to lead the people out of the bondage of Egypt (Ex 3:1–12). God chose Israel to be in a special Covenant relationship with him (Deut 7:6–11). These Israelites, who were later called the Hebrews and the Jews, are still today called God's Chosen People. God called the prophets to speak the word of God (Jer 1:4–10). These prophets promised there would be a messiah, a chosen one, who would restore justice and lead the people to God (Isa 11:1–4).

Christians believe that Jesus is the Messiah, the Christ, the chosen of God. He is the Son of Man who has forgiven sin and healed and redeemed humanity. Jesus specifically chose his Apostles to witness his ministry, death, and Resurrection.

Finally, all the baptized are also Christ's chosen ones, empowered to proclaim Jesus as Lord, to live the Good News of God's justice and everlasting love, and to witness the Reign of God to every generation. See also **Covenant.**

CHRIST: A Greek equivalent for the Hebrew word *messiah,* or "anointed one." The original messiahs were the warrior kings of Israel who led their people to liberation and established a rule of justice. King David was seen as the ideal king and messiah. After David's death, some of the prophets promised that a descendant of David would come to lead the people to freedom and restore justice to the oppressed (Isa 61:1). This promise was fulfilled in Jesus Christ, whose followers proclaimed him as the Messiah (Mk 8:29).

Christ is not Jesus' last name. Rather, Jesus is his human name, and Christ is his title. Jesus Christ literally means, "Jesus, the Anointed One," or "Jesus, Our Savior." See also **Messiah.**

CHRISTIAN: A follower of Jesus of Nazareth. In Antioch in Syria, the Jesus community was first called Christian (Acts 11:26). Christians believe Jesus is the Messiah, the Christ of God. Christians are united with the body of Christ in Baptism. They share Christ's mission to proclaim the kingdom of God and bring truth, healing, and justice to the world.

CHRISTOLOGY: The study of Jesus as the Christ and of the titles by which he was called.

CHRONICLER (kron´i-kluhr): The name given to group of Judean scribes who, around 400 BC, composed and compiled 1 and 2 Chronicles and possibly the books of Ezra and Nehemiah. Some people think parts of the worldview of Haggai and Zechariah seem similar to the work of the Chronicler. The

Chronicler emphasizes the importance of the House of David and the worship that David and Solomon established at the Temple in Jerusalem.

CHURCH: English translation of the Greek word *ecclesia,* which means "gathering" or "assembly." The Scriptures referred to the Church as a spiritual as well as a physical reality. In the spiritual sense, the Church was spoken of as being married to Christ, who was her faithful husband (Eph 5:22–27). The Church was also called the Body of Christ (1 Cor 12:12–31), which had many members but only one head, Christ. And when the faithful were gathered in homes to celebrate the Eucharist, they were called church (Rom 16:5; Col 4:15).

In the physical reality, the Scriptures also referred to the local community of Christians as the Church. Paul often began his letters that way, for example, "To the church of God that is in Corinth" (1 Cor 1:2).

The Church today is the people who have embraced the New Covenant—the new priestly, prophetic, and royal people of God who participate in the mission and life of Christ through the celebration of the sacraments and the proclamation of the Gospel. The Bible does not use the word *church* to refer to a building, which comes later in Christian history.

CIRCUMCISION (sur´kuhm-sizh´uhn): A ritual honored on the eighth day after the birth of a Jewish boy. The child has the loose fold of skin at the end of his penis removed as a consecration to God, in honor of the Covenant (Gen 17:10–12). The rite represents a cutting away of the past and bonding in blood. Circumcision becomes the seal of the Covenant and the sign of the Israelites' commitment to God.

In the New Testament, the rite of circumcision became the focal point of an early controversy that almost split the Church. Some of the first Christians insisted that to be a follower of Christ, one also had to follow Jewish laws and rituals. This meant that any adult male who wasn't a Jew would have to be circumcised to be a Christian. Paul and other Church leaders strongly argued against this requirement. The issue was decided at the Council of Jerusalem, when it was agreed that following all the Jewish laws and rituals was not a requirement for following Christ (Acts 15). See also **Covenant.**

CLAUDIUS (klaw´dee-uhs): Roman emperor who followed Caligula in AD 41. In AD 49, Claudius banished the Jews and Christians from Rome (Acts 18:2). During his reign, persecutions and hostilities broke out in Jerusalem under Herod Agrippa, resulting in many deaths and causing alienation between Christians and the Jewish people. Stephen and the Apostle James, brother of John, were among the martyrs of the period (Acts 7:53–60, 12:2). See also **Caesar.**

CLEOPAS (klee´oh-puhs): After the death of Jesus, a disciple named Cleopas and another unnamed disciple fled Jerusalem in anguish. They walked the seven miles to their home in Emmaus, asking one another how the events of Calvary could have happened. The resurrected Jesus joined them. Cleopas and his partner looked right into Jesus' face and spoke with him but couldn't recognize their Lord until the breaking of the bread (Lk 24:13–35). See also **Emmaus.**

CLOUD, PRESENCE OF GOD: Clouds were often connected in the Scriptures to the presence of God. Within a cloud, Yahweh led the Israelites across the deserts of the unknown (Ex 13:21–22), appeared to Moses on Sinai (Ex 19:16), and gave direction and correction (Num 11:25, 12:5).

Daniel envisioned the Son of Man as coming on the clouds of heaven (Dan 7:13–14). At the Transfiguration, God spoke to Peter, James, and John from within a cloud to proclaim Jesus as the beloved Son of God (Mt 17:5). At the end of the age, the Son of Man will return, joined by the angels on the clouds of heaven (Mt 24:30; Rev 14:14).

COLOSSAE (kuh-los´ee): A city in Asia Minor located near the Lycus River valley, 110 miles east of Ephesus on the road to the Euphrates River. Colossae was known for the dyeing of cloth and the production of red wool. Saint Paul's Letter to the Colossians was written to the church founded there.

COMFORTER: See **Paraclete.**

COMMANDMENT: The commandments were the rules of life that the Chosen People followed to be in right relationship with God according to the Covenant God made with them. These commandments, also called the Law of Moses, were given in the books of Exodus, Leviticus, Numbers, and Deuteronomy. These books, together with the Book of Genesis, are also called the Torah. The Torah is summarized in the Ten Commandments, also called the Decalogue (Ex 20:1–18). See also **Law of Moses; Ten Commandments.**

COMPASSION: From the Hebrew word for "womb." To be compassionate is to be as loving as a mother to the child in her womb. God's compassion for God's people reveals God's abundant, faithful love for humanity (Ps 106:45, 145:9). Compassion required pity, forgiveness of debt, and care for those in special need (Zech 7:9–10).

Jesus taught that God was a compassionate, loving Father (Mt 7:10). The parables revealed the mercy and unconditional love of God in the image of the Father in the parable of the prodigal son (Lk 15:11–32), in the care that the good Samaritan offered to the stranger (Lk 10:30–37), and in the image of the king who released the debts of his unworthy steward (Mt 18:27).

Jesus offered a mirror by which Christians examine themselves against the virtue of compassion. Be as perfect, as merciful, and as just as God, challenged Jesus (Mt 5:48). Forgive "seventy-seven times" (Mt 18:22). The Christian's dedication to Christ is to be measured against the level of compassion shown one another. Compassion is to be a way of life (Jn 20:23).

CONCUBINE (kon´kyoo-bin): A woman used as a sexual partner or breeder. A concubine did not have the rights of a wife and was usually a slave or a woman captured in war. Her main role was as a surrogate mother, who hopefully would bear sons for the tribe (Gen 35:22; Judg 8:31, 19:25). See also **Bilhah.**

CONFESSION: An opening of one's soul before God and an admission of one's sin. The Bible contains some wonderful examples of confession (Ezek 9:5—10:1; Psalm 51; Dan 9:3–12). Confession is a profession of faith in God's forgiveness. It is an admission of our responsibility for wrong behavior, and it is a prayer asking for God's healing (Jas 5:16). The sacrament of Penance and Reconciliation was called confession before Vatican Council II. See also **Sacrament.**

CONFIRMATION: The sacrament that celebrates the complete initiation into the Body of Christ and the outpouring of the Holy Spirit. Along with Baptism and the Eucharist, Confirmation is a sacrament of Christian Initiation. It empowers one to faithfulness to Christ and the Church. It provides gifts of the Spirit and the grace to do the work of the Gospel: to proclaim the Reign of God and to preach Good News, heal the broken-hearted, proclaim liberty to captives, and release those in bondage (Lk 4:17–21). The biblical roots of Confirmation are found in a story in which Peter and John laid hands on Christians in Samaria who were already baptized, and they received the Holy Spirit (Acts 8:15–17). See also **Sacrament.**

CONSCIENCE: The inborn sense of right and wrong; the inner voice of the Spirit that develops character and evaluates desires, actions, and ethics (Acts 24:16). God created us with a natural law that directs our spirits toward goodness, but our conscience needs to be trained and directed (Titus 1:15; 1 Thess 5:20–22). See also **Repentance.**

CONVERSION: An awakening to joy through the acceptance of God's unconditional love; a change of heart and mind that leads the soul to reject all sinful and unloving behaviors, have faith in the one, true God, and believe in Jesus as savior and Lord. True conversion causes the realization that love of God is the highest value and worth more than the pleasures and powers of earth. The soul responds to conversion as a new creature, with new eyes, new hope, new understanding, and a commitment to justice (Acts 26:18).

The Apostles, Mary Magdalene, and the other male and female disciples all had conversion experiences in which they came to know and love Jesus as friend and Messiah. A dramatic conversion story in the Bible is Saint Paul's conversion told in Acts 9:1–19. Paul was a very religious Pharisee who had been actively persecuting Christians. Christ appeared to Paul, and Paul came to believe in him as the Messiah. Paul turned from a persecutor of Christians into the most famous Christian missionary in history. See also **Mary Magdalene; Paul.**

CORINTH (kor´inth): A Greek city located about forty-eight miles west of Athens. It had a turbulent history. The Romans destroyed Corinth in 146 BC, and the city lay desolate for more than a century. In 46 BC, Julius Caesar rebuilt the city and named it for himself, Corinth—the praise of Julius. Corinth was noted for wealth, luxury, immorality, and the vicious habits of the people.

In the time of Saint Paul, Corinth was a successful Roman port and the ad-

ministrative center of the Roman proconsul, or administrator, of Achaia (Acts 18:12–16). Paul was in Corinth in AD 51–52. There he met the Christian missionaries, the tentmakers Aquila and Priscilla, as well as Apollos (Acts 18:1–18). During later missionary journeys, Paul wrote several letters to the Christians in Corinth, which we have as the First and Second Letters to the Corinthians.

COVENANT (kuhv′uh-nuhnt): A solemn vow and contract in which God is witness. The Hebrew word for covenant means "a cutting," which alludes to covenants often having been sealed by a sacrifice, or the shedding of blood. Covenants were made between individuals, such as the covenant between Laban and Jacob (Gen 31:44–54). They were also made between nations, such as the covenant between Abraham and Abimelech (Gen 21:22–32). A covenant was a binding oath and a commitment to a new way of being community.

The most important covenants in the Bible were covenants made with God. The first covenant was the covenant God made with Noah never again to destroy the earth with a flood (Gen 9:1–17). It was a promise that God would never abandon humanity.

The second covenant God made was with Abraham (and by implication, also with his wife Sarah). In this important covenant, God promised to provide them with descendants who would become a great nation (Gen 12:1–3, 15:1–21). This covenant was to be marked by the circumcision of all male descendants of Abraham and Sarah.

God renewed the covenant with Abraham's descendants, the Israelites, on Mount Sinai. This Covenant, called the Sinai Covenant, established the Israelites as God's Chosen People (Ex 19—20). An elaborate system of laws and rituals of sacrifice were the outward signs of the Sinai Covenant. This Covenant was reaffirmed with King David—an affirmation that included the promise that the House of David would stand forever (2 Sam 7:8–17).

These Old Testament covenants revealed God's longing to restore humanity's lost relationship with God. They were an expression of God's love for sinful humanity. See also **Abraham; Chosen; Circumcision; Covenant, New; House; Law of Moses; Moses.**

COVENANT, NEW (kuhv′uh-nuhnt): The word *testament* is another word for covenant. Thus, the Old Testament records the story of the original covenants. The New Testament is the story of the New Covenant God made with the entire human race through Jesus Christ. In its weakness, humanity did not follow the Covenant God established with Abraham's descendants, so God sent Jesus to live among us—God's love in flesh (Jn 1:14–18). Through the life, death, and Resurrection of Jesus Christ, God established a New Covenant with humanity (Heb 9:15). The New Covenant was marked by the shedding of Christ's body and blood (Lk 22:19–20). Jesus, the New Covenant, binds us to the love of God the Father through the Holy Spirit and makes us a new people of God. See also **Covenant.**

COVET: To be obsessively desirous of or jealous over another person's wealth, relationships, power, or prestige. Covetousness is a cold-hearted attachment to possessions. This greed is sinful because it is the opposite of what God intends for human life. It is alienating and destructive to relationships, steals joy, suppresses satisfaction, and places the self in bondage to sin (Ex 20:17; Col 3:5; 1 Tim 6:9–10).

CREATION: The act by which God willed into existence everything that is (Ps 89:11). The Creation stories in the Bible are in Genesis 1 and 2, although there are many other references to God's creative power throughout the Bible. These two chapters actually contain two accounts of Creation. The first account has God creating the world in an orderly fashion, in six consecutive days (Gen 1:1—2:3). The second account is very different, with God acting much more spontaneously. In this account, God created the man and the garden, and then when the man was lonely, God created the animals and finally, woman (Gen 2:4–25).

In other ancient Middle Eastern creation stories, the creation of the world was almost accidental, a by-product of the gods battling each other. The Bible's Creation stories are very different; there was just one God, who wanted to be in a loving and caring relationship with his creation. The Genesis Creation stories are mythic; they are not intended to be historical. They teach us truth about God: that God exists apart from created things, that God is all-powerful, that God's love is expressed in and through Creation, and that God wants to be in a loving relationship with the human beings God created in God's image and likeness. See also **Earth; Eden.**

CREED: In Latin, the word *credo* means "I believe." A creed is a religious oath. When Christians chant the creed at Mass, they affirm their bond with Christ and their stance on issues that affect the world. Christian creeds are a profession of faith that affirms belief in God as Holy Trinity, in the saving work of Jesus Christ, in the Church, and in our own resurrection.

In 1 Corinthians 15:3–11, Saint Paul recorded an early creed. Later creedal statements of the early Church were reflected by the speeches of Saint Peter (Acts 4:10–12) and Saint Paul (Acts 13:26–33) in the Acts of the Apostles.

At the Council of Jerusalem (AD 60), the Apostles who were still alive, the evangelists, and some early missionaries gathered to clarify their beliefs in Christ (Acts 15). The Apostles' Creed—although not specifically created at that council—is a profession of their faith. It is a prayer that proclaims the essential statements of the faith they passed to all Christians and that are already found in the Scriptures. Here is the Apostles' Creed with biblical citations for its statements.

> I believe in God, the Father almighty, creator of heaven and earth (Gen 1). I believe in Jesus Christ, his only Son, our Lord. He was conceived by the power of the Holy Spirit and born of the Virgin Mary (Lk 1:34–35). He suffered under Pontius Pilate, was crucified, died, and was buried (Mt 27:32–61). He descended into hell (Eph 4:8–10). On the third day he rose again (Mt 28:1–10). He ascended into heaven and is seated at the right hand of the Father (Lk 24:50–51). He will come again to judge the living and the dead (Mt 25:31–46). I believe in the Holy Spirit (Jn 14:15–17), the holy catholic Church, the communion of saints (Rev 7:9–10), the forgiveness of sin (Jn 20:23), the resurrection of

the body, and the life everlasting (1 Thess 4:16–17). Amen.

CRETE (kreet): One of the largest islands in the center of the Mediterranean Sea. Crete is graced with tall, rugged mountains, gentle slopes, and plateaus. It lies along the Aegean coastline to the north and the Libyan Sea to the south. In ancient times, Crete had a rich culture, and the island supported more than 100 cities. Historians believe that Crete was the original home of the Philistines.

Crete was an economic center that exported food products, cypress wood, wine, currants, olive oil, wool, cloth, herbs, and purple dye. The people of Crete traded as far as Spain, Britain, central Europe, and Iran. Saint Paul visited Crete on his voyage to Rome (Acts 27).

CROSS: An instrument of Roman torture and death. Death by crucifixion was meant to cause the victim humiliation, terror, shame, and extreme pain. The cross was two timbers of wood fastened horizontally and vertically. The body of the victim was nailed or tied to the wood. The victim's death often took days. The dead bodies were usually left on the cross to rot and be eaten by wild animals. The bodies served as a warning not to disobey the Roman governors.

However, with Jesus' death and Resurrection, the cross became the sign of the glorious Christ and the journey of his followers on earth. There is no resurrection without a willingness to sacrifice one's life. Jesus said, "Whoever does not take up the cross and follow me is not worthy of me" (Mt 10:38). To remind themselves of this, Catholics begin prayer with the rite of the sign of the cross, blessing themselves with the words, "In the name of the Father, and of the Son, and of the Holy Spirit." See also **Crucifixion.**

CROWN: In the ancient Middle East, kings, high priests, and royal persons wore a type of headdress to mark status (2 Sam 1:10). The crown was a wreath of precious metals that signified accomplishment, conquest, or honor. It could be a tiara, a garland of flowers, vines, turban, or miter.

The Romans and Greeks used the crown as a symbol of victory and reward. Conquerors wore wreaths of oak, olive, herb, or laurel leaves. The Romans awarded the "civic crown" to a soldier who fought the good fight and saved the life of a citizen.

CROWN OF THORNS: Jesus was scourged, crowned with thorns, dressed in royal purple, handed a scepter, and mocked as a king by the Roman guards (Mk 15:19). The crown of thorns was especially cruel, woven from a vine with half-inch-long thorns and pressed into the top of Jesus' head to cause great pain and bleeding. All this was intended to humiliate Jesus and mock the claim that he was the king of the Jews. The irony is that, because of his faithfulness, even to death, Jesus has become our divine king at whose name "every knee should bend" (Phil 2:8–11).

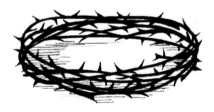

CRUCIFIXION (kroo′suh-fik′shuhn): Criminals, political prisoners, activists, rebels, or anyone—male or female—accused of even a minor infraction against Roman authority could be sentenced to crucifixion. The victim was stripped and beaten, then tied or nailed by the hands and feet to a cross. As a means of deadening pain and thus prolonging the public spectacle, the Roman soldier executioners offered the condemned drugged wine or vinegar laced with gall and myrrh (Mt 27:34).

Death was slow, taking many hours, even days. Death was by suffocation, since a person hanging by the arms cannot fill the lungs with air. When the victim no longer had the strength to push up with the legs for a breath, that person would die. Sometimes, the victim's legs were broken to speed the process of death (Jn 19:31). In most cases, the corpse was left exposed to the elements and eaten by animals, then thrown in a mass grave or garbage heap. Jesus and Peter were crucified.

On any given day, on any public roadway or town square in the Roman Empire, the torture and humiliation of the crucified was displayed to the population. Crucifixion was not only a form of capital punishment, but also a technique for control, terror, and manipulation by the Roman state. Anyone who had witnessed a crucifixion would think twice about disobeying Roman law. See also **Cross; Golgotha.**

CUBIT (cy*oo*ʹbit)**:** An inexact measurement used in ancient times, the length of a man's forearm from the elbow to the tip of the middle finger. It is estimated to be approximately 17 to 20 inches.

CURSE: The word has various meanings. A curse can be the direct opposite of a blessing; one petitions a spirit to harm, condemn, and intend evil or suffering on a victim. The curse could refer to the cult words of a sorcerer, who used a formula to cast curses or spells (Deut 18:10–11). When connected to the black arts of divination, speaking a curse was condemned in the Scriptures.

A curse could also be a punishment and condemnation by God (Gen 3:14). It could be a shaming device (Gen 9:25) or a condemnation against injustice and crime (Gen 49:7). The curse could serve as a prophetic warning, a priestly teaching against idolatry (Deut 27:15), or a warning to obey a conqueror's orders (Josh 6:26).

The Law of Moses forbade cursing the innocent, a father or mother (Ex 21:17), lawful authority (Ex 22:28), the infirm, or those who could not hear the warning (Lev 19:14). Among the most serious blasphemies was a curse against God (Lev 24:10–16; Job 2:9). Today, the word also refers to socially inappropriate speech, or "cussing."

CYCLE OF REDEMPTION: A description of a theme that runs through the Old Testament. The priests and scribes who compiled much of the Hebrew Scriptures after the devastation of the Babylonian Captivity looked at their history and realized they had lost everything: the people, the land, the nation, and the blessings. They concluded that this was the inevitable result when the people were unfaithful to the Law of Moses by worshipping other gods and committing acts of injustice.

Under the inspiration of the Holy Spirit, the priests and scribes made a commitment to record everything: the teachings, history, glories, and mistakes. As the priests and scribes wrote, they saw a pattern that described their history—the cycle of redemption. This pattern occurs in the historical books of the Bible. It goes like this.

- God creates or enters into a covenant, and it is good.

- Humanity falls into idolatry, resulting in disease, war, and grief.

- God sends teachers, kings, prophets, or others who lead the people to repentance.
- The people return to following the Covenant.
- Peace and God's healing return to the people.

See also **Deuteronomist.**

CYPRUS (*si´*pruhs): An island of the Mediterranean Sea, about sixty miles west of the Syrian coast. In ancient times, Cyprus was a Phoenician territory known as Kittim in Israel (Num 24:24). By 477 BC, it was known as Kypros of Greece. By 58 BC, it was a Roman province that exported corn, wine, oil, minerals, and timber.

Barnabas, a Jew of the Diaspora, was a landowner and native of Cyprus (Acts 4:36). Saint Paul, Barnabas, and John Mark ministered on the island (Acts 13:4–6).

CYRENE (*si*-ree´nee): In 630 BC, the Greeks founded this colony in North Africa. Today, it is known as Tripoli, in Libya. Cyrene had a large Jewish population from the time of the Ptolemaic (Greek) rulers. The city had connections to the early Christian mission. Simon from Cyrene helped Jesus carry his cross (Mt 27:32; Mk 15:21). Jews from Cyrene were in Jerusalem at Pentecost (Acts 2:10). They were among the first Christian converts, and some even became missionaries to other lands (Acts 11:20).

CYRUS OF PERSIA (*si´*ruhs): The Persian emperor who conquered Babylon in 539 BC. Cyrus was different from other ancient rulers who destroyed a conquered nation's temples and shrines. Cyrus restored the temples of conquered peoples and returned their gods to their shrines. He had the political wisdom to finance rebuilding campaigns, which created goodwill among the people he had conquered. Of course, he also installed overseers who collected tribute and maintained loyalty in his realm.

In 538 BC, as the Persians took over Chaldea, many Judeans were slaves in Babylon. The conquest of Cyrus brought good news. He decreed liberation and ended their exile (Ezra 1:1–4). He ordered the defeated Babylonians to provide the travelers with silver, gold, goods, and animals. Cyrus even returned the sacred vessels Nebuchadnezzar had stolen as booty from the Temple in Jerusalem (Ezra 1:7) and purchased with his own money cedar from Lebanon for the reconstruction (Ezra 3:7). The Jews celebrated Cyrus as a hero and saw his actions as part of God's divine plan. See also **Babylonian Captivity; Exile; Ezra; Nehemiah.**

D

DAGON (day´gon): A deity of Assyria and Babylon originally brought to the Philistines by the Chaldeans. Dagon was a fierce fertility god, the god of corn, beans, and grain imaged by the body of a fish and the head and hands of a man. Dagon had temples in Gaza and Ashdod. The Philistines in the Samson and Delilah story worshipped Dagon (Judg 16:23–24), and the ark of the Covenant was brought to Dagon's temple as booty after the Philistines' victory in the time of Samuel (1 Sam 5:2–6).

DAMASCUS (duh-mas´kuhs): The ancient capital city of Syria located sixty miles east of the Mediterranean Sea and on the far northern edge of Palestine. Abraham rescued Lot and his family from peril near Damascus (Gen

14:15–18). Over the centuries, Damascus went in and out of Israelite control. In the Syro-Ephraimite War (734–732 BC), the Assyrians destroyed Damascus (Isa 8:4) and then used it as an administrative center. In AD 65, Saint Paul walked the road to Damascus, encountered Christ, and accepted his mission as Apostle to the Gentiles (Acts 9:1–30).

DAN: The son of Jacob and Bilhah, Rachel's slave (Gen 30:6), and the patriarch of one of the Twelve Tribes. The tribe that carried Dan's name was the clan of Samson (Gen 49:16; Josh 19:40–48). In later ages, the tribe of Dan claimed the land west of Ephraim and Benjamin to the sea. See also **Twelve Tribes.**

DANCE: A woman's art of movement to music that was a fertility rite held when families gathered to choose mates for their children. Marriages were made between cousins of the father's line.

Sacred dance was a form of prayer. Miriam the prophet danced in thanksgiving for victory (Ex 15:20), as did the sadly fated daughter of the warrior Jephthah (Judg 11:34). King David danced naked before the Lord, shocking his wife Michal, the daughter of Saul (2 Sam 6:14).

Celebrations called for dancing, but men and women danced separately in Jewish tradition. Women performed a type of belly dance to mark coming of age and to attract a husband. It was an honorable and private affair, held in the security of one's tribe. When the daughter of Herodias (named Salome by the historian Josephus) danced at a public affair to please her mother and amuse her stepfather, Herod (Mt 14:6), it would have been a scandalous display.

DANIEL: His name meant "My judge is God." The folk hero Daniel was a wise man, whom people held up as a model of virtue and wisdom. Scripture lists Daniel with Noah and Job as righteous men (Ezek 14:4).

The Book of Daniel was written during the cruel rule of the Syrian warlord Antiochus (167 BC). Scripture scholars debate whether Daniel was a historical person or a fictional folk hero. In either case, his story is set during the Babylonian Captivity but was written down four hundred years later to encourage faith during the Greek persecutions of the Jewish faith.

In the story, Daniel was taken into the Babylonian Captivity under Nebuchadnezzar. He studied the arts of the Chaldeans, dream interpretation, astronomy, and healing. He became a famous seer (Dan 2). The jealousy of court officials caused Daniel to be sentenced to death and thrown in the lions' den. His faith in the God of Israel saved him from the beasts (Dan 6). Daniel is also the hero of the story of the faithful Susanna, falsely accused of adultery (Dan 13). See also **Babylonian Captivity.**

DARIUS OF BABYLON (duh-ri´uhs) (bab´uh-luhn): The name of various Mede or Persian kings. The sons of Ahasuerus were known as Darius, the seed of the Medes (Dan 9:1). Darius the Mede followed Nebuchadnezzar in the rule of Babylon (Dan 5:30). Darius Hystapes also ruled Babylon following Cyrus of Persia's conquest and extended aid to the Jews in rebuilding the Temple (Ezra 6:1–12).

DAUGHTER OF JERUSALEM: Across the ages, the title Daughter of Jerusalem has symbolized the people of Israel, the holy city of David, and in the Christian era, the Blessed Mother Mary.

To the Hebrew prophets, the Daughter of Jerusalem functioned as the witness of God's victory over injustice. She saw through the pomp and pride of the oppressors and recognized the true king of Israel. "Rejoice . . . O daughter Zion! / Shout aloud, O daughter Jerusalem! / Lo, your king comes to you; . . . / victorious . . . / riding on a donkey" (Zech 9:9).

DAVID: The youngest son of Jesse of Bethlehem and his wife, Nahash. David became the greatest king in Israel's history. David's rule spanned 1000–961 BC. As a young man, he was handsome and a skilled musician. He was a mighty warrior, a skilled military leader, a shrewd politician, and a lover of God. He also had flaws and committed a serious sin (2 Sam 11:2–27). His sincere sorrow and repentance, however, are the scriptural model of forgiveness and reconciliation (Ps 51).

To the surprise of everyone, Samuel anointed David future king to the exclusion of his older brothers, even though King Saul was still alive and in power (1 Sam 16:1–13). God directed David's life. David entered Saul's court as a harp player and became the king's favorite (1 Sam 16:14–23). His father sent him to bring provisions to his warrior brothers, and David ended up killing the dreaded Philistine giant, Goliath, with his sling and became the hero of the people (1 Sam 17).

King Saul became insanely jealous and tried to hunt down and kill David. David eluded Saul, and after Saul's death at the hands of the Philistines, David became king of Israel. He united all Twelve Tribes under one rule and extended the kingdom to include most of Palestine. 1 Samuel 16 through 1 Kings 2:10 tells his exploits. The Chronicler tells David's story in 1 Chronicles 11–29.

The life of David was filled with contradictions. When he followed his own will, his choices were deadly; when he followed the will of God, they were richly blessed. David was remembered for his lust for power and his desire to possess the woman Bathsheba, the wife of Uriah the Hittite, the warrior whom he had had murdered to conceal his crime (2 Sam 11:2–27). David was also remembered for his passionate love for God and his repentance and complete conversion to the will of God (2 Sam 7:18–29). God loved David, forgave him, and promised that David's dynasty would be eternal (2 Sam 7:1–17). Through Jesus, it is. See also **Bathsheba; Goliath; King; Nathan; Saul of the Hebrews; Solomon; Uriah.**

DAY OF ATONEMENT: See **Atonement.**

DAY OF JUDGMENT: The biblical name for the time when God's justice will prevail, also known as the Day of the Lord or the Day of Wrath. In the Old Testament, the prophets proclaimed a Day of the Lord, in which all of humanity will share the bounty of the earth and "beat their swords into plowshares and make war no more" (Isa 2:2–4). The prophets also declared that the Day of the Lord was a time when God's wrath would be brought against those who practiced idolatry and injustice (Zeph 2:1–3).

In the New Testament, the Day of Judgment came to mean the final judgment, when Jesus Christ will judge each person (Mt 10:15, 12:36). God misses nothing. On the Day of Judgment, those who have committed injustice and failed to attend to the needs of their brothers and sisters will be held accountable for their sin, lack of faith, and lack of compassion and will be banished from God's presence. Those with faith, however, who live justly and are attentive to the needs of others will experience the glory, joy, and peace of living in God's presence for all eternity (Mt 25:31–46; Rom 2:5–11). See also **Parousia.**

DEACON: Taken from the Greek word *diakonia,* which means "service." In the early Church, deacon was a title given to men and women, like Stephen (Acts 6:5–6) and Phoebe (Rom 16:1), who performed a ministry of service. Their qualifications are described in 1 Tim 4:14–15. Today, the title is used for men who receive the sacrament of Holy Orders and are ordained into the order of deacons, or the diaconate. See also **Holy Orders.**

DEAD SEA: The body of water lying sixteen miles east of Jerusalem. The Dead Sea has been called by many names: sea of the Valley of Siddim (Gen 14:3), Salt Sea, the East Sea (Ezek 47:18), the Sea of Lot, and the Dead Sea. It is fifty-three miles long and ten miles wide, with no natural outlet. The heat of the desert causes constant and rapid evaporation. Although the Jordan River empties six million tons of water into the sea every day, the Dead Sea's depth always stays the same.

The water is heavy in mineral salts, seven times that of the ocean, causing objects to float easily on the surface. Nothing can live in the Dead Sea. Fish that enter from the Jordan instantly die. The banks, however, do support many varieties of birds that eat the doomed fish.

DEAD SEA SCROLLS: From the time of King David (1000 BC), Jewish rebels and refugees sought shelter in the caves cut into the limestone cliffs along the left bank of the Dead Sea. The site had been a ruin since the Romans destroyed Jerusalem in AD 68–70.

In the spring of AD 1947, Bedouin goatherds explored the caves near the plateau at the dry steambed, or wadi Qumran. The shepherds discovered the most profound scriptural archeological site of the twentieth century.

In the caves, the shepherds found clay jars filled with ancient writings hidden by a group we call the Essenes. The find included the Dead Sea Scrolls, a Hebrew canon of Scripture (except Esther) from 250 BC, older than any Old Testament in existence by 1,000 years. The Dead Sea Scroll collection also included Essene writings in Hebrew, Aramaic, and Greek. See also **Qumran.**

DEATH: The cessation of all physical response in the body. Death is the corruption of the flesh and the end of physical life. Many people fear death as the end of individual existence, but the Christian faith teaches that God holds the mystery of death in the divine heart (Job 28:22–23). Most of the Old Testament authors did not hint at any life after death. However, some of the Old Testament wisdom writers asserted that death was not the end (Wis 5:15).

The New Testament is very clear that Christ's death and Resurrection have won the victory over death (1 Cor 15:50–57). His sacrifice on the cross has provided atonement and paved the way for eternal life after death. See also **Eternal Life; Resurrection.**

DEBORAH: A judge, prophet, and "Mother of Israel" (Judg 5:7). Deborah's name meant "bee." The prophet Deborah was the fourth judge of Israel, a fiery woman, full of courage and determination. She sat under her palm tree between Ramah and Bethel in the hill country of Ephraim and imparted wisdom to the leaders of her people (Judg 4:5). When the Canaanites attacked and pillaged Israel, God commanded Deborah to proclaim war against Jabin and his general, Sisera. Deborah made Barak her general and called together 10,000 men to battle for Israel on Mount Tabor.

Like Saint Joan of Arc, Deborah was a charismatic leader who led the army to victory. Like Miriam, Deborah sang a victory song in which she praised God and his servant, the woman Jael—the tent-dwelling woman who defeated Sisera with holy trickery and saved the Israelite people (Judg 5). See also **Barak; Judge; Wise Woman.**

DEBT: The owing of service, funds, taxes, or property to another person. The word *mercy* in the time of Jesus was a plea to a patron begging release from the burden of debt. Debt was feared in biblical times, because it could result in slavery to the person to whom the debt was owed. The idea of lending was ac-ceptable in the Israelite world, but interest could be charged only to foreigners. Usury, or extracting exorbitant profit for the debt, was condemned (Ezek 18:7–8).

On the Jubilee, all debts were cancelled (Deut 15:1–11). Collateral was accepted for debt, but with mandated protections for the poor. One's millstone could not be held, for it was essential to grind grain, and its loss could jeopardize the life of the debtor (Deut 24:6). One's cloak could be taken in pledge, but justice demanded that the cloak be returned at night so the debtor could survive the cold (Ex 22:26–27). See also **Jubilee.**

DECAPOLIS (di-kap´uh-lis)**:** The "ten cities," a Greek area on the southeast side of the Sea of Galilee that the Romans had rebuilt in 65 BC (Mk 5:20).

DEDICATION, FEAST OF THE: After Judas Maccabeus and his sons defeated the Syrian tyrant Antiochus and his troops in 167 BC, the Feast of the Dedication honored the purging and reclaiming of the Temple. Antiochus had committed an abomination of desolation by erecting an altar to Zeus in the Temple, thereby polluting and desecrating the holy sanctuary. The original festival or rededication lasted eight days. Today, the feast is connected to Hanukkah, the Jewish Festival of Light.

DEIFICATION (dee´uh-fuh-kay´shuhn)**:** A rite in which one becomes a god. Many of the emperors of Rome made it law that they and their dead ancestors be worshipped as Summus Pontifex ("one with the gods").

The deification rites were political and religious and gave Caesar ultimate power. By law, soldiers had to swear a loyalty oath, or *sacramentum*, to the "divine" Caesar, and the citizenry—on pain of death—were ordered to publicly offer sacrifice to a statue of the emperor with the words "My lord and god." Jews and Christians often accepted martyrdom rather than commit such idolatry. See also **Caesar.**

DELILAH (di-li´luh): The woman who brought defeat to the mighty Samson. Scripture identified no family line for Delilah, only that she lived between the Philistine and Hebrew territories. She married the legendary strongman Samson and betrayed him to the enemy for a large sum of money (Judg 16:5). Her name is a play on words. It sounds like the Hebrew word for night, while Samson's name is related to the Hebrew word for sun. See also **Samson.**

DELUGE: See **Flood.**

DEMON: In Hebrew, the word *demon* was related to the words for "goat" or "satyr," which represented the wood spirits of Canaan. The words *devil* or *demon* represented the personification of idolatry and unclean spirits who were connected to foreign gods (Deut 32:16–17).

The Old Testament taught that God did not create demons. All of life was created good (Gen 1—2). God created an angel of light who chose darkness, and his glorious nature decayed into an unclean spirit. The angelic beauty became a fallen, unclean devil who lusted to be worshipped as a god (Isa 14:12–15; 2 Pet 2:4).

The Christian Scriptures affirm that the demon is an unclean spirit, a fallen entity who exists outside redemption by its choice of evil (Mt 12:43–45). The demon retains the intelligence—but not the grace—of its created nature. The demon is set against God and intends harm to creation and humanity (1 Pet 5:8; Rev 12:7–9). See also **Azazel; Exorcism; Satan; Unclean Spirit.**

DEMONIAC (di-moh´nee-ak): A person possessed by an unclean spirit or demon (Mk 5:15). Diseases both physical and psychological were labeled demonic possessions. People believed that physical challenges such as blindness, epilepsy, dumbness, and various forms of mental illness were caused by demons. Jesus and the Apostles healed and exorcised those possessed by demons. See also **Exorcism.**

DESCENT INTO HELL: This article in the Christian Creed is based on the Scripture's writing that in the time between the death and Resurrection of Jesus, he went to Sheol, or the dwelling-place of the dead, where he proclaimed the Good News and released the captives (Mt 27:51–53; Eph 4:9–10). This place where the spirits of the just existed before Jesus' death and Resurrection was envisioned as a place of waiting. It was a place of purging, a type of purgatory or existence in limbo, not the hell of damnation (2 Macc 12:44–45). When these spirits trapped between the dimensions of heaven and earth encountered their Redeemer, Christ freed them to continue their journey into eternal life (1 Pet 3:18–19). See also **Sheol.**

DESERT: An arid, dry, desolate land also called the wilderness. The deserts in and around Palestine are not absolute deserts; that is, they receive some rain during the winter and support a variety of animal life. They are more pebbles, rocks, and stone than sand.

Often in the desert, the people of God have had significant spiritual encounters. In the desert in Sinai, the Hebrews received the Covenant from God. They wandered for forty years in the desert as a consequence of their lack of faith before entering the Holy Land (Num 14:26–35). John the Baptist prepared people for the coming of the Messiah by preaching in the wilderness (Mt 3:1). Jesus prepared for his public ministry by fasting in the wilderness for forty days and nights (Mk 1:12–13), and Satan tempted him there.

DESERT WANDERING: See **Wandering in the Desert.**

DEUTEROCANONICAL BOOKS (dy*oo*′tuh-roh-kuh-non′i-kuhl): Seven books that are part of the Catholic Old Testament but are not included in many Protestant Bibles. The deuterocanonical books were part of a Greek-language collection of the Jewish Scriptures called the Septuagint. The Catholic Church uses this collection of the Jewish Scriptures as the basis for the Old Testament. The seven deuterocanonical books in the Old Testament canon are Tobit, Judith, 1 Maccabees, 2 Maccabees, Sirach, Baruch, Wisdom of Solomon, and parts

of Esther and Daniel. Catholics believe them to be the inspired Word of God.

During the Protestant Reformation (AD 1517–1570), Protestant leaders removed the deuterocanonical books from Protestant Bibles. They preferred a Hebrew-language collection of the Jewish Scriptures that did not include these seven books. Today, Protestants refer to this collection of books as the Apocrypha and sometimes include them in a special section in their Bibles. See also **Apocryphal Books; Canon; Old Testament; Septuagint.**

DEUTERONOMIC REFORM (dy*oo*′tuh-ruh-nom′ik): The reign of King Josiah of Judah spanned 639 to 609 BC (2 Kings 22:1). His reign is known to history as the time of the Deuteronomic reforms. He was a loyal ruler, devoted to LORD Yahweh and dedicated to eliminating idolatry in the land of Israel and Judah (2 Kings 22:1—23:30; 1 Chr 34:1—35:27). Josiah began reconstructing the Temple of David (2 Kings 22:8–10), during which time the scroll of Deuteronomy was discovered. With the Scripture in hand, Josiah reaffirmed monotheism and loyalty to the Covenant throughout his reign. See also **Josiah.**

DEUTERONOMIST (dy*oo*′tuh-ron′uh-mist): The term used for the person or group responsible for writing the histories contained in the Old Testament books of Deuteronomy through 2 Kings. The Deuteronomist emphasized that God's just punishment occurred whenever the people sinned and broke their Covenant with God. The Deuteronomist also emphasized that if the people repented and returned to obedience to the Law of Moses, God's favor would return. See also **Chronicler; Cycle of Redemption; Priestly Tradition.**

DEVIL: See **Beelzebub; Demon; Lucifer; Satan; Unclean Spirit.**

DIASPORA (di-as´puh-ruh): A word meaning "dispersion" or "scattered ones." After the destruction of the kingdom of Israel by Assyria in 721 BC and the Babylonian defeat of the Kingdom of Judah followed by the Captivity of 586 BC, communities of Israelites existed outside the Holy Land. These communities were referred to as the Diaspora. See also **Babylonian Captivity; Esther; Exile.**

DINAH: Her name meant "judgment." Dinah's story is told in Genesis 34. Dinah was the only daughter of Leah and Jacob. She joined the Canaanite women at a banquet and was raped or seduced by Shechem, the Hivite prince. The sexual indiscretion shamed the family of Jacob.

The father of Shechem planned a marriage, and the men of the community even submitted to circumcision as a sign of goodwill. The sons of Leah—Simeon and Levi—were enraged by the defilement. As the men of Shechem recovered from their circumcisions, Simeon and Levi murdered them and reclaimed their sister. Their revenge caused ages of distrust and alienation between the Canaanites and the Israelites. Jacob grieved these sons' actions and cut them from his blessings (Gen 49:5–7).

DISCIPLE: A student who follows the instruction of a particular rabbi or school. It was the custom in Palestine for seekers of spiritual wisdom to give their loyalty to a chosen teacher; they were then disciples of that teacher. John the Baptist had disciples (Mt 9:14; Mk 2:18), as did the Pharisees and other rabbis at the time (Mt 22:15–16).

Jesus of Nazareth was a famous teacher who was followed by a large group of disciples including the Apostles, his mother, family members, and many other men and women (Lk 6:17). Jesus even welcomed tax collectors, prostitutes, the ill and infirm, and all sinners as his disciples—and was criticized because of it. Jesus loved his disciples. He called them family, brothers and sisters, and made them his church (Mt 12:49–50).

To be a disciple of Jesus, one commits the mind, soul, past life, and future life to the devotion of the Christ. Disciples of Jesus never graduate from his instruction, but rather commit themselves to live his teachings as their way of life (Acts 2:37–47) until he comes again.

DIVINATION: Practice of occult arts that attempt to foretell the future, also called augury. Scripture condemns divination because it presumes that the future is set. In essence, the practitioner steals the person's right to free will and influences the choices that form the future (Lev 19:26; Deut 18:10–12). See also **Magic; Sorcery.**

DIVORCE: In ancient times, women were considered the property of men. According to the Law of Moses, men were free to divorce a woman to whom they were bound, but women were not free to make that decision (Deut 24:1–4).

Jesus did not accept the common practice that granted men the right to put a woman away for trivial grounds. A divorced woman was sentenced to a life of poverty, shame, and the loss of her children. Jesus challenged his followers to protect women and the sacrament of marriage by taking marriage as a lifelong, sacramental commitment (Mt 5:31–32, 19:1–9). See also **Marriage.**

DORCAS: See **Tabitha.**

DOWRY: Bride price, or fee paid to a girl's father by an intended husband. This nuptial present was a sum of money, animals, and so on, offered in trade for the woman. Sometimes services were exchanged, such as recorded in the Jacob stories (Gen 29—34). In the case of seducing a virgin, the man had to pay the father a dowry to keep the woman as his own (Ex 22:16–17). See also **Leah; Rachel.**

DRACHMA (drak´muh): A coin equivalent to a day's wage. Often translated as "silver coin" (Lk 15:8).

DRAGON: In the Bible, the dragon appears as a symbol of a powerful enemy whom God defeats (Ps 74:13–14; Isa 51:9). The image brought to mind the goddess Tiamat—the ancient serpent dragon god of chaos in Semitic myth. The dragon showed up again in the Book of Revelation as an allegory for the personification of evil, Satan (Rev 12:1–17). See also **Leviathan.**

DREAM: Dreams can be simple remnant memories, vestiges of the day's events—or messages from God. Scripture recorded many examples of a dream revealing God's will, a call to service, or a warning. Jacob dreamed of angels (Gen 28:10–19). Laban received warnings in dreams (31:24). Joseph saved the nation by interpreting a dream (Gen 41:14–36). God used dreams to confront Abimelech with his adultery (Gen 20:3–7) and to empower Daniel before Nebuchadnezzar.

In the New Testament, the Magi were warned in a dream not to trust the lies of Herod (Mt 2:12). When Herod ordered the slaughter of the Holy Innocents, Saint Joseph was warned in a dream to take the Holy Family and flee to Egypt (Mt 2:13). Claudia, the wife of Pontius Pilate, received a troubling dream and warned her husband to have nothing to do with the crucifixion of Jesus (27:19). Saint Paul had several nighttime visions through which God directed and encouraged him (Acts 16:9, 18:9, 27:23–24).

DRUNKENNESS: In the biblical world, the moderate use of wine was a source of joy and wisdom (Ps 104:14–15; Eccl 9:7) and of celebration and ritual (Deut 14:26). Idolatrous cults, however used alcohol to honor the gods and goddesses in rituals that often became drunken orgies. Because of this connection to idolatry and because drunkenness makes people act foolishly and irresponsibly, both the Old and New Testaments condemn it (Prov 20:1; Rom 13:13).

DUNG: Human and animal feces, also called manure. In Egypt and Canaan, dung was dried, made into bricks, and burned as fuel. Israelites, however, considered this practice unclean and against the laws of purity. For this reason, God had the prophet Ezekiel cook over dung, to make the point that the Israelites would be driven to unclean practices because of their sin (Ezek 4:12–15). Dung was also used as a fertilizer (Lk 13:8).

E

EARTH: The planet earth is a gift from God created to sustain humanity as home (Gen 1:26–30; Ps 115:16). The Hebrew word for human, *adamah,* means a creature made from the soil of earth and the breath of God (Gen 2:7). The Scriptures teach that God has given human beings the responsibility to serve as stewards and caretakers of the earth (Gen 1:28). See also **Adam, Adamah; Creation.**

EAST: In the world of the Scripture, the East was a place of mystery that the Israelites viewed with suspicion. The enemy armies of Assyria and Babylon invaded from the East. It was the direction of the rising sun and from where the hot, dry, destructive winds raged (Job 27:21; Jon 4:8). The East was also the land of the Magi, the Wise Men from the land of wisdom (Mt 2:1).

EASTER: The name for the Christian celebration of the Resurrection of Christ. The first celebrations of Easter were tied to the Jewish feast of the Passover. The first Passover celebrated the Israelites' freedom from the bondage of Egypt in 1300–1250 BC (Ex 12:1–28). During the Passover celebrations in AD 30, Jesus suffered, died, and was resurrected (Lk 22:15). Jesus' followers saw him as the new Paschal Lamb who was sacrificed but was resurrected from the dead so that all people would be free from the bondage of sin and death, once and for all.

The word *Easter* comes from the name of the goddess Eostre, whom the pre-Christian Anglo-Saxons worshipped with feasts celebrated in spring. When the Anglo-Saxons converted to Christianity, the festival time was dedicated to Christ, but the name remained. See also **Resurrection.**

ECLIPSE: When a shadow blocks the sun or the moon from sight from the perspective of earth. In ancient times, people thought an eclipse was a sign of God's anger (Joel 3:15; Job 9:7). At the Crucifixion of Jesus, the darkness of an eclipse covered the land (Mt 27:45).

EDEN (ee´duhn)**:** Word meaning "delight" or "the land of bliss." Eden was the garden in which the Creator God placed the first humans (Gen 2—3). It symbolized the world as God meant it to be, with God, humans, and the rest of creation in perfect harmony and intimate relationship. See also **Adam, Adamah; Creation; Eve; Fall; Original Sin; Tree of the Knowledge of Good and Evil.**

EDOM, EDOMITE (ee´duhm, ee´ duh-m*i*t)**:** Name meaning "red." Edom referred to the territory and people south of Judah. The Edomites were the descendants of Isaac and Rebekah's son Esau. The Edomites' name revealed their hunger for red cereal (Gen 25:30). As the Israelites escaped Egypt in the Exodus, the Edomites refused the refugees entry through their land (Num 20:14–21), and they and the Israelites remained enemies (2 Kings 8:20). Edom fell in the Babylonian Captivity and disappeared from historical memory. See also **Esau; Edomite.**

EGYPT: An ancient land of northern Africa known in Scripture as two lands. The northern delta area was called Lower Egypt, or Mazor. The southern area was called Upper Egypt, or Pathros.

Ancient Egypt was one of the great civilizations of the world. It was also the grain basket of the Mediterranean world, because of the fertility of the Nile River valley. It was a land of plenty that provided refuge in times of famine or upheaval; but it was also a land of power and usury. The Israelites had mixed feelings about Egypt. They fled to Egypt in times of famine but also needed liberation when Egypt unjustly enslaved them as an involuntary labor force.

The Exodus escape from the slavery of Egypt under the leadership of Moses was a most significant experience for the Hebrew people and has perpetually been memorialized in the Seder of Passover (Ex 12). After the Israelites escaped, Egypt's power and influence diminished.

EHUD (ee´huhd): The second judge of Israel. Ehud, son of Gera, of the tribe of Benjamin, was left-handed, a trait associated with the use of trickery. Ehud used trickery in the conquest of the Moabites. Ehud paid tribute to the king, pretended to share a secret, and murdered him by sword (Judg 3:12–30). Ehud served for eighty years, and the people thrived, but at his death idolatry returned to the land of Israel. See also **Judge; Moabite.**

EL: In the ancient Semitic languages, *El* was either a proper noun for "God" or used as a common noun for any one of the many gods worshipped by the Canaanites. The Canaanites called their high god El. A lion or a sacred tree or pole symbolized his consort wife, Asherah, the goddess of fertility and eroticism.

In the ancient Hebrew language, the word *El* was also used for God, as seen in some of the names used for God in the Old Testament: El Shaddai and Elohim. *El* can also be seen as part of personal and place names such as in Elijah, Michael, Bethel, or El-paran. See also **Elohim; El Shaddai.**

ELAM (ee´luhm): Assyrian name meaning "high" or "highlands." Elam was the territory east of the Tigris River in Babylon, the legendary homeland of Noah's son Shem and his descendants (Gen 10:22).

Elam was a warlike nation, adept with the bow and chariot. Ashurbanipal destroyed the Elamite capital of Susa in the Assyrian conquest of 646 BC, a punishment prophesied by Jeremiah during the exile in Babylon (Jer 49:34–39). Elamites were present when the Spirit-filled Apostles preached the Gospel at the Feast of Pentecost (Acts 2:9).

ELIJAH (i-li´juh): A mystical prophet from the ninth century BC, whom God sent to defeat the idolatrous Ahab of Israel and his wife Jezebel (1 Kings 17:1—2 Kings 2:12). The life of Elijah was filled with wonders. When he hungered, ravens fed him. When homeless,

the widow Zarephath of Sidon opened her home to him. When her son died, Elijah raised him to life. When famine struck the land, he miraculously fed the people. When the land was plagued with drought, Elijah defeated the prophets of Baal and Asherah on Mount Carmel and brought rain back to the land (1 Kings 18:1–46) .

In revenge, Jezebel ordered him killed (1 Kings 19:1–13). As he hid from her wrath, angels fed and cared for him (1 Kings 19:1–10). God appeared to Elijah on Mount Horeb and asked him to anoint Hazael king over Syria and Jehu king over Israel (1 Kings 19:9–18). Elijah named Elisha his successor and then was taken from this world in a fiery chariot (2 Kings 2:11–12).

John the Baptist was seen as a type of Elijah (Mt 11:11–14). Elijah appeared with Moses in the Transfiguration of Jesus (Mt 17:1–13). See also **Ahab; Elisha; Jezebel; Idolatry; Prophet.**

ELISHA (i-li′shuh): In the ninth century BC, Elisha was called to succeed Elijah as a miracle worker and a prophet of Israel (1 Kings 19:19–21). His story is intertwined with the stories of four kings in the northern kingdom of Israel: Joram, Jehu, Jehoahaz, and Jehoash. Elisha changed poison water into pure water (2 Kings 2:19–22) and led the thirsty to drink and the poor to oil (2 Kings 3:9–20; 4:1–7). In stories that point to Jesus' miracles in the New Testament, Elisha multiplied bread for the hungry (2 Kings 4:42–44), cured a leper (2 Kings 5:1–14), and raised the dead to life (2 Kings 4:18–37).

Elisha offered hope in times of need, anointed kings, and faithfully served the Lord for more than sixty years. At Elijah's death, King Joash of Israel wept. With his dying breath, Elisha counseled the king in future victories (2 Kings 13:14–19). See also **Elijah; Prophet.**

ELIZABETH: Her name meant "God is her oath." The righteous Elizabeth of the house of Aaron married the priest Zechariah. Like Sarah in the Old Testament, Elizabeth was elderly, barren, and faithful to God. An angel's visit brought Zechariah and Elizabeth the promise of hope through the birth of child—just as with Abraham and Sarah (Lk 1:5–25). The Gospel of Luke used this event to show that, just as the Old Covenant began with the birth of a child to an elderly, barren woman, so also the time of the New Covenant began with the promise of new life.

Elizabeth was the one the Blessed Virgin sought for counsel. After the archangel Gabriel asked Mary to mother the Messiah, she raced to the home of her cousin Elizabeth and discovered that Gabriel had announced to Elizabeth that she, too, carried a child in her womb (Lk 1:39–46). Before taking his first breath, John the Baptist recognized the presence of Christ (Lk 1:5): As Elizabeth held the young Mary in her arms, the baby in Elizabeth's womb leapt for joy (Lk 1:39–63). In the rosary, this scene is honored as the mystery of the Visitation. See also **Barren.**

ELOHIM (el′oh-him): A Semitic name for God. The people of northern Israel described Elohim as an ultimate power, the one in whom humanity and all of creation stood in awe. The scribes who wrote of Elohim were the Elohists. They lived in seventh- to sixth-century BC Israel. Later writers edited the Elohists' writings—the E tradition—into sections of the Pentateuch. See also **El; God.**

EL SHADDAI (el-shad′i): An ancient Hebrew name for the Creator, meaning "the Lord God almighty of the mountaintops." See also **El; God.**

EMMANUEL (i-man´yoo-uhl)**:** A Hebrew word meaning "God is with us." Emmanuel is a central teaching to Jews, Christians, and Muslims. Across the ages, the Hebrew people prayed for the coming of the Promised One, a savior, a king who would unify, protect, and lead the people to freedom. Isaiah prophesied that such a leader would be called Emmanuel, or Immanuel (Isa 7:14). Christianity embraced this prophetic title and applied it to Jesus Christ, proclaiming that God is with us in the incarnation of Jesus (Mt 1:23). See also **Jesus Christ.**

EMMAUS (i-may´uhs)**:** A village located seven miles from Jerusalem. It is remembered as the destination of Cleopas and an unnamed disciple who unknowingly journeyed with the Christ as they walked on the road to Emmaus. They recognized him in the breaking of the bread (Lk 24:13–35). See also **Cleopas.**

ENMITY: Word referring to a distance, separation, and hatred such as the boundary God placed between humanity and the evil serpent or between God's holiness and sin (Gen 3:15; Jas 4:4).

ENOCH (ee´nuhk)**:** His name meant "initiated." The legendary Enoch was the eldest son of Cain (Gen 4:17). Cain built a city and named it after Enoch. Scripture says that Enoch walked with God for 365 years (Gen 5:22–24). According to early Jewish legends, Enoch escaped death and was caught up into the heavens (Heb 11:5–6). Enoch was a popular figure in the early Christian period and is referred to in the New Testament Letter of Jude (Jude 1:14).

ENVY: A feeling of resentment at the good fortune of another. When we hang on to envious feelings, a wound forms in the human heart that leads to sinful thoughts and actions (Mk 7:21–22).

EPHESUS (ef´uh-suhs)**:** A port city in Turkey that served as the western capital of the Roman Empire. The emperor Domitian built a temple to his own divinity in Ephesus and mandated that the populace worship him as god. The city was graced with a temple to the goddess Artemis—considered a wonder of the ancient world—and an open-air theater that seated 50,000.

The New Testament attests that Ephesus and its people heavily influenced the mission of the early Church. The Book of Acts says that Saint Paul founded the first Ephesian Christian community and ministered there with Aquila, Priscilla, and Timothy (Acts 18:19–21, 19:1–41).

By AD 80 or 90, an unknown disciple wrote the Letter to the Ephesians and named it in honor of Paul and the community. By the end of the first century (AD 90–110), scholars believe, the beloved disciple wrote the Gospel of John while in Ephesus.

EPHOD (ee´fod)**:** An ancient Hebrew priestly garment worn over a robe and hung from the neck like an apron. The ephod was clasped by golden pins and gathered at the waist by a belt of gold, purple, and precious stones. The Urim and Thummim were breastplates that connected to the ephod. See also **High Priest; Urim and Thummim.**

EPHRAIM (ee´fray-im)**:** His Hebrew name meant "fruitful." Ephraim and his brother, Manasseh, were the sons of Joseph and his wife, Asenath of Egypt (Genesis 41:50–52). Ephraim's grandfather, Jacob, blessed Ephraim and his brother, and these descendants of Joseph became the ancestors of two of the Twelve Tribes of Israel (Gen 48; Num 1:32–35). See also **Manasseh; Twelve Tribes.**

EPIPHANY (i-pif´uh-nee): The manifestation of a new star. The feast of Epiphany celebrates the birth of Christ as the Light of the World and honors the visitation of the eastern Magi, who came in search of a new king (Mt 2:1–12). See also **Magi.**

EPISTLE (i-pi´suhl): See **Letter.**

ESAU (ee´saw): The elder son of Isaac and Rebekah and the twin brother of Jacob. Esau was the first to come from his mother's womb, so as the elder, he was the heir to the birthright—a birthright Jacob tricked him out of (Gen 25:25). Later, Esau was called Edom, which means "red." He was called such for the red color of the bean stew for which he sold his birthright to his brother (Gen 25:29–34). The stories of Jacob and Esau became allegories explaining the bitter feelings between the nations of the Edomites and the Israelites. See also **Birthright; Edom, Edomite; Isaac; Jacob; Rebekah.**

ESSENES (es´eenz): A group of pious, ultraconservative Jews who left the Temple of Jerusalem and began a community beside the Dead Sea that was known as Qumran. Originating in 100 BC, the Essenes thrived until AD 70, when the Romans violently put down a Jewish rebellion. The Essene community copied, wrote, and preserved the library of texts known today as the Dead Sea Scrolls.

ESTHER (es´tuhr): The beautiful heroine Esther was the daughter of the Benjamite Abihail and part of the fourth-century BC Judean diaspora community in Persia. Her story is told in the Old Testament Book of Esther. Her Hebrew name was Hadassah (the myrtle), but when she was sent to the harem of King Ahasuerus (486–465 BC), she was given the name Esther, or star, and was made his queen.

Haman, grand vizier of the king, had a special hatred for Esther's uncle Mordecai, who refused to honor him. Haman created a plot to convince Ahasuerus to kill all Judean people in the empire, so Esther kept her faith a secret at first. At that time, women were not permitted to speak to men in public— let alone to approach a king. Ultimately, Esther courageously pleaded with the king to spare her people and thus prevented Haman's genocidal plot. The Jewish feast of Purim memorializes the event (Est 9:29–32). See also **Ahasuerus; Diaspora; Mordecai; Purim; Queen; Vashti; Xerxes, Artaxerxes.**

ETERNAL LIFE: From the beginning of time, God called humanity into life. The biblical story of the garden of Eden tells us that humans were destined to live in love and happiness in eternal life. Death was not part of God's will for humanity but entered the world as a result of Adam and Eve's original sin. God sent his only son, Jesus Christ, to restore God's original plan for human beings— to live eternally with God in love, joy, and happiness (Jn 17:1–3). See also **Death; Heaven; Hell; Immortality.**

ETHIOPIA: The country south of Egypt where the White and Blue Nile rivers join. The Hebrew name for Ethiopia was Cush. Ethiopia was the land of rivers, the land of burnt faces and of tall, smooth, black-skinned peoples, the descendants of the legendary Ham (Isa 18:1–2).

ETHIOPIAN EUNUCH: The steward of the treasury of Candace, queen of the Ethiopians. The eunuch had come to Jerusalem to worship. As he sat in his chariot reading the prophet Isaiah, he encountered the evangelist Philip, who had been led to the eunuch by the Holy Spirit. Philip explained the meaning of the Scriptures and shared the Gospel of Jesus Christ. The Ethiopian asked for baptism as soon as they reached a water source (Acts 8:26–39).

Ancient legends hold that after his conversion, the eunuch returned to his home and led Candace to faith in Christ. The legends further say he preached throughout Ethiopia, Arabia, and India and was eventually martyred for his love of Jesus. See also **Eunuch; Philip, the Evangelist.**

EUCHARIST (yoo´kuh-rist): The sacrament of the Eucharist is the central mystery and source of the Catholic faith. Catholics believe that in the Eucharist, Christ is fully present—body, blood, soul, and divinity. Through the Holy Eucharist, we are fed the bread of life and cup of salvation (Jn 6:35–58).

Jesus instituted the sacrament of the Eucharist at the Last Supper (Mt

26:17–30; Mk 14:22–26; Lk 22:14–23; 1 Cor 11:23–26). The night before Jesus suffered, he gathered his Apostles to celebrate the Passover meal and remember the Exodus, when God called the Israelites out of the bondage of Egypt. On this feast, Jesus offered himself as the Paschal Lamb and instituted the bread of life.

Today, as on the first Holy Thursday, the action of the priest consecrates bread and wine into the body and blood of the Lord. Christ is present on the altar, in the Blessed Sacrament, within the community gathered, in the living word of the Scripture, and within the person of the priest who presides at the liturgy. The Eucharistic celebration is called the Mass, from the Latin word *missa,* which means "mission" or "the sending." See also **Altar of Christ; Blood of Christ; Bread; Bread of Life; Last Supper; Passover; Sacrament; Unleavened Bread; Worship.**

EUNUCH (yoo´nuhk): A male slave who had been castrated. It was thought that this mutilation would remove sexual desire and produce loyalty in personal service of the slaveowner, as well as in harem duty. Eunuchs were often employed as chamberlains, serving in the bedroom or in the personal affairs of their masters (2 Kings 9:32; Esth 2:3). Some attained wealth and status. In Egypt, court officials, castrated or not, were called eunuchs.

The Law of Moses excluded eunuchs from the congregation (Deut 23:1), but the Book of Wisdom blesses them (Wis 3:14). In the Gospel of Matthew, Jesus acknowledged that some people were born as eunuchs, some had suffered mutilation, and some had committed themselves to living like eunuchs—that is, without being sexually active—for the sake of the Kingdom of God (Mt 19:12). See also **Ethiopian Eunuch.**

EUPHRATES (*yoo*-fray´teez): The great river of the Fertile Crescent, running through Eden—as did the Tigris and the mythic rivers Pishon and Gihon. The Euphrates River was the boundary of the Promised Land (Gen 2:14; Deut 11:24) .

The prophets described the Euphrates as a symbol of Assyrian power (Isa 8:7; Jer 2:18). It runs 1,700 miles through present-day Turkey, Syria, and Iraq and empties into the Persian Gulf.

EVANGELIST: One who proclaims the Good News of Jesus and the Reign of God. An evangelist is a preacher of the Gospel, one who works as a missionary for Christ (Acts 21:8; Eph 4:11; 2 Tim 4:5). The authors of the Gospels of Matthew, Mark, Luke, and John are called the four Evangelists (with a capital *E*).

EVE: Her name sounded like the Hebrew word for "life." Eve was the mythic first woman, the "mother of all living" (Gen 3:20). Like Adam, God created Eve in holiness and asked her to be a steward of Creation. God created her and Adam to be each other's helpmates (Gen 2:18–25).

Eve led the way to the fall from grace, as the serpent stole into Eden and turned Creation into chaos. Instead of eating from the Tree of Life, the tree that the Lord God created for her, she allowed the serpent to tempt her, and she ate from the Tree of the Knowledge of Good and Evil, offering its fruit also to her husband (Gen 3:1–7). Both she and Adam were equally guilty of the first sin, which we call original sin. See also **Adam, Adamah; Eden; Original Sin; Tree of the Knowledge of Good and Evil.**

EVIL ONE: See **Satan.**

EXEGESIS (ek´suh-jee´suhs): The writers and editors of the Bible lived in various countries and cultures, wrote in several different languages, and wrote about events that spanned thousands of years. Faithful scholars have dedicated their lives to understanding the languages, symbols, culture, history, and meanings intended by those who wrote the Bible. The search into the Scripture is called by a Greek word, *exegesis,* which means "to draw out" or "to explain." The work of scholars assists Church leaders in their interpretation. Catholics interpret Scripture in union with the Tradition and the magisterium of the Church.

Modern scholars use a number of different methods to deepen understanding of the Bible. These methods are often called criticisms, not in the sense of being critically negative, but in the sense of taking a disciplined approach to the Bible as literature. See chart **Biblical Exegesis.**

EXILE: The name given to the most tragic event in Israelite history. In 587 BC, the Babylonians pillaged Judah, destroyed the Temple and the city of Jerusalem, then exiled the people in chains to serve as slaves in Babylon (2 Kings 24:10—25:21). This travesty is remembered as the Babylonian Captivity or simply, the Exile. The Judean people remained captive for a generation (586–539 BC). This event could have been the end of the Chosen People and the Jewish religion. God, however, heard their cries and again delivered them from captivity through King Cyrus of Persia.

The Book of Lamentations and Psalm 137 reveal the people's grief in captivity. The people wept when they thought of home, hung up their harps, and couldn't sing (Ps 137:1–2). They promised they'd

Biblical Exegesis

Type of Method	Description	Questions This Method Asks
Textual Criticism	Scholars attempt to recover the most original version of biblical books, since no originals exist, only copies. These scholars compare different translations of the Scripture to understand more clearly the meaning of a given passage.	• Of the many ancient copies and fragments of Bible books, which ones are the oldest? • Can we identify why there are differences between different copies of the same book? • Can we identify why different translations use different words in passages?
Historical Criticism	Scholars work to uncover the historical situation, or *Sitz im Leben*, of the writer at the time a particular book or story was written.	• What was the historical situation during the life of the author/editor or of the author/editor's community? • How did the historical situation influence the author's writing?
Literary Criticism	Scholars look at the Scripture and seek to understand it as a work of literature.	• Did the writer use a particular literary form or device such as a poem, a historical story, a prophecy, a letter, a gospel? • Did the passage use metaphors, puns, parables, exaggeration, a midrash or other literary devices? • How did these particular literary forms or devices function in an ancient society?
Source Criticism	Scholars attempt to identify if the biblical authors used an existing story, myth, or other literature as the basis for their work.	• Are other writings from ancient cultures outside Scripture similar to a biblical passage? • What is the meaning of the differences between the way a story is told in the Bible and the way it is told in other sources?
Redaction Criticism	Scholars look at the role of the editor who compiled various writings to produce the final version of a biblical book.	• How did the inspired editor use two or more versions of a story and blend them into one lesson? • Why did the editor choose particular symbols and wording—and reject other symbols and wording—in the final version? • How has the editor tried to address current events by using older stories of faith connected to the ancestors of old?

never forget Jerusalem or give up the hope that God would send them a savior to free them from bondage (Ps 137:5—137:9). See also **Babylonian Captivity; Cyrus of Persia; Nebuchadnezzar.**

EXODUS (ek´suh-duhs): A Greek word meaning "to go out." The Exodus was one of the pivotal events in the Old Testament (Ex 12:1–49). It revealed God's compassion and God's desire to be in relationship with the Israelites in a special and unique way. God's power was revealed when the nation of Israel was freed from the bondage of Egypt in awe-inspiring and wondrous ways. Moses led the Israelites across the waters of the Red Sea into the desert of purification, where the Law was revealed on Mount Sinai. After forty years of wandering in the desert, the Israelites were ready to enter the Promised Land.

Since the first night when Moses led the people out of Egypt, the Passover Seder has been celebrated across the centuries to revere the events of the Exodus. The Exodus is remembered because it so clearly symbolizes that Yahweh hears the cries of God's people and delivers them from whatever enslaves them. Exodus is also the name of the book of the Bible that tells of these events and their meaning. See also **Burning Bush; Manna: Moses; Passover; Pharaoh; Plague; Promised Land; Rameses; Red Sea; Sinai; Wandering in the Desert.**

EXORCISM: The expulsion of evil spirits and the healing of those who suffer from demonic possession or influence. In ancient times, anyone acting in wild or uncontrollable ways was thought to be demon possessed. Sometimes, sickness and disease were seen as indications of demonic influence or possession. In New Testament times, the Roman occupation of Palestine was also interpreted as a type of possession by an evil power. Today, we might diagnose the same people as suffering from mental or spiritual illness or disease.

Whatever the source of the illness, Christ ministered to those suffering from possession, and his power to exorcise evil spirits showed his power over the devil (Mt 8:22; Mk 5:1–20; Lk 6:17). Jesus accomplished his exorcisms of evil spirits with a simple command, "Be silent, and come out of him" (Mk 1:25). After his Resurrection, Jesus' name has been powerful enough that unclean spirits flee at the sound of it (Mk 16:17; Acts 16:18). Today, the Church still uses exorcisms to drive away the power of evil. See also **Demon; Demoniac; Satan; Unclean Spirit.**

EZEKIEL (i-zee´kee-uhl): An Old Testament prophet who lived from 595 to 573 BC. His name meant "God will strengthen." Ezekiel was a priest from Jerusalem, taken captive in the Babylonian Captivity. He settled on the banks of the River Chebar, a tributary of the Euphrates River. While in captivity, Ezekiel had a vision of a heavenly chariot. The heavens opened, and he heard God ask him to serve as a prophet to the Judean refugees (Ezek 2:1–5).

The captives felt abandoned by God and became bonded to Babylonian ways and gods. Ezekiel explained that God's Law was the key to their Israelite identity. He taught that idolatry had caused the captivity, and repentance would offer the pathway home. Commitment to the Sinai Covenant would restore the House of David. Ezekiel's vision of the dry bones became a source for the Israelite hope in resurrection and life after death. Today, the people of Baghdad still honor his tomb in Keffil. See also **Prophet.**

EZRA (ez´ruh): His name meant "God helps." Ezra the scribe was a son of Seraiah and a descendant of Phinehas, of the house of Aaron (Ezra 7:1–5). He was a priest and teacher of Torah. His story is recorded in the book that carries his name.

As the Judean refugees were freed from Babylon (539 BC), Ezra led the tribes of Judah and Benjamin back to Jerusalem to begin reconstructing the Temple and nation. In an attempt to preserve Israelite identity, he organized the reading of the Torah (Neh 8:1–8), ordered the abandonment of Gentile wives by the men of Judah (Ezra 10:1–5), and led the public confession of sin and the renewal of vows to God. See also **Babylonian Captivity; Cyrus of Persia; Nehemiah; Zerubbabel.**

F

FAITH, HOPE, AND CHARITY: The building blocks of the Christian life. With the practice of these virtues, one recognizes wisdom (1 Cor 13:12–13). Faith is a grace that opens life to the possibility of realities beyond the present experience. Hope creates a vision of the future that includes God's compassion and offers the potential of healing and joy (Rom 8:24). Charity is another word for love. Love offers both hope and faith and is the path of all virtue. Charity is the mission of the Christian life. The Catholic Church calls these three virtues the theological virtues, meaning they enable us to know God, and they lead us to union with God. See also **Charity.**

FALL: The image of lost paradise and the pain caused by the alienation from God because of sin. The Scriptures teach that humanity was created in holiness and grace, that all of creation was good. The first parents, Adam and Eve, chose sin and experienced the fall from grace and the expulsion from the garden of Eden as a result. Now, all humanity suffers from that fall from grace. The Old Testament pictures the Fall as a collapse, an exile, the loss of the Promised Land and the people longing for a messiah to bring them home.

Jesus Christ offered his life to heal the alienation between God and humanity. The redemption offered through his cross and Resurrection raised humanity from the Fall and provided the way home to the Kingdom of God and eternal life with God in heaven. See also **Eden; Original Sin.**

FAMINE: Shortages of food and the resulting starvation and death that have scarred human history. In the lands of the Bible, famine, long-term drought, and crop failure often caused famine. The prophets taught that injustice caused turning away from God, collapsed covenant protections, and resulted in famine and war (Ezek 14:13; Bar 2:24–25). The Book of Revelation saw famine as the result of sin and a judgment from God (Rev 6:8, 18:8).

FAST: To restrict food, luxuries, or habits as a sacrifice offered to God. Fasting was a spiritual and physical discipline designed to elevate one's consciousness in sympathy with the plight of the poor and an act of compassion performed by the healthy to ensure that the weak, young, and infirm would eat (Lev 23:26–32; Zech 7:1–7). Fasting today is also used as a preparation for mission, an expression of interior penance in imitation of the fast of Jesus for forty days in the desert (Mt 4:1–2).

FATHER: The male head of a family, clan, tribe, or even religious group (as with Abraham). In the biblical world, the father provided material and spiritual support and sustenance for his wife or wives, children, and slaves. The father instructed his children and prepared them for life (Prov 4:1). The father arranged for the marriage of his daughters, and Israelite fathers circumcised their male sons.

In the Bible, one of the primary images of God was the loving Father. Father God protected the widow and orphan (Ps 68:5). For the Psalmist, God was "my Father, / my God, and the Rock of my salvation" (Ps 89:26). Jesus taught about God's love by using the image of the compassionate Father who sent his Son to redeem the world (Lk 15:11–32; Jn 6:57).

FEAR OF THE LORD: A gift of the Holy Spirit that empowers reverence before God rather than pride in the ways of the world's political or spiritual powers (2 Cor 5:11; Prov 8:13). Fear of the Lord is to stand in wonder before the truth of God's glory (Ex 3:6) and in awe and trembling in the overwhelming presence of God (Ps 19:9; Phil 2:12).

FEAST, FESTIVAL: A celebration of hospitality (Gen 19:3; 2 Kings 6:23); an occasion of joy and family honor (Lk 15:23; Gen 21:8). Feasts were celebrations to mark birth, marriage, victory, and occasions of festive joy (Gen 40:20; Judg 14:10). A time of feasting included festive eating, drinking, dancing, camaraderie, and honor to God.

The Israelites celebrated a number of religious feasts, also called festivals, that are described in the chart below and other entries. These feasts recall God's power, love, and faithfulness. Jewish people still celebrate these feasts today.

Old Testament Feasts and Festivals

Feast or Festival	Description	Reference
Sabbath	The seventh day, a day to honor God, to rest, and to honor family. No work is permitted.	Lev 23:1–3
Sabbatical Year	Every seventh year, there is no farming so the land can recover. Gleaning is permitted, slaves freed, and debts with fellow Israelites forgiven.	Deut 15:1–6
Jubilee Year	The fiftieth year is proclaimed a year of repentance, to return the nation's priority to the poor and outcast. All property is returned to its original owner, slaves are set free, and debts are erased.	Lev 25

Feast or Festival	Description	Reference
Trumpets (Rosh Hashanah)	This most important of the new-moon festivals marks the first day of the lunar month. Trumpets is celebrated by feasting and a day of rest.	Num 29:1–6
Day of Atonement (Yom Kippur)	The festival of forgiveness for sin and new life. The high priest confesses the sins of the community and pledges repentance. Azazel, the scapegoat, is driven into the wilderness as a symbol of sin.	Lev 16:7–31
Feast of Passover (Feast of the Unleavened Bread)	This Feast memorializes the night before the Exodus from Egypt. A young lamb is slaughtered and its blood brushed on the doorpost of a house. The story of Passover is told amid prayers for Jews across the world, and the Seder meal is shared. On Passover, Jesus gathered his disciples together to celebrate the Seder and offer himself as the Bread of Life and Lamb of God	Ex 12:1–27
Feast of Weeks (Pentecost)	The Feast of Weeks begins seven weeks after the first sheaf of grain is offered to God in thanksgiving for the gifts of the harvest. Over time, it became known as Pentecost and is now celebrated fifty days after the Passover. It is celebrated with feasting and family gathering for prayer and celebration.	Lev 23:15–21
Feast of Tabernacles or Booths	Hebrew feast celebrated in autumn at the gathering of the harvests on the fifteenth through the twenty-second days of the seventh month. The Feast of Booths commemorates when Israel lived in the wilderness.	Lev 23:33–43
Purim	This holy day honors Esther and her cousin Mordecai and their defeat of a plot for the genocide of the Judean people. The feast is honored with fasting, feasting, and prayers.	Esth 9:26–28
Festival of Lights (Hanukkah)	The Feast of the Dedication of the Second Temple honors the victory of the Maccabean War (165 BC) and cleansing and rededication of the Temple. The festival is honored with gift giving, feasting, and family celebrations with friends.	1 Macc 4:38–56

FELIX (fee´liks): His name was Latin for "happy." Felix was the Roman governor of Judea during the time of Saint Paul and was very involved personally and politically with the House of Herod. When Saint Paul was arrested for treason against Rome, he was sent to Felix for judgment. Instead of rendering a quick judgment, Felix kept Paul imprisoned for two years, hoping for a bribe (Acts 23:23—24:27).

FERTILE CRESCENT: The ancient cradle of western civilization that was between the Nile valley in the west, up through Palestine, through Syria to the two rivers of the Euphrates and the Tigris to the Persian Gulf.

FESTUS (fes´tuhs): The Roman governor of Judea who followed Felix. Festus sent Paul to Rome when Paul insisted on his right as a Roman citizen to be tried before the emperor.

FIG: The fruit of large shade trees that were plentiful in Palestine. The leaves of the fig tree covered the nakedness of Adam and Eve in Eden (Gen 3:7). The fruit was a sign of blessings and fertile bounty, a sign of peace and prosperity (1 Kings 4:25; 1 Macc 14:12). Figs could be eaten fresh or dried and were commonly made into cakes. Jesus cursed a fig tree for not bearing fruit; some scholars think this may have been symbolic of the Temple in Jerusalem, which was not bearing religious fruit (Mt 21:19; Mk 11:21).

FIRMAMENT: The Scripture's image of the expanse of sky like a dome that covered the earth. This dome was called the firmament, and it divided the waters of the heavens from the waters of earth (Gen 1:6–8). The firmament was thought of as the house of God, and through its windows and doors, rain and snow fell to earth (Gen 7:11; Mal 3:10).

FIRSTBORN: See **Birthright.**

FISH: Saltwater and freshwater gilled animals. Fish were common in the watered areas of Palestine and an important source of food. Fish with fins and scales were considered one of the clean foods and approved for the Israelite diet (Deut 14:9–10). A plentiful catch of fish was a sign of prosperity (Ezek 47:9–10). Several of Jesus' Apostles were fishers, and Jesus used the symbol of fishing to represent their new mission (Mt 4:18–22). Jesus multiplied loaves and fish to offer as food to the multitude gathered to hear his teachings (Mk 6:30–44). After Jesus was resurrected from the dead and appeared to his Apostles on the seashore, he ate fish with them (Lk 24:42–43; Jn 21:9–13).

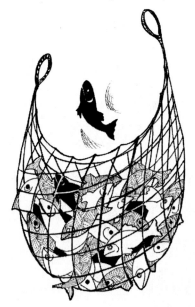

An outline of a fish became an early symbol for Christianity. The letters of the Greek word for fish, written in English as *ichthus*, were also the first letters in the Greek words of the phrase "Jesus Christ, God's Son, Savior."

FLESH: A word with many meanings in the Bible. Flesh referred to the body, its hungers, weakness, and glorious ability to offer life to the next generation (2 Chr 32:8; Ps 78:39). Flesh was considered vulnerable, soft, and weak and was a metaphor for the struggle between earthly passions and the needs of the spirit (Rom 6:19, 7:5, 7:8). The word *flesh* symbolized the family relationship (Judg 9:2), referred to human nature (Jn 1:14), and referred to the Incarnation of Jesus, the Word made flesh who reconciled humanity with God (1 Tim 3:16; Rom 1:3).

FLOOD: In the Bible, a flood was a symbol for chaos and is the opposite of the order of creation. The story of the great Flood is a worldwide allegory for human sinfulness set in mythic time. In the Bible, the hero of the deluge story was Noah, who built an ark. The cycle of violence and humanity's sinfulness had infected the whole world (Gen 6:11–12). God grieved for the creation and intended to wash it clean with the Flood but saved Noah and his family from it (Gen 6—10). See also **Ararat; Myth in the Bible; Noah.**

FOOL: In the Bible, one who was without wisdom or who rebelled against or denied the existence of God or God's law of life (Prov 10:8, 17:24).

FOREIGNER: A non-Israelite stranger passing through, or even temporarily residing in, Israelite territory, also called an alien or stranger. The Law demanded that the foreigner receive hospitality, but a foreigner could not participate in Israelite religious rites (Ezek 44:9). In business with foreigners, the Law permitted an Israelite to charge interest on loans (Deut 23:20). The Israelites considered foreigners suspect because of their worship of other gods. The Israelites were concerned that they would be corrupted by having too close contact with foreigners. However, Jesus honored foreigners as a model of gratitude (Lk 17:18). The mission of Christ eliminated alienation among all people, including those considered aliens and strangers (Eph 2:19).

FORESKIN: In the Jewish ritual of circumcision, the loose skin on the top to the penis of a male infant is surgically removed when he is eight days old (Lev 12:3). The circumcision of the foreskin is a symbol of the Covenant relationship between God and the people of Israel (Gen 17:11). The need for circumcision became a point of contention in the early Church. See also **Circumcision.**

FORGIVENESS: A healing gift from God that restores unity. Forgiveness provides release from the burden of guilt and liberates humans from the bondage of sin. Jesus offered his very life so that humanity could know the grace of forgiveness (Mt 26:27–28). Jesus commissioned his Apostles to offer others his forgiveness (Jn 20:22–23; Mt 16:19). The followers of Jesus were called to forgive one another (Mt 5:23–24) and to turn to God with contrite hearts (Ps 51:17).

As the Gospel of Christ spread throughout the world, the Church offered forgiveness and absolution through the sacraments of Baptism and of Penance and Reconciliation (Col 1:14; 2 Cor 5:17; Eph 1:7).

FORNICATION: Sexual intercourse between unmarried partners. In the Old Testament, an unmarried couple who entered into a sexual relationship had to marry (Deut 21:28–29). Fornication was a sin condemned in the New Testament (Acts 15:29; 1 Cor 6:18).

FORTITUDE: A virtue that refers to courage, firmness, and conviction of one's values and beliefs. Fortitude is strength of character and is listed as one of the seven gifts of the Holy Spirit (Wis 8:7).

FOWL: Edible birds. Hens, cocks, chickens, quail, and other birds that were not scavengers were considered clean. Eagles, vultures, buzzards, ravens, hawks, owls, and other scavengers were considered unclean (Deut 14:11–20). Jesus used the image of the hen gathering her chicks under her wing for his desire to protect and hold safe the ancient city of Jerusalem (Lk 13:34).

FRANKINCENSE (frang´kuhn-sens): Perfumed resin collected from trees in Arabia and Palestine (Ex 30:34). Frankincense was offered as sacrifice in religious rites (Lev 2:1, 6:15). When burned, frankincense released a beautiful fragrance and was offered as a sacrifice of sweet-smelling smoke to God. It was one of the gifts the Wise Men gave to the infant Jesus (Mt 2:11). The smoke rising from frankincense was seen as a symbol of prayers rising to God (Ps 141:2; Rev 5:8, 8:3).

FRUIT OF THE SPIRIT: When one has opened one's heart and life to God, the Holy Spirit blesses that person with the gifts of the Spirit. Those gifts produce fruit, that is, positive virtues in a person's life. The Letter to the Galatians named the fruit of the Spirit: "love, joy, peace, patience, kindness, generosity, faithfulness, gentleness, and self-control" (5:22–23). See also **Gifts of the Spirit.**

FULLER: A slave or freedman who worked in cloth and leather. The fuller was a craftsman who collected urine from the homes of the populace and mixed it with lye and other chemicals to bleach cloth white (Mk 9:3). The fuller was considered lower class—untouchable and unclean.

G

GABRIEL (gay´bree-uhl): His name meant "God's strength." Gabriel was an archangel who appeared several times in the Bible. Gabriel explained to Daniel the meaning of the prophecies of the coming of the Son of Man (Dan 8:16, 9:21–27). Gabriel announced to Zechariah that Elizabeth would give birth to John the Baptist (Lk 1:18). Gabriel appeared to the Virgin Mary, announced that the time of Emmanuel was at hand, asked if Mary would mother the Messiah, and revealed that Mary had found favor with God (Lk 1:26). See also **Annunciation; Archangel.**

GALATIA (guh-lay´shuh): In 280 BC, the king of Bithynia bade a Celtic people, the Gauls, to migrate to Macedonia to serve as soldiers against Asia Minor. The territory became known as Galatia. By 25 BC, Galatia had become a Roman province that also included other southern territories. Paul, Silas, and Timothy ministered in Galatia (Acts 16:6; Gal 4:13; Acts 18:23). Saint Paul's letter to the Christian community in Galatia is revered as one of the most significant documents of early Christianity.

GALILEE, GALILEAN (gal´uh-lee) (gal´uh-lee´uhn): A small region in northern Palestine, west and north of the Sea of Galilee. The people of Upper Galilee (Acts 9:31), who were once called Israelites, were called Galileans. They were far away from the priestly rulers who resided in Jerusalem of Judea in the south. The Galileans had spent much of their history as marginalized peasantry, small villagers without resident authority. In the time of Jesus, Galilee was the headquarters of Herod Antipas, who was the tetrarch, one of the four Jewish rulers, of Galilee and Peraea.

In the time of Jesus, all of Palestine was an occupied territory of Rome. Rome particularly disliked the Galileans, as they repeatedly asserted their independence and vowed their loyalty to their Jewish traditions and to God. Rome thought of them as rebels, anarchists, and prophets. Jesus and his disciples, with the exception of Judas Iscariot, were all from Galilee (Mt 4:15; Lk 22:59). See also **Galilee, Sea of; Herod the Great.**

GALILEE, SEA OF (gal'uh-lee): In the time of Jesus, northern Israel was called Galilee. The great lake of the region—fed by the Jordan River—was called the Sea of Galilee. Its shore and waters were filled with life. Jesus made the sea and its surrounding communities the focus of his early mission. On the shores of Galilee, Jesus called Peter, Andrew, James, and John to be fishers of humanity (Mk 1:16–20). The Sea of Galilee was also known as the Lake of Gennesaret and Sea of Gennesaret (Lk 5:1), as well as the Sea of Tiberias (Jn 6:1). See also **Galilee, Galilean.**

GAMALIEL (guh-may'lee-uhl): The much-revered Rabbi Gamaliel was renowned for his loyalty to God and to the teachings of Torah. He is forever honored for unknowingly nurturing the birth of the Christian church. At Pentecost, as Peter and the Apostles proclaimed Jesus as resurrected Lord, they were arrested and dragged before the Sanhedrin. The Sanhedrin demanded immediate execution of these Apostles.

Rabbi Gamaliel recommended caution and suggested that the group free the Apostles (Acts 5:34–40). He said that if their mission was from God, there would be no way to stop it; and if not, it would vanish from the earth. Gamaliel's protection of the original Apostles from an untimely death protected the future of the mission of Christ.

GAME: People of all cultures and ages enjoy entertainment. The Scripture described various games that children played (Zech 8:5; Mt 11:16), games designed to hone the skills of combat (Judg 20:16; 1 Chr 12:2), and games that were hosted as public spectacles (Ps 19:5; Eccl 9:11).

Public games were core to Greek and Roman social life, a source of national pride. Athletic feats of wrestling and racing were considered noble ventures. In the time of Christ, the games of Rome were called spectacles. The Romans supported the circus, the gladiatorial competitions with wild beasts, and cultic blood baths between human beings. Paul often used athletic images to encourage others (1 Cor 15:32; Phil

2:16; 1 Tim 6:12).

GAZA (gay´zuh): A city on the shores of the Mediterranean Sea. As early as 1600 BC, Gaza had economic and political connections to Egypt (Gen 10:19; Josh 15:47). Gaza was Philistine territory remembered for its idolatries (Jer 25:20). In Gaza, Samson pulled down the temple of Dagon, killed the Philistines, and then met his death (Judg 16:21–30). In the New Testament, the Holy Spirit told the evangelist Philip to take the desert road from Jerusalem to Gaza (Acts 8:26), where he met an un-named Ethiopian eunuch.

GEHENNA (gi-hen´uh): A word used as a simile for hell. The valley of Hinnom, where children were burned in the fires of Baal Molech, was called Gehenna (Lev 20:2–5; Jer 19:2–6). In the time of Jesus, Gehenna was the name of an eternally burning dump outside Jerusalem where bodies of animals and criminals were cast into the flames. Jesus used the image of Gehenna as the unquenchable fires of hell, the ultimate destiny for those who refused to repent of evil (Mk 9:43–47; Mt 5:22–30). See also **Hades; Hell.**

GENEALOGY: A type of family tree. More than a bloodline, a genealogy was a literary form used as a proclamation to make connections with important ancestors. The genealogy of Jesus not only proclaimed his ancestry, but also placed him and his followers in the family of Abraham. The early Christian community chanted the genealogy to affirm that salvation history—beginning with Abraham—was fulfilled in Jesus (Mt 1:1–17). The genealogy of Jesus connects all Christians with a family of honor; we have become brothers and sisters with the saints of the Old Testament in the great family of Christ (Rom 4:16–17).

Catholics across the world proclaim the genealogy of Christ in the Vigil mass on Christmas. See also **House.**

GENTILE (jen´til): A non-Jewish person. In Scripture, the Gentiles were the uncircumcised, those who did not honor the God of the Torah. In the New Testament, Saint Paul and other evangelists reached out to the Gentiles, baptizing them into the family of God.

GERIZIM, MOUNT (ger´uh-zim): The site of the Samaritan temple erected in the fourth century BC. Gerizim was the highest mountain in Samaria, and pilgrimages to the Gerizim temple rivaled pilgrimages to the Jerusalem Temple. For the Jews outside Samaria, however, it was considered a site of blasphemy, for non-Samaritan Jews felt that true worship could be held only in the Temple in Jerusalem.

When Jesus met with the woman at a well in Samaria, this very temple on Mount Gerizim was her concern (Jn 4:20). She reminded Jesus of the ancient hostilities between Jerusalem and Samaria. Jesus proclaimed that a new age was coming when people would worship in neither place but would worship in "spirit and truth" (Jn 4:22–24).

GETHSEMANE (geth-sem´uh-nee): A Hebrew name meaning "the oil press." The garden of Gethsemane was a grove near the Mount of Olives where Jesus gathered with his disciples to pray and prepare for his Crucifixion on Calvary (Mk 14:32; Jn 18:1). John's Gospel placed Gethsemane across the Kidron valley near Jerusalem on the western slope of the Mount of Olives.

GIDEON (gid´ee-uhn): His name meant "the cutter." Gideon was the fifth judge of Israel, also known as Jerubbaal. When Gideon encountered the angel of the Lord, he converted from worshipping foreign gods to worshipping the true God of Israel (Judg 6:11–24). With zeal, Gideon destroyed the altars of Asherah and poles of Baal. The people planned to kill Gideon, but his father, Joash, quelled the crowd, pointing out that if Baal was really a god, he'd deal with Gideon himself (Judg 6:28–32).

Gideon was not a model of faith. His story shows the results of backsliding into idolatry. When Gideon's faith was strong, he united the tribes, listened to the advice of angels, and conquered the Midianites; but when he lost faith and made idols to Baal, the people followed him into idolatry (Judg 8:22–28). See also **Judge.**

GIFTS OF THE SPIRIT: The Holy Spirit empowers humanity with grace, power, and tools that support spiritual growth, happiness, and the wisdom to build just societies. In ancient times, the gifts of the Spirit were recognized as understanding, knowledge, counsel, piety, fortitude, wisdom, and fear of the Lord (Isa 11:1–3). The early Christian experience added speaking with tongues, casting out devils, and healing (1 Cor 12:27–31). See also **Fruit of the Spirit.**

GILEAD (gil´ee-uhd)**:** Word meaning "rugged." Gilead described the land east of the Jordan River. Gilead was situated on a major trade route traveled by caravans of Ishmaelites. The balm of Gilead became legendary in its value as a precious commodity for perfume, anointing, and restorative medicinal salve (Jer 8:22).

GLEAN: According to the Law of Moses, the edges of fields were to be left untouched so the poor could harvest the remnant crops (Lev 19:9; Ruth 2:2). This gathering of the leftover harvest was called gleaning.

GLORY, GLORIFY: The root of the word *glory* means "weight" or "importance." So to have glory is to have weight or importance; thus, God has glory. God's glory could be seen in the cloud and fire that led the Israelites out of Egypt (Ex 24:16–17), and it was seen in the tabernacle and the Temple (Ps 24:7–10). Christians proclaim that Jesus is the very face of the glory of God (Jn 1:14).

All created beings are called to give glory to God (Ps 29:1). To glorify God means to honor God by showing praise, love, and commitment (1 Cor 6:20, 10:31). Jesus' presence in believers causes them to reflect God's glory (Col 1:27).

GOD: The Supreme Being, the Creator, the Sustainer, the Governor, and the Preserver of all that is (Ps 136:2–9). God is the awe-inspiring Elohim of the Israelites and Lord of Life, the "I AM WHO I AM" (Ex 3:14), the Yahweh of Judah. God is the author of Revelation and the source of all salvation, mercy, and justice (Jer 31:31–34). God is love (1 Jn 4:16). Jesus is God revealed as love in flesh (Jn 15:9–10). Christians believe that there is one God, who exists as a Trinity of divine Persons in relationship: the Father, Son, and Holy Spirit (Mt 28:19). See also **Adonai; Elohim; El Shaddai; Trinity; Yahweh.**

GOG: The word *gog* evolved from the name of a king of Lydia from the seventh century BC. Gog evolved into an apocalyptic figure, a terror from the north, a personification of evil who battles the forces of God (Ezek 38—39; Rev 20:8).

GOLDEN CALF: Symbol of idolatry and slavery and how foolish people can be when they fear the unknown. While waiting for Moses to return from Mount

Sinai after a long absence, the Israelites began to grow fearful. They appealed to Aaron to make them a god to worship. Aaron created a golden calf from their jewelry. The people worshipped and offered sacrifice to the idol and celebrated at the very foot of Mount Sinai, the sacred mountain. Upon his return, Moses was greatly angered upon seeing this idolatry and broke the tablets of the Law he had brought from the mountaintop (Ex 32). God threatened to withdraw his presence from the people because of their idolatry (Ex 33:3), but Moses interceded for mercy and forgiveness (Ex 33:12–16).

GOLGOTHA (gol´guh-thuh): A Hebrew word meaning "place of the skull." Golgotha was an execution site outside the walls of the city of Jerusalem where the Romans crucified insurgents and criminals. Golgotha was the site where Jesus died on the cross (Mt 27:33). See also **Crucifixion.**

GOLIATH (guh-li´uhth): The Philistine warrior from Gath whom young David killed with a sling. The conquest took place in the Valley of Elah where the shepherd faced the well-trained Goliath. Two ancient versions of the story exist: one says Goliath was four cubits tall, or 6 feet, 9 inches; the other version says his height was six cubits, or 9 feet, 9 inches. Either way, David faced a grown man and is remembered as victorious (1 Sam 17). See also **David.**

GOMER (goh´muhr): Her name meant "complete." Gomer was the unfaithful wife of the prophet Hosea. The story of her unfaithful love was an allegory for God's faithful love of the people of Israel despite their infidelity. See also **Hosea.**

GOMORRAH: See **Sodom and Gomorrah.**

GOOD AND EVIL: The historic monotheistic religions—Judaism, Christianity, and Islam—understand good and evil as separate realities. Goodness bonds humanity to God and humans to one another. Evil is the fruit of idolatry and injustice (Wis 14:27). Evil is sin. It alienates humanity from God (Ps 15) and fractures human relationships (Gen 3:12). Evil even wounds the created order (Gen 3:18).

Although great lessons are learned from failure, the Scriptures teach that God does not will evil (Gen 1). Only goodness exists in the will of God. Evil is outside God's creative order and needs redemption. Justice, faithfulness, and love are needed to heal the corruption that evil causes (Mic 6:8).

GOSHEN (goh´shuhn): The land of the eastern Nile delta of Egypt where Joseph settled the family of Jacob (Gen 45—50). During the Exodus from Egypt, the land of Goshen was spared from the plagues because it was still home to the Israelites (Ex 8—9).

GOSPEL: An English translation of the Greek word *euangelion,* which means "good news." In the ancient world, a gospel was an announcement proclaiming that a new age had dawned, a new king was born, or enemies had been conquered. It represented justice, freedom, and protection from harm; good times were at hand (Isa 61:1).

Christians use the word *gospel* to refer to the Good News revealed through Jesus Christ: his life, teachings, death, and Resurrection. *Gospel* also refers to the four books written by the Evangelists Mark, Matthew, Luke, and John. They announce the Good News that Jesus Christ is Lord and savior and has conquered sin and death. See chart **Gospel Comparison.**

GOVERNOR: In the New Testament, a ruler of a Roman province. Rome appointed governors who had military and judicial control of the province they governed. Pontius Pilate was the governor of Judea when Jesus was arrested and crucified (Mt 27:2). Felix and Festus were governors of Judea when Paul was arrested (Acts 24:1—25:12).

GRACE: Concept referring to the covenant relationship of favor with God (Gen 6:8; Acts 20:24). The Hebrew concept of God, as well as Jesus' proclamation of the Kingdom, includes the awe-inspiring idea that God is in intimate relationship with humanity (Ex 33:11; Jn 15:1–17). God's grace is a free gift, given in love to sustain our being and to bring us to eternal life (Rom 5:12–21).

GREECE: A coastal country of southern Europe, located between the mountains of southern Europe, the Aegean Sea, and the Black Sea. Several hundred years before the birth of Christ, Greece was a collection of powerful city-states. They were centers of science, culture, and athletics. Rome conquered Greece in 146 BC.

The Greeks were very religious and devoted to their numerous gods. Greeks also worshipped an unknown god to make sure they hadn't forgotten any gods (Acts 17:23). Greece was one of the earliest centers of Christianity Paul ministered to. It was home to Luke's community (Acts 17:16–34).

GROVE: Some ancient peoples worshipped in groves of trees. The tree held its branches in the heavens and its roots securely within the earth. Trees were sacred; a group of sacred trees was called a grove, an Asherah, or a garden. *Asherah* was also the word for a wooden idol or sacred pillar. Asherah and Astarte were names for the Canaanite goddess—represented as a tree. See also **Asherah.**

GUILT: A word with many meanings in the Bible. One meaning was being responsible for committing a sin, an act of evil. Another meaning was the feeling of remorse for having committed a wrong. Sometimes, guilt applied just to a single person, at other times to a whole group of people, even an entire nation. The prophets often condemned the whole nation for being guilty of idolatry.

Sinful behavior created the need to be washed clean through reconciliation and restitution. In the New Testament, Saint Paul taught that all people were guilty before God (Rom 1:18—2:16). The breach between people and God caused by sin needed the love of Christ to

Gospel Comparison

	Mark	Matthew	Luke	John
Date Written	AD 65–70	AD 75–80	AD 80–85	AD 90–110
Writer	A second generation Christian, possibly a follower of Peter; traditionally, the John Mark mentioned in the Book of Acts.	An unknown Jewish Christian, traditionally, the Apostle Matthew.	A Gentile Christian, traditionally, Luke the physician and Paul's traveling companion.	The Beloved Disciple, the Apostle John, or his disciple.
Images of Christ	The Suffering Servant of God, Son of Man, Son of God, Messiah and Lord.	Teacher and prophet like Moses, Son of God, Son of Man, Messiah and Lord.	Great Healer, merciful, compassion for the poor, Son of God, Son of Man, Messiah and Lord.	Logos, Word of God, Son of God, Son of Man, Lamb of God, Redeemer, Messiah and Lord.
The Author's Community	A Gentile Christian community (in Rome?) undergoing persecution.	A Jewish Christian community (in Antioch, Syria?).	Written to Theophilus (meaning "lover of God"), who possibly represents any Christian.	Community of Jews, Gentiles, and Samaritans.
Theological Themes	Jesus shows that the suffering in our lives can be a source of grace when united to the sufferings of Christ.	Jesus teaches what it means to be a member of the Kingdom of God. He prepares his followers to continue his teaching and ministry.	Jesus heals longstanding divisions among people. He calls his followers to have a special compassion for those excluded from wealth and power.	Jesus is the divine Son of God, the image of God in flesh. Salvation is available for those who believe in Jesus and commit their lives to him. You are either for him or against him, you must decide.
Historical Situation	The Romans subdued armed Jewish rebellions. Christians experienced persecution in Rome.	Written after Romans had destroyed Jerusalem, including the Third Temple.	Written when the persecution of Jews and Christians was intensifying.	Emperor Domitian deified himself and mandated that all people worship him. Jewish leaders banned Christians from the synagogues.
Caesars	Nero (AD 54–68)	Vespasian and Titus (AD 70–81)	Domitian (AD 81–96)	Domitian (AD 81–96), Nerva (AD 96–98), and Trajan (AD 98–117)

cleanse our souls from guilt and shame and to reconcile us with God and each other (Rom 5:1–11).

H

HABAKKUK (huh-bak´uhk): An Old Testament prophet, contemporary with the prophets Jeremiah and Zephaniah. Habakkuk lived between 650 and 627 BC. He warned of the coming Babylonian Captivity (Hab 3:8).

The Book of Daniel contains a legendary story: Habakkuk was visited by an angel who told him to feed Daniel in the lion's den. The angel carried Habakkuk by his hair to Babylon, where he fed Daniel and his companions. Then the angel returned Habakkuk to his home (Dan 14:33–39).

HABIRU (hah-bee´roo): See **Hebrew.**

HADES (hay´deez): A Greek image of hell, the fiery pit, the abyss (Wis 1:14). See also **Gehenna; Hell.**

HAGAR (hay´gahr): Her name meant "wanderer" in Arabic and "splendid one" in Ethiopian. The Egyptian Hagar was Sarah's personal slave. Because of Sarah's

barrenness, she offered Hagar to her husband, Abraham, as a concubine (Gen 16—21). Sarah treated her with contempt, and Hagar ran away to the wilderness of Shur. There she met an angel who told her that her son would have a special destiny. Hagar returned to Abraham and Sarah, where she gave birth to Ishmael. God called Hagar to be the matriarch of the great nation of the Arabs. She is the first person after Abraham to have an encounter with God. Her son Ishmael became the patriarch of the Arab peoples (Gen 16, 21:8–21). See also **Ishmael.**

HAGGAI (hag´i): A Judean prophet of the sixth century BC. Haggai is remembered for encouraging the Hebrew remnant population in the rebuilding of the Temple at Jerusalem.

HALLELUJAH (hal´uh-loo´yuh): Word formed from combining a short version of *Yahweh* with the root word *hallel*, which means "to give praise." Thus, *hallelujah* is a liturgical religious cry of joy that means "praise to our God" (Rev 19:1–8). *Hallelujah* is found most often in the Psalms, where it is translated "Praise the Lord." The Greek form of the word is *alleluia.*

HAMAN (hay´muhn): See **Esther.**

HANDMAID: A female servant or personal slave, also translated as "slave girl" or "servant" (Gen 16:1; Ruth 3:9; Lk 1:48).

HANNAH (han´uh): Her name meant "grace and compassion." Hannah lived in the last years before the Israelite monarchy (1100 BC). Hannah was barren at a time when a woman's primary value was in childbearing. To add to Hannah's despair, Peninnah, the second wife of Hannah's husband, Elkanah, mothered children and was quite boastful about her good fortune.

In Shiloh, during the annual sacrifices, Hannah prayed with such passion that the priest Eli accused her of being drunk. Hannah believed that God heard her prayer. She vowed that when she conceived, she'd dedicate the child as a Nazirite (1 Sam 1—20). Her son, Samuel, became a judge and prophet who anointed Hebrew messiahs and kings (1 Sam 1:1—2:10). The "Song of Hannah" was a proclamation of justice and praise that affirmed God's preferential heart for the poor and forgotten ones (1 Sam 2:1-10). The New Testament prayer known as the Magnificat or the "Song of Mary" was composed in the tradition of Hannah's song (Lk 1:51-53). See also **Barren; Nazirite; Samuel.**

HARAN (hair´uhn): A city on the Balikh River in southern Turkey. In ancient times, Haran was an oasis for nomads on caravan who prepared to cross the Euphrates River on their way to Damascus in Syria. Haran is central to the story of the Hebrews. Abraham and Sarah left Haran and followed God's call to the Promised Land (Gen 12:5).

Years later, when Abraham sought a wife for his son, Isaac, he sent his servant to Haran, where he found Rebekah (Gen 24). In the next generation, Rebekah directed her son Jacob to escape to Haran to hide from his brother Esau's rage over the issue of a stolen birthright blessing. There, Jacob was tricked and worked fourteen years of servitude in Haran to pay the bride price for Rachel and Leah (Gen 29).

HARLOT: See Prostitute.

HASMONEANS (haz´muh-nee´uhnz): Judas Maccabeus was the Jewish hero who resisted the abuse of the Syrian war-lord and Seleucid (Greek) king Antiochus Epiphanes (175–164 BC). Judas, whose family name was Hasmon, led the Jews to freedom. The rulers who followed in his family line were known as the Hasmoneans. They ruled Judea as high priests and kings from 142 to 63 BC. The Herods continued the Hasmonean line. See also **Maccabees; Mattathias Hasmon.**

HEAVEN: In the Old Testament, the expanse of space beyond the orbit of planet earth is called the heavens. The word *heaven* also expresses the ultimate destiny of those who are saved to spend eternal life with God. In heaven, we will be forever in God's presence, and all pain and sadness will be washed away (Rev 21:1–7). Souls in heaven will be in perfect communion with the Lord, the heavenly angels, and all the saints (1 Thes 4:13–18). See also **Eternal Life; Hell; Immortality.**

HEBREW (hee´broo): A descendant of Abraham and Sarah. The word *Hebrew* refers to the tribes of Semites who migrated from Ur to Haran, and into Egypt and Canaan. They were known in the ancient world as sojourners in the land. No one knows for sure where the word *Hebrew* comes from, but it may be related to the word *habiru*, which means "the unlanded wanderers" or "the foreigners." The Hebrew people were wandering tribal herders before settling in the Promised Land.

After the Exodus and the escape from Egypt, the Chosen People called themselves Israelites. At various times and places, however, including in some New Testament passages, the word *Hebrew* has still been used to designate someone who maintains the traditional Judaic heritage. See also **Israel, Israelite.**

HEBREW LANGUAGE (hee´br*oo*): A class of Semitic languages in which the Hebrew Scripture—or the Old Testament—was written. It is the language of Canaan spoken by the Israelites. Semitic languages were spoken throughout Palestine. In the time of Jesus, Hebrew was reserved for worship. Aramaic and Greek were spoken at home and in business. As a written language in biblical times, Hebrew had twenty-two consonants and no vowels. It was and still is read right to left.

HEBREW SCRIPTURES (hee´br*oo*): See **Old Testament.**

HEBRON (hee´bruhn): In Hebron, Abraham, Sarah, and Hagar lived under the oaks of Mamre (Gen 13:18). Sarah was buried near Hebron in a cave of Machpelah (Gen 23:17–20). Hebron was a city of Judah that lay twenty-three miles southwest of Jerusalem and Bethlehem on the main road to Beersheba. The Hebrew word *Hebron* is related to the word *haver,* or "friend," in honor of the patriarch Abraham, who was called "friend of God" (Jas 2:23). Hebron was also where King David made his home and was anointed king over Israel (2 Sam 2:1–4, 11).

HELL: The state of eternal separation from God. Hell is not mentioned in the Old Testament, but it is mentioned several times in the New Testament as a place of punishment for sin (Mt 5:22, 23:15; 2 Pet 2:4). Hell is often thought of as a place of eternal fire and suffering (Isa 66:24). This may be partially because Jesus based his images of hell on Gehenna, the eternally burning city dump outside the walls of Jerusalem. Revelation contains images of an eternal lake of fire (Rev 20:14–15).

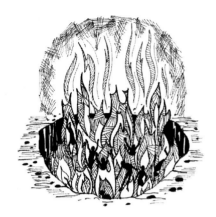

Jesus taught that without repentance, sin steals a person's joy and destiny with God in paradise. Ultimately, hell is a state of existence in which people exclude themselves from God by the choices they make. See also **Eternal Life; Gehenna; Hades; Sheol.**

HELLENISM (hel´uh-niz´uhm): Word referring to the acceptance of Greek culture, language, and traditions. After Alexander the Great conquered the Mediterranean Sea and Middle Eastern world, his reign resulted in Greek culture, religion, customs, and language being spread across the West. This Hellenization lasted 600 years. One result was the translation of the Hebrew Scriptures into the Greek language, a version called the Septuagint. The New Testament was written in Greek because of the influence of Hellenism. See also **Septuagint.**

HEROD (her´uhd): The family name of the Judean rulers of Palestine in power from 55 BC until the end of the first century AD. Antipater was the grand patriarch of the Herods. He served as military commander (103–76 BC) under the Hasmoneans. His son Antipater, or Antipas, was a soldier and diplomat who won favor with Julius Caesar, for which he was given the rule of Judea in 47 BC. Antipas and his wife, Cypros, had four sons and a daughter. One of the sons was Herod the Great, who was appointed King of the Jews. See also **Herod Antipas; Herod the Great.**

HEROD AGRIPPA I (her´uhd uh-grip´uh): Herod Agrippa (AD 37–44) was the son of Aristobulus and Bernice and the grandson of Herod the Great. He was tetrarch, one of the four rulers, of Palestine and used the title king. He was an enemy of the early Church, martyred the Christian leader James the elder, and imprisoned Saint Peter (Lk 3:1; Acts 12:1–19).

HEROD ANTIPAS (her´uhd an´tee-puhs): Antipas (4 BC–AD 39), the son of Herod the Great, was educated in Rome. He is not to be confused with the first Herod Antipas, who ruled before Christ's birth. In the time of Christ, Antipias served as tetrarch (king) of Galilee and Peraea (Lk 23:7). While married to Phasaelis, Antipas met and seduced his half brother Philip's wife, Herodias. John the Baptist condemned the adultery (Mt 14:3–4).

Scripture suggests that Antipas abused and shamed his stepdaughter Salome and used her dancing to satisfy his lust, leading to the arrest, imprisonment, and murder of John the Baptist (Mt 14:1–12). Herod Antipas is remembered as the Judean puppet of Rome who judged, mocked, and turned Jesus over to Pontius Pilate to be condemned to death (Lk 23:7–12). See also **Herod; Herod the Great.**

HEROD THE GREAT (her´uhd): King of Judea from 37 to 4 BC by decree of Rome. Herod's reign was one of economic prosperity, social stability, and major building campaigns. He built numerous cities, palaces, and military forts including Masada, Antonia, and Herodium; the cities of Caesarea and Sebaste, in honor of Augustus; structures in Hebron; and numerous towers and fortifications in Jerusalem. He rebuilt and refurbished the Temple of David. Herod is remembered in the Scripture as the cruel tyrant who orchestrated the Slaughter of the Innocents in an attempt to murder the infant Messiah (Mt 2:1–22).

When he died, eaten internally by worms, Herod's kingdom was divided among his sons. Philip ruled the land east of the Jordan River, Caesarea Philippi, and Bethabara. Antipas had Galilee and Peraea. Archelaus ruled Samaria and Judea. See also **Herod Antipas; Galilee, Galilean; Salome.**

HERODIAS (hi-roh´dee-uhs): The daughter of Aristobulus and Bernice. Herodias married Herod Philip I and had a daughter, Salome. While in Rome, her husband's brother, Herod Antipas, seduced her to leave Philip and become his illicit wife. John the Baptist condemned the marriage as unlawful. Herod Antipas had John imprisoned. At Herod's birthday party, Herodias had Salome dance and ask for the head of John the Baptist (Mt 14:1–11).

HEZEKIAH (hez´uh-ki´uh): The twelfth king of Judah (the southern kingdom), the son of Ahaz and Abijah (727–698 BC). Hezekiah's name meant "God strengthens." Hezekiah was a model king: "There was no one like him among all the kings of Judah" (2 Kings 18:5). Hezekiah was a reformer who worked to heal ancient wounds between Israel and Judah. He sent couriers throughout all Israel and Judah, inviting the people to return to the Lord and welcoming them in Jerusalem to celebrate Passover (2 Chr 29—31).

A testament to Hezekiah's goodness and faithfulness was God's faithful response to Hezekiah. During an Assyrian invasion, the angel of the lord defeated 185,000 Assyrian warriors in response to Hezekiah's prayer (2 Kings 19:35–36; 2 Chr 32:20–22). Hezekiah was also remembered for drilling the tunnel of Siloam that protected Jerusalem's water supply while under siege (2 Kings 20:20; 2 Chr 32:3–4).

HIGH PLACE: Both the Hebrews and the Canaanites established places of worship on high ground (Gen 12:7–8; 1 Kings 13:32). The Caananite high places often included practices of the fertility rites and human sacrifices offered to Baal Molech and Asherah. Over the centuries, the Hebrews destroyed the high places of the Canaanites (Deut 12:2–3).

HIGH PRIEST: Priests were Israelite religious officials who offered sacrifices to God on behalf of the people. The high priest held the most important position; he supervised the other priests and presided over the most important religious ceremonies. Aaron was the first high priest, set apart for this call (Ex 29:4–7). He wore special vestments, including the ephod with the Urim and Thummim (Ex 28). Only the high priest was worthy to enter the holy of holies, which was the sacred center of worship in the Temple. The high priest entered the holy of holies only once a year, on the great Day of Atonement (Lev 16). The Letter to the Hebrews described Jesus as the perfect high priest, who by offering himself has fulfilled the high priest's role for all time (Heb 7:26–28, 8:23–28). See also **Annas and Caiaphas; Ephod; Priest; Urim and Thummim.**

HISTORICAL CRITICISM: See **Exegesis.**

HITTITE (hit´tit): One of the three tribes of ancient Palestine and Syria. The Hittites were a tribe of warriors credited with inventing iron weapons. They ruled most of Syria down through modern-day Lebanon from 1650 to 1200 BC. The invasion of the Sea Peoples (Philistines) led to the Hittites' demise. During the Israelite monarchy, the Hittites lived north of Galilee in the mountains of Judah and in the region of the Euphrates River and Damascus. They were not a major power.

HOLOFERNES (hol´uh-fuhr´neez): Assyrian general decapitated by the Hebrew hero Judith (Jdt 13:4–8). See also **Judith.**

HOLY ONE: Title referring primarily to God, the Holy One of Israel (1 Sam 2:2; Isa 1:4). Sometimes, the title referred to angels or messengers of God (Deut 33:2–3). In the New Testament, the demons and Peter identified Jesus as the Holy One (Mk 1:24; Jn 6:69).

HOLY ORDERS: One of the seven sacraments of the Catholic Church. The source of the sacrament in the Scriptures was the moment when Jesus gathered his Apostles to himself, breathed on them, and said, "Receive the Holy Spirit" (Jn 20:22). In this way, he set them aside for a special service of evangelism and sacramental ministry. In Holy Orders, men are ordained as priests and deacons for the service of the Church. They are set apart by anointing with holy oil and the laying on of hands. They are called to give their lives to Christ, to serve the church, to heal the sick, and to free those in bondage. See also **Bishop; Deacon; Priest; Sacrament.**

HOLY SPIRIT: The second person of the Trinity. The Father, Son, and Spirit are revealed in Scripture as one God. In the Old Testament, the Holy Spirit was sometimes called "wind" or "breath," all variations of the same Hebrew word, *ruah*. Thus in the Old Testament, the Spirit was the creative aspect of God (Gen 1:2; Ps 33:6; Ezek 37:1–10), a source of inspiration and power (1 Sam 11:6; 2 Chr 24:20; Isa 61:1), and God's presence in the community (Ezek 36:26–27).

In the New Testament, the Holy Spirit was more clearly seen. The Spirit was the Paraclete and Advocate, who empowered, inspired, and formed the mission of the Apostles (Lk 2:25–27; Jn 14:16–17; 1 Jn 2:1). This Comforter and Spirit of Truth will counsel and lead the Church until the end of time (Jn 14:26, 16:7–14).

The presence of the Holy Spirit can be experienced through the manifestation of the Spirit's gifts: fortitude, wisdom, understanding, knowledge, fear of the Lord, counsel, and piety (Isa 11:1–3), and praying in tongues, healing, and casting out demons (Mk 16:17–18; Acts 19:6; 1 Tim 4:14). See also **Paraclete; Spirit; Trinity.**

HOMOSEXUALITY: A nonbiblical word that originated in modern times to describe sexual attraction to and sexual activity with a person of one's own gender. In the Bible, homosexual behavior was condemned (Lev 18:22; Rom 1:26–27). There is, however, considerable scholarly debate about how to interpret these condemnations in their cultural context. Today, the Church distinguishes between homosexual orientation and homosexual activity—a distinction not made in the Bible. Homosexual orientation is sexual attraction to the same sex and is not considered wrong if it is not acted upon.

HONOR AND SHAME: In the world in which Jesus lived, the possession of honor and the avoidance of shame were essential core values that drove private and public interaction. To possess honor was of the highest value. Without honor, a person had no dignity.

Mediterranean cultures developed strategies to preserve the insider as honorable and outsider as shamed. One shaming strategy was to ask an opponent a question he could not answer. This explains why the scribes and Pharisees were always trying to ask Jesus questions he couldn't easily answer. If they could take away his honor, they would also take away his popularity. However, they actually allowed Jesus to gain more honor, since he often answered their questions with clever replies—something that increased a person's honor in other people's eyes.

HOREB, MOUNT (hor´eb): An alternative name for Mount Sinai. The northern people from Israel used Mount Horeb (Ex 3:1), while the southern people from Judah called God's holy mountain Mount Sinai (Ex 19:18–25). See also **Sinai, Mount.**

HOSANNA (hoh-zan´uh)**:** A well-known proclamation meaning "Lord save us!" When Jesus of Nazareth triumphantly entered Jerusalem as Messiah, the multitude waved palms and begged the Redeemer to save them from the occupation of Rome as they chanted "Hosanna"(Mt 21:9). Two thousand years later, on Palm Sunday, the congregations of every Christian church across the earth wave palms and chant "Hosanna."

HOSEA (hoh-zay´uh)**:** A prophet of Israel who, after the destruction by Assyria (721 BC), relocated to Judah and wrote the wisdom parables known as his prophecies. God told Hosea to marry the adulterous Gomer, who bore him three children. Their names reveal Hosea's heartache to come. The first son was named Jezreel, meaning "God sows"; his daughter was named Loruhamah, meaning "not pitied"; and his second son was named Lo-ammi, meaning "not my people" (Hos 1:4–9).

The story functioned as an allegory for the love between Israel and God. Hosea became the symbol for the Holy One, the betrayed lover. Gomer became the symbol for Israel in shame. Her betrayal symbolized the history of Israel's idolatry and injustice and adultery against God (Hos 5:3–4). The images of wounded love revealed Yahweh's compassion for Israel and Judah.

Hosea's love for Gomer, as God's love for Israel, was unconditional (Hos 11:8). If the people simply repented and returned to God, God offered redemption from death and rebirth (Hos 14). See also **Allegory; Gomer; Prophet.**

HOSPITALITY: Travelers and wanderers in the desert deserved access to water and food. Hospitality was a matter of life and death. The stranger, the outsider, the foreigner, or the sojourner who didn't have family was cared for within the Old Testament laws of hospitality (Deut 10:17–19). These laws were designed to protect travelers from death and to provide basic needs: food, water, and shelter.

HOST: A huge number of people or an army. The host of heaven was the stars of the skies. Ancient peoples, especially the Babylonians, thought the stars were gods. The Israelites knew them to be creations of God (Deut 4:19). Yahweh was called the Lord of Hosts (1 Sam 4:4), meaning that God the Creator held all of existence—including those whom the foreign nations feared as gods—in his hands.

HOUSE: A place to live. In the Bible, people lived in caves, tents, or buildings made of limestone, clay, straw, or other materials. Sometimes, these were two-story houses, with animals living downstairs and the people upstairs. In hot weather, people slept on the houses' flat roofs. The houses of the wealthy contained multiple rooms, courtyards, and walls with frescoes.

House also designates a family line. The House of David is the royal family line of the Jewish people. To share honor, especially with women, one would say that she was, or would become, a house. Tamar became a house in the line of Judah (Gen 38:6–30; Mt 1:3); Rahab became a house of the line of David (Josh 6:17; Mt 1:5), as did Ruth for her kindness to Naomi and faith in God (Ruth 4:18–21; Mt 1:5). See also **Genealogy.**

HULDAH (huhl´duh)**:** Like Miriam (Ex 15:20) and Deborah (Judg 4:4), Huldah was among the three women in the Old Testament called a prophet. She was a Temple prophet who spoke in the name of Yahweh during the reign of Josiah, the reformer (640–609 BC). King Josiah sought the counsel of Huldah to validate as the word of God a scroll that was found. Josiah feared the apocalyptic tone of the writing. Huldah proclaimed the text genuine and comforted the king (2 Kings 22:14–20). See also **Josiah.**

HUSBAND: In the ancient world, marriage was a contract between families that awarded the husband the possession and ownership of his wife or wives and children. The husband was responsible for their survival and held legal and moral control over his household. This is not to suggest that these unions were loveless, as Scripture offered the husband as a model of protection and loyalty (Gen 29:20). The image of a loving husband was used to describe God's longing for union with Israel. God's love for humanity was compared to the longing of a husband for the beloved wife (Hos 2:16).

In the New Testament, wives were counseled to submit to, be subject to, or obey, their husbands. This may sound strange in our culture, which emphasizes the partnership between husband and wife, but the counsel reflected the culture of the time. The same passages, however, also counseled husbands to love their wives as Christ loved the Church—an idea that would have been countercultural in its time (Eph 5:22–33; Col 3:18–19). See also **Wife.**

HYPOCRITE: An actor; a person who wears a mask and portrays a character that may or may not connect to the person's internal life. In the Gospel of Matthew, Jesus used the word *hypocrite* to refer to the Pharisees (Mt 23:13). He also warned his followers against all kinds of hypocrisy for effect and social approval, including giving alms, praying, and fasting (Mt 6:1–18). He also warned against the hypocrisy of judging others while ignoring one's own faults (Mt 7:1–5).

I

I AM: "I AM WHO I AM" was the name God called himself when talking to Moses from the burning bush (Ex 3:14). It expressed that God simply is, God has no beginning and no end, and everything else exists because of God. Yahweh, the most common name for God in the Old Testament, was probably based on that phrase.

The New Testament contained suggestions of this title in connection with Jesus. Jesus asked Peter, "Who do you say that I am?" And Peter said, "You are the Messiah, the Son of the living God" (Mt 16:16). In the Gospel of John, Jesus had a series of "I am" statements. He said, "I am the bread of life" (Jn 6:35), "I am the light of the world" (8:12), "I am the gate for the sheep" (Jn 10:7), "I am the good shepherd" (Jn 10:11), "I am the resurrection and the life" (Jn 11:25), "I am the way, and the truth, and the life" (Jn 14:6), and "I am the vine, you are the branches" (Jn 15:5). See also **Burning Bush; Moses; Yahweh.**

IDOL: An object of desire and worship, or the image of a deity. The Hebrew words we translate as "idol" meant "nothingness," "vanity," "a carved image," or "shameful entities." Statues of gods were commonly present in places of worship and often were also kept in places of honor in people's homes. While the statue or image was clearly not understood as being the god itself, it was often worshipped and treated as if it were the god. The commandments warned that relationships with idols were empty and worthless (Josh 24:14–18). Further, the worship of the idol known as Baal was connected to the detestable practices of human sacrifice and impure fertility rites (Ezek 16:36, 20:8, 37:23).

IDOLATRY: The worship of false gods or the love of anything more than the one, true God. Idolatry is a sin against the first commandment (Ex 20:2–6). The Scriptures reveal that humanity was created to find happiness in relationship with the one, true, living God and with one another (Deut 32:6).

Idolatry was a special concern in the Old Testament and connected to sins against justice. When the Israelites settled in the Promised Land, they were surrounded by peoples who worshipped gods other than Yahweh. These gods were sometimes called "the gods of the nations." The prophets condemned the practices of the gods of the nations because they offered no covenant love, demanded human sacrifice, and practiced cultic prostitution. Yahweh offered the Law to free the people: "Loving the LORD your God, obeying him, and holding fast to him . . . means life to you" (Deut 30:19–20). See also **Asherah; Baal.**

IDUMAEA (idy*oo*-mee´uh)**:** The land of Edom of Judea, southwest of the Dead Sea. Found in the Septuagint, *Idumaea* is the Greek form of *Edom.* Herod the Great was an Idumaeanite. See also **Edom, Edomite.**

IHS: The letters *IHS* are an ancient symbol for Jesus Christ. These are the first three letters of the Greek spelling of Jesus' name. They are also the first three letters of the Latin phrase *Iesus Hominum Salvator,* which means "Jesus, Savior of Humanity." Early Christians

used the letters *IHS* as a symbolic way of honoring the Lord as Redeemer.

As a symbol, the letters *IHS* are usually pictured with a cross. The symbol can be found in Christian art, as illustrations in the Scriptures and embroidered on sacred vestments worn by bishops, priests, and other ministers. See chart **The Titles of Jesus.** See also **Jesus Christ.**

IMAGE OF GOD: Our attempts to describe God are limited by human nature. As human beings, we have a tendency to project our own image onto the image of God. The nature of the Holy One is the greatest mystery, yet we by necessity perceive and speak of God in human terms, ideas, and language.

The Bible offers a variety of images of God that humans can understand: God is our rock (2 Sam 22:2–3), a good shepherd (Ps 23), a mother (Ps 131:2), a bridegroom (Isa 62:5), and a loving Father (Mt 6:9). These are only some of the many images used for God in the Scriptures. The Scriptures also tell us that God is reflected in the glories and power of the creation all around us (Ps 19; Rom 1:20). It is important to remember that all of these images of God are incomplete and imperfect—the reality of God is infinitely more than any one human image can describe.

We do have two images of God that stand above all others in the Bible. The New Testament tells us that the most perfect description for God is love (1 Jn 4:8) and the most perfect image of love is Jesus. Jesus Christ is the "image of the invisible God" (Col 1:14). To know Jesus is to know God because "in him all the fullness of God was pleased to dwell" (Col 1:19).

IMMANUEL (i-man´yoo-uhl): See **Emmanuel.**

IMMORTALITY: Eternal life or life after death. The Bible reveals a type of immortality that begins with the resurrection from the dead for those with faith in Christ Jesus. The Gospels teach that Jesus is the Resurrection and the Life who will call the righteous out of the grave on the last day (Jn 6:40; 1 Thess 4:13–18). The righteous will live with the Lord in heaven for all eternity, where God will dry all tears and death will be no more (Mt 22:23; Lk 18:29–30; Rev 21:4). We are reassured that our departed loved ones are with the Lord where we shall someday join them (1 Thes 4:13–18). See also **Eternal Life; Heaven; Resurrection.**

INCARNATION (in´kahr-nay´shuhn): From the Latin, meaning "to become flesh." *Incarnation* is the word for the biblical Revelation that Jesus is both fully God and fully human (Rom 8:32; 1 Tim 3:16; Heb 2:14–15).

INERRANCY: Without error in passing on the truth God reveals for our salvation. The Scripture is the word of God written in the words of human beings. The Spirit guided the original writers and editors who created the Scriptures to preserve the truth across the centuries.

This does not mean the Bible is completely without error in certain nonreligious facts. The human authors retained their full humanity in writing the books of the Bible, including the limitations of human knowledge and culture. Scholars have discovered inaccuracies or discrepancies in certain historical and geographical facts. This type of accuracy is not necessary for our salvation; the religious and moral truth God reveals is still inerrant.

Another element to inerrancy is that the Scripture is part of the Tradition of the Church, and the Church interprets the Scripture. Inerrancy also means the Holy Spirit will guide the Church through its leaders to interpret the Bible without error for each new generation of believers. See also **Apostolic Tradition; Inspiration.**

INHERITANCE PRACTICES: See **Birthright.**

INSPIRATION: Word meaning "breathed into" or "spirit filled." Throughout human history, the Holy Spirit has moved certain men and women to be God's instruments of grace to the world. In the case of Holy Scriptures, the Holy Spirit filled certain authors and editors and inspired them to write down the stories of faith that became the Bible. Through these authors, God revealed what God wanted the human race to know for its salvation. The Spirit also inspired the early Church in the selection of which books would become the Bible as we know it today. The Spirit continues to inspire people throughout history to see God speaking to us in the words of Scripture. See also **Canon; Inerrancy.**

ISAAC (i´zik): The son of Abraham and Sarah, the promised son of the covenant. Isaac's name meant "God's joke" or the "laughter of God," since he was born in his parents' old age. His very existence was a sign of God's continual love and favor toward the people of Israel. Isaac's life became a symbol of the uniqueness of the Hebrew people and their relationship to the God of life. Even so, Abraham was willing to sacrifice Isaac out of obedience to God (Gen 22), making Isaac a sign pointing to the sacrifice of Christ in the New Testament. God stopped Abraham from sacrificing Isaac, teaching that Yahweh did not desire child sacrifice like the false gods of other nations.

Isaac married Rebekah of Haran, and the two had twin sons, Jacob and Esau (Gen 21—25). The story of Isaac and Rebekah mirrored that of Abraham and Sarah. When famine struck the land, Isaac and Rebekah migrated to Gerar of the Philistines. Isaac presented Rebekah as his sister to King Abimelech, just as his father had done with Sarah in Egypt (Gen 26). These matriarchs were described as so beautiful that their men's lives were in danger because more powerful men might want to take them by force.

Isaac lived a long life, blessed his sons (Gen 27), died at Mamre, and was buried in the cave of Machpelah alongside his mother and father (Gen 35:27–29). See also **Abraham; Esau; Jacob; Patriarch; Rebekah; Sarah.**

ISAIAH (*i*-zay′yuh): The prophet Isaiah and his prophet wife lived in Jerusalem between 742 and 701 BC, as Assyria pillaged the northern kingdom of Israel (Isa 8:3). He feared that the land and the people would be destroyed.

Isaiah was called to serve in a most profound, mystic encounter with God: a vision of the Lord surrounded by seraphim who sang "Holy, holy, holy is the LORD of hosts; the whole earth is full of his glory" (Isa 6:3). In humility,

Isaiah proclaimed that he and the people had "unclean lips" (Isa 6:5). The angel purified his mouth with a fiery coal (Isa 6:6–7), and Isaiah heard the LORD ask, "Whom shall I send?" (Isa 6:8). Isaiah accepted the call and became a speaker of the truth, one who had the courage to call the kings to loyalty and obedience to God.

Isaiah's prophecies are among the great treasures of the Christian faith. The kingdom of Judah feared that it, too, would fall to foreign invaders. Isaiah proclaimed that a child would be born, Emmanuel, or "God with us" (Isa 7:14). In the promise of Emmanuel, Isaiah affirmed that God would protect and guide the Jewish people.

For hundreds of years after Isaiah's death, his disciples continued in his tradition, writing prayers, oracles, and stories of faith. Isaiah's original prophecies, along with his disciples' later work, constitute the Book of Isaiah in the Old Testament. See also **Prophet.**

ISHMAEL (ish´may-uhl): His name meant "God hears." Ishmael was born at Mamre to Abraham and the slave Hagar. Ancient law provided barren Sarah with offspring through the service of Hagar as concubine (Gen 16:3).

When after twelve years, Sarah gave birth to Isaac, she became jealous of the young Ishmael and his mother. Sarah turned them out into the desert of Beersheba with no more than a skin of water and some bread. As Hagar prepared for death, God heard Ishmael's cry (Gen 21:16–17). Hagar was comforted with an angelic visitation in which she was told that Ishmael would be the father of many nations. The two thrived in the wilderness of Paran between Canaan and the mountains of Sinai (Gen 21:8–21).

Ishmael became an expert with the bow and married an Egyptian wife, whom Hagar chose for him (Gen 21:21). He became a great desert chief and a father of the twelve Arab nations (Gen 25:12–18). His spiritual descendants are Muslims, the followers of the Islamic religion. See also **Hagar.**

ISHTAR (ish´tahr): Goddess worshipped in Mesopotamia from early times. Ishtar blended into many female deities in the Middle East. She was the goddess of war and eroticism and the source of the image of the serpent in the garden of Eden story. Her fruit was death. Over time, the word *Ishtar* became a common noun for "goddess." See also **Queen of Heaven.**

ISRAEL, ISRAELITE (iz´ray-uhl) (iz´ray-uh-l*it*): At the ancient site of Bethel, God affirmed the promises of the Covenant and gave Jacob a new name: Israel (Gen 35:9–15). Jacob, or Israel, became the symbol for the struggles of the Hebrew peoples across the millennia (Gen 35:14–15). His Hebrew descendants became known as Israelites.

Later, when David united the Twelve Tribes to form an independent nation, it was called Israel. After the civil war at the end of Solomon's reign, the northern tribes separated and became known as the kingdom of Israel. The southern tribes became known as the kingdom of Judah. Assyria destroyed the kingdom of Israel in 721 BC (2 Kings 17:5–18). See also **Hebrew; Jeroboam; Judah, Judea.**

ISSACHAR (is´uh-kahr´): The ninth son of Jacob, the fifth by Leah. Issachar is the ancestor of one of the Twelve Tribes of Israel. The tribe settled between the Jezreel valley and the Jordan River valley.

J

JACOB (jay´kuhb): The patriarch of the Israelites, the second son of Isaac and Rebekah, the twin brother of Esau, and the father of the Israelite nation. In Hebrew, Jacob's name means "wrestles with God" (Gen 32:22–32). He is the symbol of the Israelite people who have struggled with God across their history. The name Jacob also suggests a trickster or a deceiver. At birth, he caught his brother Esau's heel and eventually overtook Esau's place as the chosen son. Jacob was the favorite son of his mother, Rebekah. Together, they plotted to steal the ancestral blessing from Esau and have Isaac bestow the inheritance and covenant blessings on Jacob (Gen 27).

While Jacob traveled to Haran to seek a wife, God first spoke to him at Bethel. There, he had a vision of angels going up and down a ladder that reached heaven (Gen 28:10–17). Years later, on Jacob's return from Haran, God reaffirmed the promises of the covenant with Abraham and renamed Jacob Israel. Jacob fathered twelve men and one woman. The patriarchs of the Twelve Tribes of Israel were his sons, mothered by four women: Rachel, Leah, Bilhah, and Zilpah (Gen 35:23–26). See also **Bilhah; Esau; Isaac; Laban; Leah, Patriarch; Rachel; Zilpah.**

JAEL (jay´uhl): Her name meant "the mountain goat." Jael was a war hero of Israel, a poor, nomadic tent woman. Her story is told within the ancient victory song of Deborah, which proclaimed Jael "most blessed of women" (Judg 5:24). Jael killed the warlord Sisera, who was fleeing for his life after his army's defeat by Deborah's troops. Jael welcomed Sisera into her tent, soothed him, comforted him, and fed him. As he slept, she took a mallet and drove a tent peg through his temple, killing him instantly (Judg 4:17–23). Thus the unlikely Jael, like David before the giant Goliath, defeated a strong and powerful warrior and became a protector of Israel.

JAIRUS (jay-i´ruhs): A leader in the synagogue at Capernaum. Jairus came to Jesus when his daughter was near death. The daughter died before Jesus arrived, but Jesus took her hand and raised her from the dead, his first miracle of bringing the dead back to life (Mk 5:22–43).

JAMES, THE APOSTLE: A common name in New Testament times. There may have been two Apostles who carried the name James. Possibly they are one and the same man.

The most frequently mentioned Apostle James is James the son of Zebedee and brother to the Apostle John (Mt 10:2). James and John are close associates of Jesus and are present with Jesus at the Transfiguration (Mt 17:1) and in the garden of Gethsemane (Mk 14:33). Jesus nicknamed James and John the "sons of thunder" (Mk 3:17). Herod Agrippa martyred James for his faith (Acts 12:1–2).

Another Apostle James was the son of Alphaeus. This could be James, called the brother of the Lord (Mt 10:3, 13:55). Little else is known about him. See also **Apostle; John the Apostle.**

JAMES THE BROTHER OF THE LORD: A James, called the brother of the Lord, was the leader of the Church in Jerusalem (Mt 13:55; Acts 15:13, 21:17–26). He may also have been James the son of Alphaeus (Mt 10:3). The exact relationship of this James to Jesus is disputed. He could have been a cousin of Jesus or even a close friend, since the definition of kinship was very flexible in New Testament times. See also **Kinship.**

JEPHTHAH (jef´thuh): The eighth judge of Israel. Jephthah personified the idolatrous history of the land and the practices of the foreign nations. He was born the son of a harlot of Astarte. He was driven away from the clan and became an outlaw in a gang of mercenaries who raided the local population. When the Ammonites attacked, the elders of Gilead called Jephthah home to command the army and rule the land.

In preparation for battle, Jephthah vowed he would sacrifice as burnt offering whatever or whoever came out of his house. The victory was Jephthah's, but his only daughter was the first person to come out of his house to greet him. He tore his clothes and grieved at what he believed was his binding vow to God.

His daughter submitted to what she considered her unchangeable fate. She asked only that she be permitted to join her women friends in the mountains to weep for her virginity. Her story ended when two months later she returned home and her father fulfilled his vow (Judg 11). See also **Judge; Vow.**

JEREMIAH (jer´uh-mi´uh): The Hebrew prophet Jeremiah was born in 645 BC to a priestly family from Judah. When Jeremiah was just a boy, God called to him with words of profound love, "Before I formed you in the womb I knew you, and before you were born I consecrated you; I appointed you a prophet to the nations" (Jer 1:1–6). Like Moses, Jeremiah was afraid to speak in front of people. "I am with you," God promised (Jer 1:8). From that day, Jeremiah spoke the word of the LORD.

Jeremiah worked with a group of professional prophets who advised the king within the Temple complex in Jerusalem. Many were paid to tell the king what he wanted to hear. Jeremiah didn't fit in, and he wasn't well liked. Jeremiah was a man of truth, and his values were radically united to those of God. Like Isaiah, he condemned the Temple rites as shallow (Jer 6:19–20), prophesied against idolatry and injustice (Jer 22:1–5, 44:1–3), and held firm in faith even as the Babylonians overtook Judah.

Jeremiah suffered through the destruction of Jerusalem, the ruin of the sacred Temple, and the exile of his people. In captivity, he wrote that the Babylonians were able to conquer Judah because of the Judeans' sins of injustice and idolatry. Jeremiah was not popular for speaking the truth. He was threatened, persecuted, and left for dead (Jer 37:11–16). He made so many enemies that after the Judeans were freed from Babylon, he fled to Egypt with his secretary, Baruch. He disappeared from the pages of history, but not from the story of salvation. See also **Baruch; Prophet.**

JERICHO (jer´uh-koh): One of the oldest cities on earth, located six miles north of the Dead Sea and five miles west of the Jordan River. A stone shrine by an ancient spring dates the area's earliest occupation to 9000 BC. The infamous walls of Jericho were standing as early as 8000 BC. In the Bronze Age (3200–2000 BC), Jericho flourished, as it did in the time of the patriarchs (1900–1500 BC).

The children of Israel feared the ancient reputation of Jericho, but when the time of their immigration took place, God placed the city into the hands of the Israelites. The angels of the Lord came to give the directions for the conquest. At the sound of the trumpet, the people gave a mighty shout, the heavens opened, and the walls came tumbling down (Josh 6). The lesson intended is clear. There is nothing to fear when we are in a covenant relationship with God, the Lord of the universe. See also **Joshua; Rahab.**

JEROBOAM OF ISRAEL (jer´uh-boh´uhm): The first king of Israel, the northern kingdom. Jeroboam (922–901 BC) was the son of the widow Zeruah and Solomon's servant Nebat. After Solomon's death, the injustice of Solomon's son Rehoboam fueled a civil war that lasted sixty years. Jeroboam's revolt took ten of the Twelve Tribes north to Israel, where 'Jeroboam was proclaimed king. The resulting division between the northern and southern kingdoms was permanent (1 Kings 11:26—12:24).

Jeroboam built shrine centers in Shechem, Tirza, and Samaria, as well as on the sacred sites in Dan and Bethel. He finalized the schism by worshipping golden calves. He closed travel to Jerusalem during holy days and festivals, so the people of the north could not worship at the Temple. The shrines that Jeroboam established flourished until the reforms of Josiah. The Bible does not remember Jeroboam kindly (1 Kings 12:25—14:20). See also **Israel, Israelite; King; Rehoboam; Samaria.**

JERUSALEM (ji-r*oo*´suh-luhm)**:** Word meaning "city of peace." Jerusalem, the Holy City of Jews, Christians, and Muslims, has a most ancient history. Overlooking the area from a ridge, Jerusalem was situated in the central hill country of Palestine on the southern slope of Mount Moriah and Mount Zion. A settlement on the site was mentioned as early as 3000–2000 BC. Its earliest name, Salim, is recorded in Elba business documents of 2400 BC.

David brought the head of the giant Goliath into Jerusalem. David claimed Zion—as Jerusalem also was called—as "the city of David" (1 Chr 11:4–8). The citadel was later made his capital, the national, religious, and royal center of the Israelite people. David ceremoniously brought the ark of the Covenant to the city as a sign of Jerusalem's worthiness (1 Chr 11:7).

Solomon built the Temple of Jerusalem to honor his father, David, on the summit of Mount Moriah, the Temple mount. The city thrived and was spared in the Assyrian destruction of Israel, but it fell to the violence of the siege of the Babylonian king Nebuchadnezzar of 587 BC (2 Kings 25). Jerusalem was restored in the fourth century (Ezra 1:2–11) but overtaken by the Greeks under the leadership of Alexander the Great (333 BC).

After the Maccabean War, the Hasmoneans and their descendants, the Herodians, restored the city. Herod the Great rebuilt the city and Temple. The Magi, the Wise Men from the East, assumed that the newborn king resided in Jerusalem. In Jerusalem, Herod first heard of Christ's birth. Jesus' mother, Mary, and his foster father, Joseph, brought Jesus to the Temple in Jerusalem for Mary's purification and Jesus' presentation. In the Jerusalem Temple, Anna and Simeon prophesied about Jesus' mission (Lk 2:25–38).

Jesus began his teaching ministry in the Temple of Jerusalem at the age of twelve, where he astonished the doctors of the law with his wisdom and where his parents lost him for three days (Lk 2:41–47).

In Jerusalem, the Pharisees and Sadducees heard of Jesus' teachings and were outraged by his presumption of relationship with God (Mt 15:1). Jesus told his followers that the Son of Man would suffer at the hands of the authorities in Jerusalem (Mt 20:17–19). At the Temple in Jerusalem, Jesus took a bullwhip and drove out the money changers for desecrating his Father's house (Mk 11:15). In the city, he was condemned to death. Jesus longed and grieved for Jerusalem (Mt 23:37–39). And in Jerusalem, Jesus was crucified, laid in the tomb, and resurrected on that first Easter morning.

While on Jerusalem's Mount of Olives, the Apostles witnessed Jesus ascending into the heavens (Acts 1:12). In Jerusalem, the Holy Spirit descended on the disciples in the upper room on that first Christian Pentecost (Acts 1:8). From Jerusalem, the City of David, the Gospel spread to the ends of the earth. And in the fullness of time, from the heavenly Jerusalem, the Bride of Christ, the Church, will embrace her long-awaited bridegroom, the risen Lord (Rev 21). See also **Zion, Mount.**

JESSE (jes´ee): The father of King David. Isaiah prophesied that the Messiah would come from the "root of Jesse" (Isa 11:10). Catholics and other Christian traditions still honor Jesse in our celebration of the Jesse Tree during Advent.

JESUS CHRIST: English name for Yeshua, or Joshua, which in Hebrew means "God saves" (Mt 1:21). Jesus was named by the archangel Gabriel when he asked the Virgin Mary to be mother of the Messiah (Lk 2:31). Jesus would be Messiah, the Anointed One, the Liberator, Savior, and Redeemer. His followers would call him the Christ, the Greek word for Messiah.

Jesus was born in Bethlehem of Galilee around 6 BC to a virgin named Mary. He was entrusted to the care of his foster father Joseph of the House of David. Two different versions of his birth story appear in Mathew and Luke. The Matthew story contains the appearances of the angel to Joseph, telling him not to divorce Mary, the visit of the Wise Men from the East, the escape to Egypt, and the Slaughter of the Innocents by King Herod (Mt 1:18—2:23). The Luke story contains the announcement of the birth of John the Baptist, the archangel Gabriel's announcement to Mary, Jesus' birth in a stable in Bethlehem, and the angel choir's announcement of his birth to the shepherds (Lk 1:5—2:40). The Gospels are silent about Jesus' formative years except for the story in Luke of the boy Jesus astounding the teachers with his questions (Lk 2:41–52).

Around the age of thirty, Jesus began his active ministry. For three years, he taught in the synagogues of Galilee and Jerusalem, proclaimed the Reign of God, healed the sick, liberated the oppressed, set the captives free, and taught the Gospel of salvation. Jesus was known as a miracle worker, an exorcist, and the leader of the Apostles. He interpreted the Mosaic Law with an emphasis on God's love, on doing good from the heart—not simply because it was required—and on being saved through faith. He was critical of the religious authorities' hypocrisy, wealth, and prestige. For these reasons, these leaders distrusted him and eventually had him arrested and brought before Pontius Pilate, the Roman governor of Judea.

After Jesus' betrayal by the Apostle Judas (Mt 10:4; Mk 3:19; Lk 6:16), the Roman authorities arrested and tortured Jesus as a traitor of the Roman state. Pilate called Jesus innocent. Yet when faced with a riot instilled by the Jewish religious leaders, he had Jesus tortured and condemned to be crucified. Mary Magdalene, the sorrowful mother Mary, Mary Cleopas, Johanna, Susanna, John the Beloved, and Salome, the mother of James and John, stood at the foot of cross. At Jesus' death, a Roman officer recognized Jesus as the Son of God. Jesus was both he who offered sacrifice and the sacrifice itself. Jesus was the Lamb of God, who offered himself for love and reconciliation of humanity.

The disciple Joseph of Arimathea secured the body of Jesus and laid it within the tomb he had prepared for himself. Then the tomb was sealed with a huge stone. On Easter morning, when Mary Magdalene and some of the holy women returned to anoint the body, they found the tomb empty. Angels sent them to tell the other disciples that Christ had risen from the dead. From that moment on, the followers of Jesus Christ proclaimed his resurrected glory until he comes again. See chart **The Titles of Jesus.** See also **Christ; Emmanuel; Messiah; Redemption; Resurrection of Christ; Sacrifice; Trinity.**

The Titles of Jesus

Title	Meaning	Reference
Alpha and Omega	The first and last letters of the Greek alphabet. Symbolizes that Jesus is the beginning and end of all creation.	Rev 22:13
Carpenter's Son	Signifying Jesus' earthly trade.	Mk 6:3; Mt 13:55
Christ	The Greek word for *messiah*.	Jn 4:25
Emmanuel	Literally means "God with us."	Mt 1: 23; Isa 42:1
Holy One	An Old Testament title used for God; now used for Jesus by humans and demons alike.	Mk 1:24; Lk 4:34
Jesus	English for *Yeshua* (or *Joshua*), which in Hebrew means "God saves."	Mt 1:21
King of the Jews	Born of David's royal line. Shepherds and angels adored him. Magi brought gifts to honor the newborn king. In mockery, Pontius Pilate called Jesus "King of the Jews."	Mt 2:2; John 19:19
Lord	An Old Testament title used for God; now used for Jesus.	Acts 16:31
Messiah	Word meaning "anointed one." The long-awaited savior and redeemer of the Hebrew people.	Mk 8:29; Mt 1:18
Prophet	One who proclaims the word of God.	Mk 8:28; Mt 21:11
Rabbi or Rabbouni	Words meaning "teacher." Jesus was a Jewish teacher and wisdom figure.	Mk 10:51; Jn 20:16
Resurrection and the Life	Through Jesus' Resurrection, eternal life is available for all who believe.	John 11:25
Savior	The one who saves us from sin and death.	Lk 2:11
Son of Abraham	Indicates Jesus is the descendant of Israel's great patriarch, inheritor of God's Covenant.	Mt. 1:1
Son of David; Root of David	Indicates Jesus is the descendant of Israel's greatest king.	Mt 1:1; Rev 5:5
Son of God	Jesus is also God, the third Person of the Holy Trinity.	Mk 3:11; Mt 27:54
Son of Man	Another title for the messiah used by the prophets. Jesus also referred to himself by this title.	Lk 18:31
Son of Mary	The son of the virgin who found favor with God.	Lk 1:26
Son of the Most High	Another way of saying Jesus is the Son of God.	Lk 1:32

JEW: The title "Jew" developed over the centuries as the name for the diverse peoples of Judea. Prior to the Babylonian Captivity, the southern kingdom had been called Judah, but in Greco-Roman times the area was called Judea. The people came to be called Judeans or Jews. The Israelite religion of these people evolved into Judaism. Judaism was based on Abraham's covenant relationship with God, the Sinai Covenant with its gift of the Law, and the study of the sacred Scripture. The core Scriptures of the Jews is the Torah—the first five books of the Old Testament. Jesus Christ himself was a Jew from Galilee.

Jewish religious practices include honoring the Lord's Sabbath, circumcision, honoring the holiness and purity codes, which include certain dietary regulations, and following the laws of justice. Special feasts, such as Passover, Pentecost, and Tabernacles, are celebrated to honor historic religious events.

JEZEBEL (jez´uh-bel): The notorious queen of Ahab, a king of Israel (869–850 BC). Jezebel was a priestess of the Baals who supported the idolatrous rites and worship of foreign gods. Ahab and Jezebel were known for their idolatrous practices and social injustice. Together, they built temples to the Baals, erected sacred poles, and sacrificed the children Abiram and Segub as a tribute to Baal while fortifying the walls of Jericho (1 Kings 16:31–34).

When famine struck the land of Israel, Jezebel ordered a slaughter of the prophets of God as sacrifice. God sent the prophet Elijah to defeat her. Despite the drought, Elijah brought rain, defeated the prophets of Baal and Asherah, and reconciled the people to Yahweh (1 Kings 18).

In revenge, Jezebel ordered Elijah killed, but he hid from her wrath. Angels fed and cared for him (1 Kings 19:1–10). Ahab was killed in battle, and eventually Jezebel's servants threw her from an upper window, and dogs ate her corpse (2 Kings 9:30–37). See also **Ahab; Elijah; Idolatry.**

JEZREEL (jez´ree-uhl): The name Jezreel identified a valley, a town, and a person. The Jezreel valley separated Samaria from Israel. In this valley, Gideon defeated the Midianites and Amalekites (Judg 6:33). The name Jezreel also referred to a Canaanite town in the hill country. King Ahab made his royal headquarters at Jezreel (1 Kings 18:45–46). It was the site of the execution of the infamous Queen Jezebel (2 Kings 9:30–37). Hosea was directed to name his son Jezreel (Hos 1:4).

JOAB (joh´ab): The best-remembered nephew of King David, the son of David's sister Zeruiah (1 Chr 2:16). Joab was the leader of David's army (2 Sam 20:23). He was a courageous warrior and calculating politician. His pragmatic advice was a good balance to King David's emotional decision making. At times, Joab could be too cold and merciless, as when he executed David's rebellious son, Absalom, against David's orders. Joab was executed when he sided against Solomon after David's death (1 Kings 2:28–34).

JOANNA CHUZA (kyoo´zuh): The wife of Chuza, the steward of Herod Antipas (Lk 8:3). Joanna was one of the women who ministered to Jesus and the Apostles. Jesus appeared to Joanna at his Resurrection (24:10). Her inclusion in the Gospel record shows the spread of the Christian message into the household of Herod.

JOB (johb): The focus of a wisdom book about suffering. Job was a righteous man who suffered disaster and personal grief. His story was an Old Testament reflection on why the innocent suffer. Using the genre of an extended debate with three friends, the Book of Job explored many possible reasons why people suffer and ultimately, it dismissed each reason as inadequate.

Finally, Job challenged God and demanded to know the reason for his misfortune and suffering. God overwhelmed Job with questions that were beyond his knowledge—saying that no human could fully understand the divine plan. Job's blessings were restored as a reward for his faithfulness. The Book of Job marked a significant step forward in recognizing that suffering does not necessarily mean God is punishing a person.

JOEL (joh´uhl): His name meant "Yahweh is God." Joel was a prophet of Judah from the late sixth century BC who wrote after a national tragedy, but before the destruction of the Temple in Jerusalem by the Babylonian invaders. Joel prophesied a great plague of locusts as the onset of the Day of the Lord (Joel 1:4). He asked the people to lament, repent, and return to their faith in God. See also **Prophet.**

JOHN THE APOSTLE: The name John was short for Johnanoan or Jehonanan. It was a common name in Jewish culture. The most noteworthy person in the New Testament to carry the name was the Apostle John. He was one of the sons of Zebedee. He had a brother, James, who was also an Apostle (Mt 4:21).

Jesus called John and James the *boanerges,* or "sons of thunder" (Mk 3:17). James and John, along with Peter, seemed to have a special place among the Apostles. They alone were present with Jesus at the raising of Jairus's daughter, at the Transfiguration, and in

the garden of Gethsemane. Jesus entrusted the care of his mother to John from the cross. An old tradition has it that John, or a disciple of his, wrote the fourth Gospel in Ephesus in AD 90–110. See also **Apostle; James the Apostle.**

JOHN THE BAPTIST: Jesus said that his cousin John, the son of Elizabeth and Zechariah, was the greatest man ever born of woman (Mt 11:11). John was a man filled with the Spirit and dedicated to God, justice, and the proclamation of righteousness. He most likely had taken a vow as a Nazirite, dedicating himself to prayer, fasting, and the contemplation of God in the desert wilderness (Num 6:1–12).

In the wilderness, John called people to repent and revere the Lord. He condemned the sins of the Sadducees, Pharisees, and Herod and demanded a radical return to the Law of God (Lk 3:7–9). The power of his conviction awed multitudes of people, who thought that perhaps he was the Messiah. They gathered at the edge of the Jordan River to receive the Baptism of Repentance, yet John said another was to come whose sandals he wasn't worthy to carry (Mt 3:11).

Imprisonment and murder by King Herod Antipas cut John's life short (Lk 3:19–20; Mk 6:17–29). John was the last of the Hebrew prophets and the beginning of Christian prophecy. See also **Baptism of Repentance; Nazirite.**

JOHN MARK: The Evangelist known as John to the Jews and Mark to the Romans. Although the name Mark never appears in the Gospels, other New Testament writings note that Saint Peter and Saint Paul have a companion called Mark (Acts 12:25; Col 4:10). Mark's family was among the earliest followers of Christ. The Church of Jerusalem met in Mark's mother Mary's home. An old tradition suggests Peter converted Mark to Christ; possibly they were of the same family (Acts 12:12). In the Letters of Peter, the scribe Silvanus wrote that Mark was with Peter in Babylon, where Peter called him "my son" (1 Pet 5:13).

John Mark worked closely with his cousin Barnabas (Col 4:10); the two joined Paul to collect famine relief for the starving in Jerusalem (Acts 12:25). Together, they had a successful mission in Cyprus. Mark abandoned the work, however, and he and Paul parted ways, evidently with hard feelings (Acts 13:13–14). They apparently later reconciled, judging from Paul's letters in Rome (Col 4:10). An ancient tradition says John Mark wrote the Gospel of Mark while in Rome (AD 65), but there is little proof for this one way or the other. See also **Mary, the Mother of John Mark.**

JOHN OF PATMOS (pat´muhs)**:** A Christian in Ephesus, in modern-day Turkey, during and following the reign of the Roman emperor Domitian and his cruel persecutions of the Church. John was exiled for his faith to the isle of Patmos, a mosquito-infested penal colony (Rev 1:9). While there, an angel of the Lord appeared to John and invited him to watch as a series of prophetic visions unfolded. Christ appeared to John and revealed his nature, "'I am the Alpha and the Omega,' says the Lord God, who is and who was and who is to come, the Almighty" (Rev 1:8).

John's apocalyptic visions described God's salvation and vindication against the evil powers of the earth. The Book of Revelation was written for a community that needed hope in the midst of great persecution for their faith. The Scripture says that God understood their suffering and would "wipe every tear from their eyes. / Death will be no more; / mourning and crying and pain will be no more, / for the first things have passed away" (Rev 21:4). See also **Alpha and Omega; Apocalyptic Literature.**

JONAH (joh´nuh)**:** In the sixth century BC, an unknown writer told the story of God's unwilling prophet—the folk hero Jonah. Jonah lived during the conquest and destruction of Israel by the Assyrians (721 BC). The conquerors ruled the people with an iron hand and organized their control from their capital city of Nineveh. God asked Jonah to proclaim judgment on the sins of Nineveh. Jonah feared Assyrian retaliation and tried to run away from the call of God. He took off in the opposite direction from Nineveh but ended up being swallowed by a huge fish—just as the Assyrians and their fish god, Dagon, had swallowed up Israel. For three days and three nights, Jonah prayed in the belly of the fish and was vomited up on the shore of Nineveh (Jon 1—2).

This time, Jonah proclaimed judgment on Nineveh and fully expected them to refuse to repent and prepared himself to watch the wrath of God rain down. The people, however, repented and were spared. Jonah was angry and resentful. God scolded Jonah for his lack of compassion for the 120,000 people who lived in Nineveh (Jon 3—4). The lesson of the somewhat humorous story is that God loves all people regardless of culture, faith, or history. See also **Nineveh.**

JONATHAN (jon´uh-thuhn)**:** The son of Saul and beloved friend of David. When Saul became insanely jealous of David and planned to kill him, Jonathan warned David and interceded with his father to spare David's life. When David was unsure about Saul's intentions, Jonathan arranged to let David know if his father still wanted to kill David. When Saul learned of Jonathan's continued friendship with David, he nearly killed Jonathan in anger. Jonathan followed through on the plan to warn David, and he and David parted in tears, swearing their friendship for each other (1 Sam 19:1–7, 20:1–42).

Jonathan died in battle along with his brothers on the fatal field of Gilboa. His grave was moved to the site of Saul's grave in Zelah, in Benjamin (1 Sam 31). David grieved at Jonathan's death. The legendary elegy "The Song of the Bow" is attributed to David to honor Jonathan (2 Sam 1). See also **David; Saul of the Hebrews.**

JOPPA (jop´uh)**:** A town between Caesarea and Gaza, thirty miles northwest of Jerusalem. This ancient town was the most significant seaport of middle Asia. All the materials for building the Second Temple were imported from Joppa (Ezra 3:7). Peter ministered in the city (Acts 9:36–43).

JOSEPH OF ARIMATHEA (air´uh-muh-thee´uh)**:** Joseph was from the town of Arimathea. He was a member of the Sanhedrin, a man of means and faith, and a secret disciple of Christ (Mk 15:43; Jn 19:38). He disagreed with the Sanhedrin over the judgment of Jesus (Lk 23:51). Joseph's influence allowed him to approach Pontius Pilate and secure the body of Jesus. Within Joseph's own tomb, Jesus was laid to rest. Joseph honored Jesus with traditional burial customs (Mt 27:57–60).

JOSEPH OF EGYPT: The favorite son of Rachel and Jacob. Joseph was the full brother of Benjamin and the half brother of Jacob's other ten sons. The stories of Joseph explained how the Hebrew people ended up in Egypt.

Jacob favored Joseph with a gift of a coat with sleeves or a coat of many colors, a garment worn by the elite (Gen 37:3). This was why Jacob's other sons hated Joseph. They planned his murder but instead settled on selling him into slavery to a caravan of Ishmaelites for twenty shekels of silver—less than the price of a slave (Gen 37).

The Ishmaelites sold Joseph to a captain of Pharaoh's guard. Joseph became a gifted interpreter of dreams, and Pharaoh himself sought Joseph's counsel to prevent famine in the land. Joseph married Asenath, the daughter of the priest On, and became an honored member of the priestly class and an advisor to the Pharaoh. Asenath and Joseph had two sons, Manasseh and Ephraim, who are thought of as the thirteenth tribe of Israel (Genesis 40—41).

When Joseph's family migrated to Egypt to survive a famine, they unknowingly pleaded to Joseph for help. Joseph concealed his identity but treated his family with compassion (Gen 42—47). His father, Jacob, and all his brothers and their families were welcomed into Egypt. With Joseph's death, the age of the patriarchs was over. See also **Patriarch; Pharaoh; Potiphar; Rameses; Twelve Tribes.**

JOSEPH THE CARPENTER: The son of Jacob of the House of David, husband of Mary of Nazareth, and foster father of Jesus. Joseph was a skilled craftsman and builder who would have taught Jesus his craft (Mk 6:3). Herod Antipas hosted the reconstruction of Sepphoris a few miles from Nazareth. Joseph and his son likely were among the crew, as their skill as stonemasons and woodworkers would have been needed (Mk 6:3; Mt 13:55).

Joseph was a man of faith, a righteous man who honored the Law and believed in the divine revelation sent through angels and dreams. He was told that Mary's pregnancy was of the Holy Spirit, and he believed. He was told to take refuge in Egypt to protect the infant Christ and the Virgin Mother, and he obeyed (Mt 1:18–24, 2:13–15).

Joseph was the model for Jesus' experience of father. Jesus' image of God as loving Father was influenced by the care of this wise and unconditionally loving man. Joseph last appears in the Gospel story when the Lord was a twelve-year-old boy, teaching the doctors of the Law (Lk 2:16). Tradition says that Joseph died in the presence of Mary and Jesus. He is considered the patron saint of a holy death.

JOSHUA (josh´yoo-uh): His name meant "the salvation of God." The story of Joshua was compiled as a national epic to show God's miraculous intervention on behalf of the children of Israel. Joshua was a teenage hero, the successor of Moses, and the leader of the people in the conquest and distribution of the land of Israel after the desert wanderings. The Book of Joshua described him as a man of faith whom God protected from harm.

Joshua was of the tribe of Ephraim. He was called Hoshea before Moses renamed him (Num 13:16). When the Israelites first came to the Jordan River about a year after the Exodus from Egypt, he and Caleb alone had faith that God would deliver the land to them. So after the Israelites wandered thirty-nine more years in the desert, Joshua and Caleb alone of the original Israelites who were in Egypt survived to cross over the Jordan to claim the Promised Land.

Joshua became the people's new leader, taking the place of Moses (Deut 34:9). Under Joshua's direction, the Israelites set up twelve sacred stones to commemorate the parting of the waters, circumcised all the children, celebrated Passover, and commemorated that they were the children of God (Josh 4—5).

After the Israelites ate the harvest of the Promised Land, the gift of manna stopped, but the wonders continued. Joshua called for the sun and moon to stand still (Josh 10:12–15) and for the walls of Jericho to collapse at the sound of the trumpets (Josh 6). See also **Caleb; Jericho.**

JOSIAH (joh-si´uh): The great reformer king. Josiah's name meant "Yahweh cures." Josiah was the fifteenth king of Judah, the grandson of King Hezekiah. He reigned from 640 to 609 BC. Josiah was eight years old when his father, King Amon, was assassinated and Josiah became king (2 Kings 22:1).

Since the time of Solomon, Judah, the southern kingdom, had worshipped the gods of the foreign nations in the Temple along with Yahweh (1 Kings

11:7). Josiah, however, was a loyal advocate of Yahweh. He condemned the fertility and death rites of the foreign gods and goddesses. He began reconstructing the Temple of Solomon, during which the ancient scroll of Deuteronomy was found (2 Kings 22).

After reading the scroll, Josiah was afraid of God's wrath, for the nation had been unfaithful to the Sinai Covenant for many generations. He sought the counsel of the prophet Huldah and began a system of reforms to renew the covenant with God (2 Kings 23). The time of Josiah was the beginning of the Deuteronomic reform. See also **Deuteronomic Reform; Huldah; King.**

JUBILEE: Word that comes from the sound of the ram's horn trumpet, the shofar. When blown, the shofar's sound signified the heavens opening and the presence of God made near. According to the Law of Moses, every fiftieth year was proclaimed a Jubilee, a year of repentance, and the people were to place their focus on the redistribution of wealth and property to the poor and dispossessed.

During the Jubilee, the land was to rest. Only gleaning of the fields was permitted. All landed property was returned to its original owners, slaves were set free, and all debts were erased (Lev 25:8–55). The Jubilee created a society of justice in which the bounty and the land were shared. It prevented abject poverty and erased lines between rich and poor. It corrected societal injustices and restored God's intended equality to human relationships. See also **Debt; Justice; Sabbatical Year.**

JUDAH, JUDEA (joo´duh) (joo-dee´uh)**:** From the Hebrew word *Yehudah,* which means "praise the Lord." Judah was a son of Jacob and Leah, a patriarch and founder of one of the Twelve Tribes of Israel. The tribe of Judah became the most powerful of the Twelve Tribes. Judah became a place-name of the southern territory of Palestine. Judah and its capital city, Jerusalem, were the headquarters for the administration of the nation of Israel, the location of religious life via the Temple, and the dwellingplace of the royal family of David. For centuries, the Temple priests and Judean kings ruled Judah. In the time of Roman rule, the area was called Judea. See also **Israel, Israelite; Twelve Tribes.**

JUDAS ISCARIOT (is-kair´ee-uht)**:** The Apostle who betrayed Jesus (Mk 3:19). Iscariot was a territory south of Hebron in northern Judea. Judas was the only non-Galilean among the twelve Apostles.

Judas held the community funds. He betrayed Jesus for thirty pieces of silver (Mt 26:14–16). When he understood what he had done, he returned the money to the priests of the treasury and hanged himself. The land that the priests purchased with the blood money became a potter's field in which to bury the poor (Mt 27:3–10). See also **Apostle.**

JUDAS MACCABEUS (mak'uh-bee'uhs)**:** The third son of Mattathias Hasmon. Judas was a second-century BC Jewish guerilla fighter who led a successful revolt against the Greek occupation of Judea. His nickname was "the hammer."

Judas was a brave warrior and brilliant military strategist and led many successful raids against the Syrians and their Samaritan sympathizers. He led the Israelites in driving the occupation force out of Jerusalem so the Temple could be rededicated (1 Macc 3—9). He continued to wage successful war, liberating many Jews from the territories surrounding Jerusalem. He eventually died in battle in 160 BC (1 Macc 9:11–22). See also **Maccabees; Mattathias Hasmon.**

JUDE: A loyal follower of Christ and one of the Twelve Apostles. Jude is a short form of Judas. The author of Luke and Acts calls him Judas son (or brother) of James (Lk 6:16; Acts 1:13). In Mark and Matthew, he is called Thaddaeus (Mt 10:3; Mk 3:18). So perhaps his full name was Jude Thaddaeus. The only other reference to Jude is in the Gospel of John, where he asked Jesus at the Last Supper why Jesus didn't reveal himself to the whole world (Jn 14:22).

The letter attributed to Jude was most likely written by a Christian writer who embraced Jude's faith in Christ and wished to honor the Apostle. Ultimately, Jude's historical identity remains a mystery. According to an early tradition, however, after Jesus' Ascension, Jude left to preach the Gospel in Judea, Samaria, Idumaea, Syria, Mesopotamia, and Libya and was a martyr for the faith along with Saint Simon in Armenia. Saint Jude is the patron saint of desperate causes. See also **Apostle.**

JUDEA: See **Judah, Judea.**

JUDGE: One of the men and women who served the Hebrew people as tribal leaders and military commanders. The judges settled disputes and proclaimed the will of God. They were not judges as we understand that role today, presiding over legal cases. Instead, they were charismatic leaders whom the Holy Spirit inspired to lead the Israelites when they were a loosely knit federation of tribes (1200–1000 BC). The judge was a clan hero who empowered the faith of the people in times of crisis and focused their attention on the promises of the Covenant.

Twelve judges of Israel were called to lead the Twelve Tribes by uniting them to God and the Law: Othniel (Judg 3:7–11), Ehud (Judg 3:12–30), Shamgar (Judg 3:31, 5:6), Deborah (Judg 4—5), Gideon (Judg 6—8), Tola and Jair (Judg 10:1–5), Jephthah (Judg 11:1—12:7), Ibzan, Elon, and Abdon (Judg 12:8–15), Samson (Judg 13—16). Some lists include Abimelech (Judg 9). Most people also consider Samuel, whose stories appear in 1 and 2 Samuel, to be the last of the judges and the first of the prophets.

Some judges were very faithful to the Covenant, some were not. God's will was accomplished through them or in spite of them. The stories of the judges link the conquest of the land of Canaan under Joshua's leadership to the period of the monarchy. See chart **The Judges of Israel.** See also **Barak; Deborah; Ehud; Gideon; Jephthah; Othniel; Samson; Samuel; Shamgar.**

This is a fragment of a fresco in the **Northern Palace of Herod the Great,** at Masada. Notice how it is painted to imitate marble. Masada was a fortress built at the top of a 1,300-foot-tall rock.

his is a view of the **Sinai desert**; notice ow it is more rocks than sand. The structure n the center may be an ancient burial tomb.

Underwater plants and fish of the **Red Sea** are viewed in an observation tube. The tube was built into the sea to allow observation of aquatic life in its natural setting.

This **olive tree** is growing in a grove of olive trees. Olives were used for food and were also pressed to make olive oil.

igs are growing on a branch of a **fig ree** in July. The fruit will be ready to at in a few weeks.

This is a view of the **Red Sea** near the Israeli city of Eilat.

This model show the temple area c **Jerusalem** as would have looked Jesus' time.

People might have seen this view of the **Sea of Galilee** while they listened to Jesus preach. The church in the foreground is the **Catholic Chapel of the Beatitudes**, built in 1939 by the Franciscan Sisters.

This excavation site shows the remains of a **house from New Testament times**. The cone-shaped rock was used to grind wheat into flour. The cylinders in the foreground were rolled over the mud roof to press out excess water!

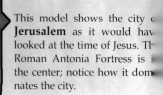

This model shows the city c **Jerusalem** as it would hav looked at the time of Jesus. Th Roman Antonia Fortress is i the center; notice how it dom nates the city.

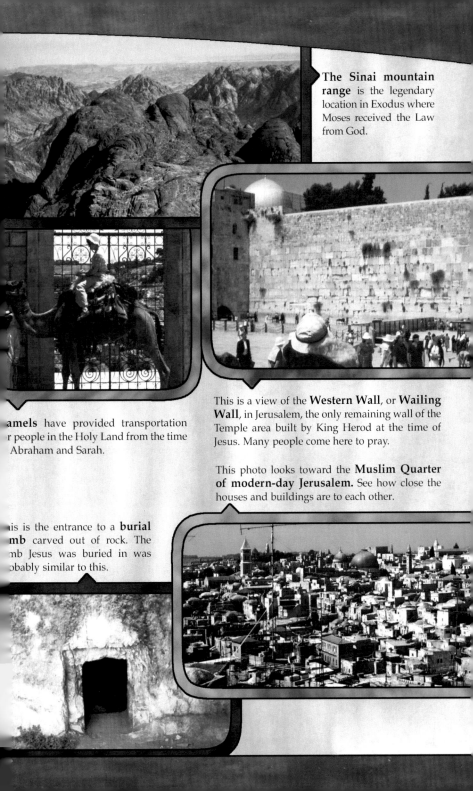

The Sinai mountain range is the legendary location in Exodus where Moses received the Law from God.

...**amels** have provided transportation ...r people in the Holy Land from the time ...Abraham and Sarah.

This is a view of the **Western Wall**, or **Wailing Wall**, in Jerusalem, the only remaining wall of the Temple area built by King Herod at the time of Jesus. Many people come here to pray.

This photo looks toward the **Muslim Quarter of modern-day Jerusalem.** See how close the houses and buildings are to each other.

...is is the entrance to a **burial** ...mb carved out of rock. The ...mb Jesus was buried in was ...obably similar to this.

This cave is one of the caves near Qumran, where the **Dead Sea Scrolls** were discovered. The Dead Sea Scrolls are said to be the greatest modern discovery for Bible scholars.

This is a wall in the garden of the Church of the Visitation near Jerusalem. Each plaque has the *Magnificat* (Luke 1:46–56) written in a different language.

MAGNIFICAT

MY SOUL MAGNIFIES THE LORD AND MY SPIRIT REJOICES IN GOD MY SAVIOR. BECAUSE HE HAS REGARDED THE LOWLINESS OF HIS HANDMAID FOR BEHOLD HENCEFORTH ALL GENERATIONS SHALL CALL ME BLESSED BECAUSE HE WHO IS MIGHTY HAS DONE GREAT THINGS FOR ME, AND HOLY IS HIS NAME. AND FOR GENERATION UPON GENERATION IS HIS MERCY TO THOSE WHO FEAR HIM. HE HAS SHOWN MIGHT WITH HIS ARM, HE HAS SCATTERED THE PROUD IN THE CONCEIT OF THEIR HEART. HE HAS PUT DOWN THE MIGHTY FROM THEIR THRONES, AND HAS EXALTED THE LOWLY. HE HAS FILLED THE HUNGRY WITH GOOD THINGS AND THE RICH HE HAS SENT AWAY EMPTY. HE HAS GIVEN HELP TO IS RAEL, HIS SERVANT, MINDFUL OF HIS MERCY EVEN AS HE SPOKE TO OUR FATHERS: TO ABRAHAM AND TO HIS POSTERITY FOREVER.

This is a close-up of the *Magnificat* in English.

The **Wadi Qelt** is located in the wilderness of Judea. Wadis are usually dry riverbeds—except during the rainy season. Wadis have steep sides, making escape impossible when the waters rush through after a heavy rain.

This spring is one of the northern sources of the **Jordan River**, near the ancient city of Dan.

hese are **mineral deposits** at the edge of the
outhern shore of the **Dead Sea**. Deposits are
ft after water evaporates in the hot temperatures,
nd they are used for a variety of health and beauty
urposes.

his view of the **Mount of Olives** is directly across
e Kidron Valley from the city of Jerusalem. This is
here Jesus
ent to pray
ith his dis-
ples before
s arrest.

Due to the high level
of salt and minerals in
the **Dead Sea**, the
human body easily
floats. The Dead Sea is
six times saltier than
ocean water.

This **ancient amphitheater** at Caesarea
was built by Herod the Great and had a seat-
ing capacity of 3,500. Caesarea was the center
of Roman government in Palestine for over
six hundred years.

is **aqueduct**, built by Herod the Great to
ng fresh water from Mount Carmel into his
wly built city of Caesarea, is nearly ten
les long.

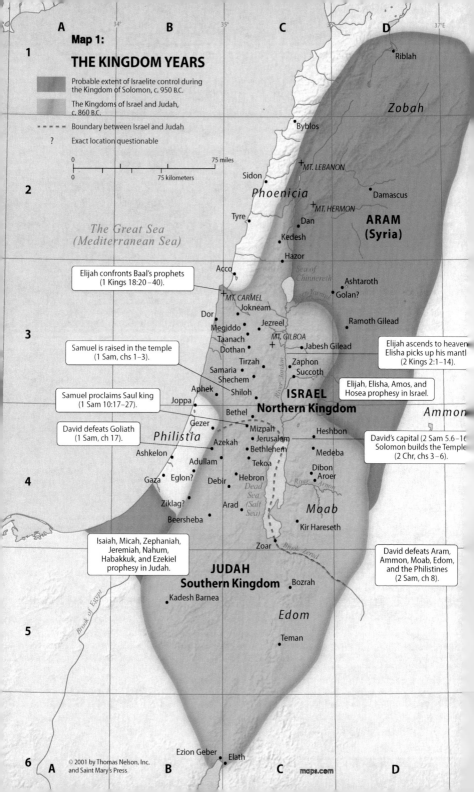

Map 1:

THE KINGDOM YEARS

Probable extent of Israelite control during
the Kingdom of Solomon, c. 950 B.C.

The Kingdoms of Israel and Judah,
c. 860 B.C.

– – – – Boundary between Israel and Judah

? Exact location questionable

0 —————————— 75 miles

0 —————————— 75 kilometers

A B C D

1 34° 35° 37°E

Riblah

Zobah

Byblos

+ *MT. LEBANON*

Sidon

2 *Phoenicia* + *MT. HERMON* Damascus

Tyre Dan **ARAM**
(Syria)

The Great Sea Kedesh
(Mediterranean Sea) Hazor

Acco *Sea of*
Chinnereth Ashtaroth

Elijah confronts Baal's prophets + *MT. CARMEL* Golan?
(1 Kings 18:20–40). Jokneam

Dor Ramoth Gilead

3 Megiddo Jezreel
Taanach *MT. GILBOA*
Dothan + Jabesh Gilead Elijah ascends to heaven
Samuel is raised in the temple Tirzah Zaphon Elisha picks up his mantl
(1 Sam, chs 1–3). Samaria Succoth (2 Kings 2:1–14).
Shechem
Aphek Shiloh **ISRAEL** Elijah, Elisha, Amos, and
Samuel proclaims Saul king Joppa **Northern Kingdom** Hosea prophesy in Israel.
(1 Sam 10:17–27). Bethel *Ammon*
Gezer Mizpah Heshbon
David defeats Goliath Azekah Jerusalem David's capital (2 Sam 5.6–16
(1 Sam, ch 17). *Philistia* Bethlehem Medeba Solomon builds the Temple
Ashkelon Adullam Tekoa Dibon (2 Chr, chs 3–6).
4 Gaza Eglon? Debir Hebron Aroer
Ziklag? Arad *Dead* *Moab*
Beersheba *Sea* Kir Hareseth
(Salt
Sea)
Isaiah, Micah, Zephaniah, Zoar *Brook Zered* David defeats Aram,
Jeremiah, Nahum, Ammon, Moab, Edom,
Habakkuk, and Ezekiel **JUDAH** Bozrah and the Philistines
prophesy in Judah. **Southern Kingdom** (2 Sam, ch 8).

Kadesh Barnea *Edom*

5 Teman

6 © 2001 by Thomas Nelson, Inc. Ezion Geber
and Saint Mary's Press Elath

A B C D

maps.com

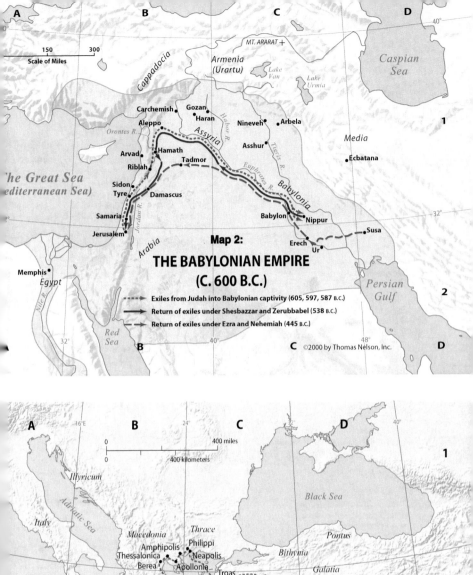

Map 2:

THE BABYLONIAN EMPIRE
(C. 600 B.C.)

- ········ Exiles from Judah into Babylonian captivity (605, 597, 587 B.C.)
- —— Return of exiles under Shesbazzar and Zerubbabel (538 B.C.)
- – – – Return of exiles under Ezra and Nehemiah (445 B.C.)

©2000 by Thomas Nelson, Inc.

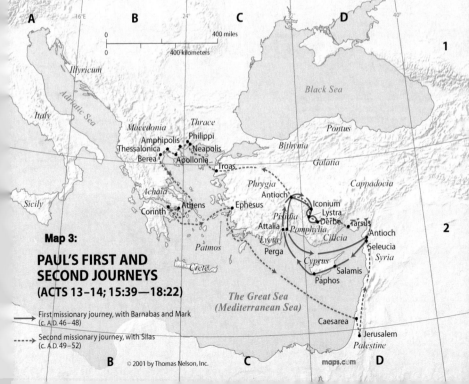

Map 3:

PAUL'S FIRST AND SECOND JOURNEYS
(ACTS 13–14; 15:39—18:22)

- —— First missionary journey, with Barnabas and Mark
  (c. A.D. 46–48)
- ········ Second missionary journey, with Silas
  (c. A.D. 49–52)

© 2001 by Thomas Nelson, Inc.

maps.com

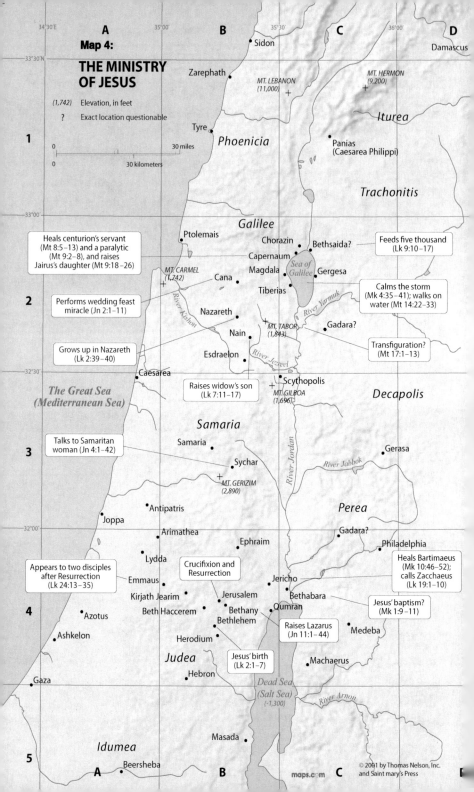

A · B · C · D

Map 4:

THE MINISTRY OF JESUS

(1,742) Elevation, in feet

? Exact location questionable

0 _____ 30 miles
0 _____ 30 kilometers

Sidon

Damascus

Zarephath

MT. LEBANON (11,000) +

MT. HERMON (9,200) +

Iturea

Tyre

Phoenicia

Panias (Caesarea Philippi)

Trachonitis

Galilee

Ptolemais

Chorazin

Bethsaida?

Feeds five thousand (Lk 9:10–17)

Heals centurion's servant (Mt 8:5–13) and a paralytic (Mt 9:2–8), and raises Jairus's daughter (Mt 9:18–26)

Capernaum

Sea of Galilee

Gergesa

MT. CARMEL (1,742) +

Cana

Magdala

Tiberias

Calms the storm (Mk 4:35–41); walks on water (Mt 14:22–33)

Performs wedding feast miracle (Jn 2:1–11)

River Kishon

Nazareth

River Yarmuk

MT. TABOR (1,843) +

Gadara?

Nain

Transfiguration? (Mt 17:1–13)

Grows up in Nazareth (Lk 2:39–40)

Esdraelon

River Jezreel

Caesarea

Scythopolis

Decapolis

Raises widow's son (Lk 7:11–17)

MT. GILBOA (1,696) +

The Great Sea (Mediterranean Sea)

Samaria

Talks to Samaritan woman (Jn 4:1–42)

Samaria

River Jabbok

Gerasa

Sychar

MT. GERIZIM (2,890) +

Antipatris

Perea

Joppa

Arimathea

Ephraim

Gadara?

Philadelphia

Lydda

Crucifixion and Resurrection

Heals Bartimaeus (Mk 10:46–52); calls Zacchaeus (Lk 19:1–10)

Appears to two disciples after Resurrection (Lk 24:13–35)

Emmaus

Jericho

Kirjath Jearim

Jerusalem

Bethabara

Jesus' baptism? (Mk 1:9–11)

Azotus

Beth Haccerem

Bethany

Qumran

Bethlehem

Raises Lazarus (Jn 11:1–44)

Medeba

Ashkelon

Herodium

Jesus' birth (Lk 2:1–7)

Judea

Machaerus

Gaza

Hebron

Dead Sea (Salt Sea) (-1,300)

River Arnon

Idumea

Masada

Beersheba

River Jordan

The Judges of Israel

Name	Major Accomplishment or Memorable Shame	Reference
Othniel	Defeated King Cushan-rishathaim	Judg 3:7–11
Ehud	Freed the Israelites from Eglon, king of Moab	Judg 3:12–30
Shamgar	Defeated the Philistines	Judg 3:31
Deborah	Recruited the warrior Barak and helped gather an army to defeat the Canaanites	Judg 4–5
Gideon	Commissioned by the angel of the Lord to defeat the people of the East	Judg 6–8
Tola	Served Israel as a loyal Israelite	Judg 10:1–2
Jair	Led the people in the faith of Yahweh	Judg 10:3–5
Jephthah	Sacrificed his only daughter as an offering for victory in battle, revealing his misunderstanding of the Law and connection to foreign gods	Judg 11:1–12:7
Ibzan	Married his children to partners throughout the tribes of Israel, creating unity among the people	Judg 12:8–10
Elon	Lived and died a loyal Israelite	Judg 12:11–12
Abdon	Lived and died a loyal Israelite	Judg 12:13–15
Samson	Wayward Nazirite married to Delilah; repented in the last hours of his life; superhumanly strong; had many victories against the Philistines	Judg 13–16

JUDITH (joo´dith): A Jewish heroine. The fictional Book of Judith is set during the time of the Assyrian invasion (721 BC). It pictures the Assyrian Holofernes in support of the king Nebuchadnezzar, who was really a Babylonian king. When Holofernes and his army were at the gates of Judith's city, the city elders planned to surrender the city to the invaders. The beautiful widow Judith chided their action as a manipulation of God, refused to surrender, and planned to deliver the city herself (Jdt 8).

Judith presented herself as a refugee from Israel and was escorted to the tent of Holofernes. She bowed before the general and prayed to the Lord. Holofernes thought that she directed the honor to him. Judith said she was a traitor. Holofernes bought the story. The general called her beautiful and wise. He promised that her God would become his own and that she would live in the palace of Nebuchadnezzar (Jdt 10–11).

Holofernes planned to seduce the beautiful Judith but drank too much alcohol at a party. He collapsed in his tent. Judith prayed for strength and decapitated him with his own sword. Judith's maid hid Holofernes's severed head in their bag. After secretly returning to their city, Judith displayed the head to the people (Jdt 13:15–16). The

Israelites took courage and prepared for battle. After they discovered Holofernes's body, the Assyrians fled in panic. Like Miriam, Judith led the people in a victory song (Jdt 12—16). See also **Holofernes.**

JUNIAS (joo′nee-uhs)**:** The woman Junias (or Junia) was honored in Saint Paul's Letter to the Romans. Paul says that she was "prominent among the apostles" (Rom 16:7) and mentioned that she knew Christ before Paul. Her inclusion indicated the prominence of women among the early Church evangelists.

JUPITER: The chief god of the Romans, worshipped by various names, such as Zeus. See also **Zeus.**

JUSTICE: A central theme that is pervasive throughout the Bible. The Hebrew and Greek words that are translated as "justice" are also translated as "righteousness" and "judgment." Justice calls for the fair and equitable distribution of life's necessities. The scriptural idea of justice is based in the truth that all human beings have dignity and worth and are children of God. God's love for all creation is shown in the emphasis God places on justice, which is love in action.

God created human beings to live in a society of justice, in which everyone would receive everything necessary for life (Gen 1:29). In the Covenant, laws to ensure justice were included (Lev 25). The prophets declared that God defended the poor and the oppressed and those who had experienced injustice (Am 5:11–12). Jesus proclaimed that the wealthy were obligated to see the poor and take care of them (Lk 16:19–31). The Beatitudes are about justice. In the Kingdom of God, the poor and hungry shall be blessed, but woe to the rich and the full (Lk 6:20–26).

Finally, God's spiritual justice was fulfilled in Jesus Christ. Through faith in Christ, we are made righteous, or just, in the sight of God (Rom 3:21–26). See also **Amos; Jubilee; Lazarus and the Rich Man; Orphan; Poverty; Widow.**

K

KETURAH (ki-tyoor′uh)**:** Abraham's wife or concubine after Sarah died (Gen 25:1–6). Abraham and Keturah had six sons, who migrated east after leaving the tribe.

KING: In the ancient world, the king was a symbol of unification and centralization of the government. From 1000 BC to the fall of Jerusalem in 587 BC, the Israelites lived as nations under a monarchy led by a king.

The prophet Samuel resisted the election of a king who would rule Israel like the other nations. The rule of Israel was to follow the vision of justice and monotheism called for by their primal Covenant relationship with God. The true king of Israel was forever to be the LORD God, King of Kings (1 Sam 2:1–2). Samuel was afraid that a human king would lead to problems (1 Sam 8:4–18). Ultimately, God instructed Samuel to give in to the people's demand for a king.

The ideal king of Israel was to be consecrated, not unlike a priest of Yahweh, and called to rule as a type of messiah, or anointed one of God (1 Sam 10:1). He was envisioned as a spiritual descendant of the ancient ancestor who worshipped with Abraham—the first king of Jerusalem, Melchizedek of Salem, a king of righteousness and peace (Gen 14:18; Heb 5:6, 7:1–4). Thus, the king of Israel would be called to make all judgments in keeping with the Law of Moses (1 Sam 12:13–15). Throughout their history, the kings of Israel and Judah fell short of that call.

Saul, David, and Solomon were the only three kings to rule over the united kingdom of Israel. Following Solomon's death, the ten northern tribes formed their own kingdom, called Israel. The kingdom in the south, which included the city of Jerusalem, was called Judah. Nineteen kings ruled the northern kingdom of Israel. Nineteen kings also ruled the southern kingdom of Judah. See also **David; Israel, Israelite; Jeroboam of Israel; Josiah; Judah, Judea; Manasseh; Rehoboam; Solomon; United Monarchy.**

The Hebrew Kings

Kings of the United Monarchy			
King	**Period**	**Successes**	**Failures**
Saul (1 Sam 9—31:13)	1020–1000 BC	Military king and warrior who suppressed the Philistines.	Worshipped the foreign gods of the nations alongside Yahweh. Failed to follow the prophet Samuel's orders.
David (1 Sam 16:1—1 Kings 2:11)	1000–961 BC	Greatest king of Israel. David's heroism, military prowess, passion for God, and willingness to repent his sins provided a model of what it meant to be king.	Lusted for power and committed adultery with Bathsheba, whose husband David had murdered to conceal his sin.
Solomon (1 Kings 1:1—11:43)	961–922 BC	Noted for his wisdom and his building projects, especially the Temple of Jerusalem.	Reign was marred by idolatry. Overtaxed the people to fund building campaigns, and enacted forced labor. At his death, the Hebrews entered a sixty-year civil war.

(The Hebrew Kings *continued on next page*)

Kings of the Southern Kingdom of Judah	Kings of the Northern Kingdom of Israel
The dates included represent a consensus of modern scholars.	

1. Rehoboam (ree-huh-boh´uhm). Last king of the united monarchy. His cruelty and taxation fueled civil war (1 Kings 11:42—14:31).
Date: 922–915 BC

2. Abijam (ah-bi´jem) or **Abijah** (uh-bi´juh). Constant warfare with Jeroboam. An unjust and idolatrous king (1 Kings 14:31–15:8).
Date: 915–913 BC

3. Asa (ay´suh) of Judah. Son of Abijam. Loyal to God, tore down the idols of Asherah and Baal. Victorious in war (1 Kings 15:8–24).
Date: 913–873 BC

4. Jehoshaphat (ji-hosh´uh-fat). Son of Asa. A diplomat and loyal to God. Worked for peace with Israel (1 Kings 22:41–50).
Date: 873–849 BC

5. Jehoram (ji-hor´uhm) of Judah. Took the throne and murdered all his siblings. Married Athaliah, the daughter of Ahab and Jezebel (2 Kings 8:16–24).
Date: 849–842 BC

6. Ahaziah (ay´-huh-zi´uh) of Judah. Unsuccessful as a king, failed in battle, was idolatrous, made a fateful alliance with Jehoram of Israel, and was killed by Jehu (2 Kings 8:24—9:29).
Date: 842 BC
Athaliah (ath´uh-li´uh). Mother of Ahaziah, she murdered all of Ahaziah's children and ruled Judah until she was killed.
Date: 844–837 BC

7. Joash (joh´ash) or **Jehoash** (ji-hoh´ash) of Judah. The son of Ahaziah. Survived the mass murders of Athaliah and was anointed king at age seven. Renewed the covenant promises and destroyed the cult of Baal (2 Kings 11:1—12:21).
Date: 837–800 BC

8. Amaziah (am´uh-zi´uh). Son of Joash. Suffered from pride and didn't destroy the high places where foreign gods were worshiped. Conquered Edom and dedicated the place to God. Later, he was captured and caused Jerusalem to be attacked and the Temple treasury taken as booty (2 Kings 14:1–20).
Date: 800–783 BC

9. Uzziah (uh-zi´uh) or **Azariah** (az´uh-ri´uh). The son of Amaziah. Began his reign at sixteen years old. Ruled in stability, victorious at war and faith (2 Kings 14:21, 15:1–7).
Date: 783–742 BC

10. Jotham (joh´thuhm). Son of Uzziah. Reigned eight years as regent, eight years as king. Contained the Ammonites, built cities, towers, and forts. Peace flourished, but the high places where foreign gods were worshiped were left intact (2 Kings 15:32–38).
Date: 750–735 BC

1. Jeroboam (jer-uh-boh´uhm). Overseer of Solomon's labor camps. Led Israel into civil war. An idolater who built shrines to foreign gods (1 Kings 11:26—14:20).
Date: 922–901 BC

2. Nadab (nay´dab). Son of Jeroboam. Evil and idolatrous. Took the throne in the second year of the reign of Asa of Judah (1 Kings 15:25–27). The dates conflict.
Date: 901–900 BC

3. Baasha (bay´uh-shuh). Warred with Asa of Judah. Built citadels and idolatrous shrines at Ramah and moved the capital to Tirzah (1 Kings 15:27—16:7).
Date: 900–877 BC

4. Elah (ee´luh): Son of Baasha. Murdered by his servant, Zimri, while drunk (1 Kings 16:6–14).
Date: 877– 876 BC

5. Zimri (zim´ri). A charioteer in the army who murdered King Elah. Mass-murdered the house of Baasha and then committed suicide (1 Kings 16:9–20).
Date: 876 BC

6. Omri (om´ri). Army commander proclaimed king. Hailed as a statesman in Assyrian documents but condemned in Scripture as an idolater (1 Kings 16:15–28).
Date: 876–869 BC

7. Ahab (ay´hab). Reigned with the evil Queen Jezebel. Together, they served Baal and blended the worship of Yahweh with the foreign gods of the nations. Ahab performed human sacrifice and slaughtered the prophets of God (1 Kings 16:28—22:40).
Date: 869–850 BC

8. Ahaziah (ay´-huh-zi´uh) of Israel. Son of Jezebel and Ahab. Worshipper of the Baals and Beelzebub. Died without an heir (2 Kings 22:40—2 Kings 1:18).
Date: 850–849 BC

9. Jehoram (ji-hor´uhm) or **Joram** (jor´uhm) of Israel. Son of Ahab. Succeeded his brother Ahaziah, who had no son. Idolatrous and unjust. The prophet Elijah condemned him as evil (2 Kings 1:17—9:26).
Date: 849–842 BC

10. Jehu (jee´hyoo). Destroyed the House of Ahab and removed Baal of Tyre from Israel. Like Jeroboam, worshiped Oisrael, the golden calf (2 Kings 9:1—10:36).
Date: 842–815 BC

Kings of the Southern Kingdom of Judah	Kings of the Northern Kingdom of Israel
The dates included represent a consensus of modern scholars.	

11. Ahaz (ay´haz). An evil, idolatrous king who sacrificed his own son in the fires of Molech and practiced the rites of Canaan in the high places. Refused to join the anti-Assyrian alliance and became a vassal of Assyria (2 Kings 16:1–20).
Date: 735–715 BC

12. Hezekiah (hez´uh-ki´uh). Son of Ahaz. A model king who worked to eliminate idolatry and tried to heal ancient wounds. Dug the tunnel of Siloam to protect the city's water supply when the Assyrians invaded (2 Kings 18:1—20:21).
Date: 715–687 BC

13. Manasseh (muh-nas´uh). Only son of Hezekiah. Idolater of the Baals who sacrificed his own son. The Assyrians took Manasseh captive. Repented in Assyria (2 Kings 21:1–18).
Date: 687–642 BC

14. Amon (am´uhn). Adulterer, unjust, and more evil than his father, Manasseh. His own servants murdered him because of his policies and dealings with the Assyrians (2 Kings 21:19–26).
Date: 642–640 BC

15. Josiah (joh-si´uh). The great reformer, the grandson of King Hezekiah. Renewed the covenant, made idolatry a crime, and restored the Temple of Solomon (2 Kings 21:26—23:30).
Date: 640–609 BC

16. Jehoahaz (ji-hoh´uh-haz) of Judah. Son of Josiah. Was twenty-three years old when he became an idolatrous and unjust king. After reigning only three months, taken prisoner by Pharaoh Neco and exiled to Egypt, where he died (2 Kings 23:30–33).
Date: 609 BC

17. Jehoiakim (ji-hoi´uh-kim). Pharaoh Neco appointed Eliakim, son of Josiah, as king and changed his name to Jehoiakim. The Egyptians demanded rich tribute, and the idolatrous, unjust Jehoiakim taxed the people heavily (2 Kings 23:34—24:5).
Date: 609–598 BC

18. Jehoiachin (ji-hoi´uh-kin). Son of Jehoiakim. Had just become king when Nebuchadnezzar attacked Jerusalem. The royal family surrendered and was exiled to Babylon with much of the population (2 Kings 24:6–16, 25:27–30).
Date: 597 BC

19. Zedekiah (zed´uh-ki´uh) or **Mattaniah** (mat´uh-ni´uh). Last king of Judah. A puppet leader for Babylon during the final years of the occupation of Jerusalem. When Zedekiah rebelled, Nebuchadnezzar destroyed the city, tortured and murdered the royal family, and put our Zedekiah's eyes. The king was led in chains to Babylon, where he died.
Date: 597–587 BC

11. Jehoahaz (ji-hoh´uh-haz). Ruled in idolatry and warfare. Prayed to the God of Israel, and God sent a savior to protect the people from the Arameans; but idolatry continued in Israel (2 Kings 13:1–9).
Date: 815–801 BC

12. Joash (joh´ash) of Israel. Son of Jehoahaz. Idolater who worshipped Oisrael as golden calves (2 Kings 13:10–11). Reign was marked with warfare (2 Kings 13:10—14:16).
Date: 801–786 BC

13. Jeroboam II (jer-uh-boh´uhm). Like his namesake, worshipped the golden calves of Oisrael. He made Israel very prosperous, but injustice and iniquity prevailed in the land (2 Kings 14:23–29).
Date: 786–746 BC

14. Zechariah (zek´uh-ri´uh). Son of Jeroboam II. Six-month rule marked by idolatry and injustice. Last of the line of Jehu (2 Kings 14:29—15:12).
Date: 746-745 BC

15. Shallum (shal´uhm). Murdered Zechariah. Was murdered himself within one month (2 Kings 15:10–15).
Date: 745 BC

16. Menahem (men´uh-hem). Killed Shallum and reigned for ten years. Became a puppet ruler of the Assyrians and was much hated by his own people (2 Kings 15:14–25).
Date: 745-738 BC

17. Pekahiah (pek´uh-hi´uh). Pro-Assyrian son of Menahem. One of Pekahiah's trusted friends, Pekah ben Remaliah, assassinated him. After Pekahiah's death, an anti-Assyrian policy began, and war with Judah escalated (2 Kings 15:23-26).
Date: 738–737 BC

18. Pekah (pee´kuh). Began rule after killing Pekahiah. Damascus, Tyre, and Philistia bonded with Pekah in anti-Assyrian resistance (2 Kings 15:25–31).
Date: 737–732 BC

19. Hoshea (hoh-shee´uh). The last king of Israel. Murdered Pekah to ascend the throne, then was forced to serve Tiglath-Pileser III of Assyria. Considered untrustworthy even by the Assyrian conquerors. Assyria overtook Israel and exiled much of the population, including Hoshea (2 Kings 17:1–6).
Date: 732–724 BC

KINGDOM OF GOD: Also called the Reign of God, the central message of Jesus' preaching during his earthly ministry. He began his ministry by announcing that the Kingdom of God was at hand by reading from Isaiah (Lk 4:16–21). Through his miracles and his parables, Jesus taught what the Kingdom of God was like. In the Kingdom of God, love reigns, sickness and death are no more, there is forgiveness, and people live in peace with each other. Everyone is welcome in God's Kingdom, including the poor, the unclean, and all other outcasts from society. We are to be ready for the kingdom to manifest itself, ready to find Jesus in our midst (Mt 25:1–13).

When we keep the two great commandments, we are very near the Kingdom of God (Mk 1:15, 12:34). The Beatitudes are a description of the Kingdom of God: the poor are blessed, the hungry are fed, those who mourn laugh, those who are mocked for the faith are cherished (Lk 6:20–23). Jesus taught that when we make the Kingdom of God our first goal, we will be given everything we need (Mt 6:33).

KING OF KINGS: A title other nations used to honor monarchs (Ezek 26:7). The Israelites, however, revered the title as belonging to God. From its birth, Israel was a religious monarchy. The true king of Israel was forever to be the LORD God, the King over all kings (1 Sam 2:1–2). Even the rulers of foreign nations would come to know the God of Abraham as "God of gods and Lord of kings" (Dan 2:47).

Jesus of Nazareth was honored with the royal titles of the House of David, as well as those of the kingship of God. In the New Testament, Jesus also received the title King of Kings (1 Titus 6:14; Rev 19:16).

KINSHIP: An important concept in the Bible that defined the relationship people had with each other. In the Old Testament, kinship referred to extended family, symbolically of the same womb. The words *brother* and *sister* equally referred to the child of one's biological parent or to a near relative such as a cousin. It could also refer to another member of one's tribe, another Israelite. Honor required that one offer compassion and special care to kin.

Throughout the Bible, humanity was the family of God, and the Lord was kin and patron, a loving Father who redeemed and offered salvation from bondage. In the New Testament, Jesus extended the concept of kinship beyond blood relatives. "My mother and my brothers are those who hear the word of God and do it" (Lk 8:21). Through Christ, we are all kin to one another, all children of God. See also **Blood; Compassion; James the Brother of the Lord.**

KNOWLEDGE: In the early writings of the Old Testament, the word *wisdom* was a gift of the Spirit of God. In contrast, the word *knowledge* referred to the understanding that came through worldly experience. To "know someone" was also used to indicate being in a sexual relationship with that person. So to "know someone" referred to an intimate relationship of total acceptance. In the Greek period, the two ideas blended. Knowledge then referred to the understanding that came through wisdom, experience, emotion, and relationship, as well as assuming faith in God (1 Jn 2:3).

L

LABAN (lay′buhn): His name meant "white" or "pale one." Laban was a clan chief of the line of Terah, the ancestors of Abraham and Sarah (1860–1740 BC). Laban was the brother of Rebekah, who married Isaac. His daughters were Rachel and Leah, who eventually married Jacob. First, though, Jacob had to pay the bride price.

Laban was a shrewd and somewhat deceitful man. Jacob worked for Laban seven years to pay the bride price for Rachel, but Jacob was tricked into marrying Laban's elder daughter, Leah. Jacob loved Rachel more than Leah, so he worked seven more years to pay the bride price for the one he truly loved (Gen 29—30). Rachel, Leah, and their maidservants, Bilhah and Zilpah, are the mothers of the twelve sons of Jacob. See also **Jacob; Leah; Twelve Tribes.**

LAMB: Sheep were an important symbol of life for the ancient Hebrews because they provided milk, meat, hides, and wool for these wandering tribes. Thus, lambs made a perfect choice for sacrifice; they were meek and innocent and symbolized the gift of life (Ex 29:38–46). The lamb's caregiver, the shepherd, became an image for God. Special celebrations in which the community gathered called for the sacrifice of a lamb: Sabbath, the New Moon, Trumpets, Weeks or Pentecost, Passover, the Day of Atonement, and Booths (Ex 28—29).

The early Christian community saw Jesus as the divine shepherd whose care, love, and passion for his lambs—the members of his Church—assured salvation (Jn 10:11, 10:14, 21:15). The writers of the New Testament connected the ancient image of the lamb of the Passover to the selfless dedication and love of Christ, even to his death, as a gift or sacrifice worthy to offer God (Lk 10:3; Rev 13:8). In every Mass across the world, we pray, "Lamb of God, you take away the sins of the world: have

mercy on us." See also **Paschal Lamb; Sacrifice.**

LAMENT: A prayer, petition, or ritual of grief that honored the death of a loved one (Sir 38:16–23); the cry of despair over disease, famine, or destruction, marked by the cry of "alas" (Isa 19:8–10; Jer 9:19–26); a ritualized wailing to memorialize loss and remorse (Judg 11:40; Jer 49:3–4).

Eventually, the lament became a literary form, a liturgy of formalized grief presided over by priests and singers who led the community in a release of emotion, a cry and pleading for mercy marked by fasting and prayers to God (1 Macc 1:25–28; Wis 18:10–14). The Book of Lamentations and many of the psalms are examples of laments recorded in the Bible (Ps 38, 51, 74). See also **Mourning Ritual.**

LAST SUPPER: The Gospel event during which Jesus instituted the Holy Eucharist. On the night before he suffered, Jesus gathered his closest friends to celebrate the Feast of Passover to honor the Exodus, in which God called the Israelites out of slavery in Egypt. The Seder and its Paschal lamb memorialized the gift of freedom and God's loving care for his people.

In this most sacred moment, Jesus identified himself as that Lamb of God who would be sacrificed for the salvation of many. At the Last Supper, Jesus took the bread and wine of Passover and consecrated them into the true presence of his body and blood, the Holy Eucharist (Mt 26:17–32; Mk 14:22–25; Lk 22:19–20; 1 Cor 11:23–26). He then washed the feet of the Apostles as a sign of their call to be servant leaders (Jn 13:5–7). Christians celebrate in a special way the events of the Last Supper during the Holy Thursday liturgy. See also **Eucharist; Passover.**

LAW IN THE NEW TESTAMENT:

The Law that was revealed to Moses was also taught by Jesus: "Love the Lord your God with all your heart, and with all your soul, and with all your mind. . . . Love your neighbor as yourself" (Mt 22:36–40; Lk 10:27–28). Rabbi Jesus affirmed everything revealed to Moses and his ancestors in faith (Mt 5:17–20).

In the time of Christ, Jewish religious leaders had reduced the Law to a rigid set of religious observances and moral laws. This may have been unavoidable due to the influence of the Greeks, for whom law meant following a strict moral code. The original Covenant was more about being in proper relationship with God and one another. Through Jesus Christ, God sealed a New Covenant with the entire human race. In this New Covenant, we are saved through faith in Christ, not by following a rigid set of religious observances and laws (Rom 3:27).

As a result, a strong theme runs throughout the New Testament that the Law alone is not the path to salvation. In the Letter to the Romans, Saint Paul provides an elaborate—and sometimes difficult to understand—analysis of the role of the Law and the gift of faith by which all people are saved (Rom 2—3).

LAW OF MOSES (moh´zis): Modern

people think of law as a written code that governs what a society may and may not do. The Law in the Bible was much more than that. It was the set of stories, religious rituals, and moral laws that defined the relationship of the Israelite people to their God. These are recorded in the first five books of the Old Testament, which are also called the books of the Law or the Torah. Yahweh gave Moses the tablets containing the Law (Ex 31:18), which is why it is also called the Law of Moses, or the Mosaic Law.

The Law was revealed to Moses as a crucial element of the Israelites' Covenant with God. Indeed, the two are so closely connected that the words *Law* and *Covenant* are often used interchangeably. The Law was a gift, a teaching of truth, and a guide to form right choices—both personal and communal. "Obey my voice, and I will be your God, and you shall be my people; and walk only in the way that I command you, so that it may be well with you" (Jer 7:23). The revealed Law is Good News. See also **Covenant.**

LAYING ON OF HANDS: A sacred

action, blessing, anointing, or consecration. Jesus laid hands on the children to bless them (Mt 19:13–15), on the sick to heal them (Mk 6:5, 8:23–25; Lk 13:13), and on the dead to raise them to life (Mk 5:23–41). The Lord laid hands on the Apostles to set them apart for ministry and assured them that they, too, had received and would impart the gift of laying on of hands (Mk 16:18).

Like Jesus, the Apostles laid hands on people to bless and heal them. They also laid hands on people to impart the Holy Spirit (Acts 8:17), which often resulted in people receiving spiritual gifts. The laying on of hands became a sacramental action within the ministry of the Church and was listed with spiritual formation, Baptism, and teaching of the mysteries of faith to be passed on by the elders in the community (Heb 6:2; 1 Tim 4:14–15).

LAZARUS (laz´uh-ruhs): His name meant "God helps." Lazarus was a beloved friend of Jesus and the brother of the disciples Mary and Martha. When Lazarus had fallen ill, the sisters sent for Jesus. By the time Jesus arrived, Lazarus had lain dead in his tomb for four days. The sisters were tormented in their belief that if Jesus had been there, Lazarus would have lived. Jesus consoled Martha with an awesome promise: "I am the resurrection and the life. Those who believe in me, even though they die, will live" (Jn 11:25).

Jesus himself was deeply moved with grief and wept. Then, he ordered the stone covering the tomb to be rolled away. After offering thanksgiving to his heavenly Father, Jesus cried, "Lazarus, come out!" (Jn 11:43). At his word, Lazarus returned to life and walked out of his tomb, alive! In the Gospel of John, this great miracle was the culminating sign of Christ's divine authority (Jn 11:1–44). Lazarus served the mission of Christ for the rest of his time on earth. Wherever he went, the crowds wanted to see the man whom Jesus called back to life. Because of his witness, many believed in Jesus, so much so that the authorities also plotted to kill Lazarus as well as Jesus (Jn 11:45–53, 12:9–11). See also **Bethany; Martha of Bethany; Mary of Bethany.**

LAZARUS AND THE RICH MAN (laz´uh-ruhs): A parable Jesus told that focused on a poverty-stricken man named Lazarus, who was starving to death and covered with sores. A rich man passed Lazarus every day and ignored his plight. The rich man ended up in hell, and Lazarus ended up in heaven (Lk 16:19–31). Jesus' point was that being wealthy was not necessarily a sign of being blessed by God; in fact, ignoring a brother or sister in need when one has the power to help is a great sin. See also **Justice.**

LEAH (lee´uh): The oldest daughter of Laban and sister to Rachel. Jacob fell in love with the beautiful Rachel and asked Laban for her hand. Laban made Jacob work seven years for Rachel's bride price, and then secretly substituted Leah in the wedding rite. Although tricked, Jacob honored their union and worked another seven years to marry Rachel (Gen 29—30).

Leah is remembered as having lovely eyes (Gen 29:17). She became a matriarch of Israel and bore Jacob six sons: Reuben, Simeon, Levi, Judah, Issachar, and Zebulun, and one daughter, Dinah. Leah's slave Zilpah bore Jacob two sons: Gad and Asher. See also **Dowry; Jacob; Laban; Zilpah.**

LEAVEN: In ancient times, fermented dough was used as a type of yeast, or leaven, in the making of bread. It takes only a small amount of leaven to make a batch of bread dough rise. Jesus used the image of the action of leaven as a sign of the Kingdom of God. When one sows love, justice, and compassion, it will spread among individuals and throughout the world (Mt 13:33).

During the Exodus, the Passover bread was made so quickly that there wasn't time for it to rise. So the Passover Feast is celebrated with unleavened bread (Ex 12:15; Lev 2:11). The hosts that are consecrated during the Eucharist are made from unleavened bread.

LEBANON (leb´uh-nuhn): In ancient times, Lebanon was the land of the Phoenicians and referred to the 100 miles of snow-capped mountains and surrounding terrain that lined the eastern coast of the Mediterranean Sea in Palestine (Jer 18:14). Lebanon was part of Canaan and was famous for its forests of cedar (1 Kings 4:33; Ps 92:12). Solomon sought out Lebanon to supply cedar for the construction of the Temple of David as well as for the construction of the royal palace.

LEGION: Six thousand Roman soldiers led by sixty centurions. The word *legion* was used twice in the Gospels. In one story, Jesus healed a man possessed by an unclean spirit that called itself "Legion," meaning there were many spirits of darkness present and that the condition of the poor soul was critical (Mk 5:1–20).

At Gethsemane, Jesus said his Father would send twelve legions of angels to his defense if asked (Mt 26:53), but Jesus freely chose to embrace the cross for humanity's salvation.

LEPER, LEPROSY (lep´uhr) (lep´ruh-see): A leper is a person with leprosy. In biblical times, leprosy identified a wide spectrum of skin disorders. Beginning with infected pustules on the eyelids and hands, leprosy spread across the whole body. The hair turned white, the skin broke out with white scales, sores, ulcers, and swellings. Eventually, the whole body decayed. Leprosy was contagious, and there was no known cure at the time.

To avoid further infection, the Law of Moses had detailed instructions for identifying leprosy and avoiding con-

tamination (Lev 13—14). Lepers were isolated from the town and forced to wear identifiable dress, leave their heads uncovered, and identify themselves as unclean. The leper was forced to live separate from the community for fear of the spread of the disease (Num 5:1–4). Only priests upon close examination could declare a person free from the disease.

In Jesus' time, many thought that leprosy was a punishment from God. Jesus showed compassion on lepers; he touched them and healed their leprosy (Mt 8:2–4).

LETTER: A written address, a literary form used for communication. The letters in the New Testament were also known as epistles. There are twenty-one letters in the New Testament. Saint Paul was the most prolific letter writer, with thirteen letters written by him or people writing in his honor. The structure of first-century letters usually followed an established format: a greeting to the intended recipient, a blessing, the main content, and a closing with final greetings and blessings.

The New Testament letters were addressed to individuals, local Christian churches in specific cities, and all Christians in general. Early Christian leaders wrote these letters to pass on wisdom, correction, and community information. By studying these letters, modern readers gain insight into the formation of the early Christian Church and gain wisdom for how we are called to be the Church today.

LEVI, LEVITE (lee´v*i*) (lee´v*i*t): One of Leah's sons fathered by Jacob (Gen 29:34). Levi became a patriarch of Israel and the head of the tribe that carried his name, also called Levites. Moses and Aaron were descendants of Levi (Ex 2:1). According to the command of God, only Aaron and his sons could serve as priests (Ex 28:1). Thus, the Levites became the tribe entrusted with sacred ministries, the caretakers of the tabernacle and the Temple (Num 1:48–54). See also **Aaron; Priest; Sacrifice.**

LEVIATHAN (li-vi´uh-thuhn): A creature common in Semitic creation myths. The Leviathan was the symbol of power and chaos, often pictured as a serpent monster or dragon. We see hints of the Leviathan in the deep waters calmed by God at Creation and in the image of the serpent in the garden of Eden. More explicit references to God having power over the Leviathan are found in Job, the Psalms, and Isaiah (Job 41:1–34; Ps 74:13–14; Isa 27:1–3). See also **Dragon.**

LEVIRATE MARRIAGE (lev´uh-rit): If a man were to die without leaving an heir, the Law of Moses provided that the dead man's brother would take the widow as his own wife. The children of this

union would be considered the descendants of the dead man (Deut 25:5–10). See also **Onan; Tamar of the House of Judah.**

LIBATION (li-bay´shuhn): An offering poured out as a sacrifice to the Holy One. A libation could be an offering of wine poured around the altar (Num 15:5), the pouring of sacred waters, or offerings of blood poured out in sacrifice (Ps 16:4).

LIGHT OF THE WORLD: The words of the prophet Isaiah echo across the ages, "The people . . . in darkness have seen a great light" (Isa 9:2). The New Testament saw this prophecy fulfilled in Jesus, the Light of the World (Jn 8:12). Christ shattered the dark night, healed the soul, and led humans to salvation and eternal life (Jn 11:9–10). Jesus called his followers to be the "salt of the earth" and "light of the world" (Mt 5:13–14). The Holy Spirit, through Baptism, empowers disciples of every age to bring the light of Christ to the world.

LITERARY CRITICISM: See **Exegesis.**

LOGOS (loh´gohs): A Greek term meaning "word." *Logos* is the Greek word used in the Gospel of John to describe Christ as the Word of God (Jn 1:1–18). In the first Creation story in Genesis 1, God's word is so powerful that simply by speaking, God caused all creation to come into existence. By calling Jesus the *Logos*, John's Gospel is saying that Jesus is God's divine son.

Logos was a beloved title in the Greco-Roman world. The people of that time believed in the power of words. The Evangelist John used *Logos* to describe Christ at the beginning of his Gospel, since he was writing for people heavily influenced by Greek culture and world-view.

LOIS AND EUNICE (loh´is) (yoo´nis): Lois was the maternal grandmother, and her daughter Eunice the mother, of Timothy, a young evangelist who became a friend and disciple of Saint Paul (2 Tim 1:5). These Jewish women were learned in the Scripture and dedicated to the faith (2 Tim 3:14–15). Although Eunice was married to a Greek, she and Lois raised Timothy within the traditions of Judaism and later, Christianity (Acts 16:1).

LORD: Socially, a title of respect for males of important status; the title *Adonai*—which meant "lord" in Hebrew—was also used for God in the Old Testament. The Greek word for lord is *Kyrios*. This became an important title for Jesus Christ for the early Christian community. Jesus was called Lord in the New Testament almost 600 times. To say "Jesus is Lord" was a statement of faith in Jesus' divinity that could only be truly proclaimed by a person who believed in Christ (1 Cor 12:3). See also **Adonai; Jesus Christ.**

LORD'S DAY: The term early Christians used to describe the day of the Lord's Resurrection, which they celebrated on Sunday, the first day of the week. The term is used only once in the Bible (Rev 1:10). The earliest Christians probably attended observances in the synagogue on the Sabbath (Saturday), and then celebrated the Eucharist on the Lord's Day (Sunday) in house churches. See also **Parousia; Sabbath.**

LORD'S PRAYER: The way in which Jesus taught his followers to pray has come to be known as the Lord's Prayer—which Catholics also call the "Our Father." The two versions of this prayer (Mt 6:9–13; Lk 11:2–4) are short summaries of Jesus' key teachings: God as Father, reverence, the centrality of the Kingdom of God, trusting God for our forgiveness, and avoiding all forms of evil.

LORD'S SUPPER: See Bread of Life; Eucharist; Last Supper.

LOT: A nephew of Abraham. When God called Abram, Lot left the tribe to travel with his uncle to the land of Canaan. After the journey into Egypt to escape famine and the group's return to Canaan, Lot separated from Abram's clan for a last time and went to Sodom (Gen 12—13).

Lot and his family became prisoners of war in the battles of the kings of Elam against the kings of Sodom and Gomorrah. Abram rescued Lot and returned him to safety. Abram offered sacrifice for Lot's safe return with King Melchizedek of Salem, who offered bread and wine as a "priest of God Most High" (Gen 14).

When judgment fell on the cities of Sodom and Gomorrah, Lot and his family were called out of harm's way on the eve of destruction (Gen 19:1–29). Lot's wife looked back as the family escaped the destruction and "became a pillar of salt" (Gen 19:26). See also **Abraham; Sodom and Gomorrah.**

LOTS, CASTING OF: A common form of divination practiced in the ancient Middle East. People threw sticks, dice, or pieces of clay on which were inscribed names or words. Casting lots was thought to reveal destiny and the will of God (Dan 12:13; Esth 3:7). The soldiers who crucified Jesus cast lots for his clothing (Jn 19:24).

LOT'S DAUGHTERS: After the destruction of Sodom and Gomorrah—and the loss of their mother, who was turned into a pillar of salt for her lack of faith—Lot and his two daughters hid together in a cave in the hills of Zoar. Fearing that the world was over and that all people but themselves had been destroyed on the earth, the two women got their old father, Lot, drunk with wine. While he was drunk, they seduced him so they would become pregnant. The children they bore were Moab, the ancestor of the Moabites, and Ben-ammi, the ancestor of the Ammonites (Gen 19:30–38). See also **Moabite.**

LOVE: The word *love* had many meanings in Scripture and identified powerful emotions of affection, reverence, and blessing. Love described the manifestation of the presence of God in creation (Ps 36:5). God's love provided feelings of safety and refuge (Ps 36:7). The steadfast *hesed*, or love God offered humanity, was unconditional and eternal (Ps 86:5). The Scriptures described the Covenant vow between the people of Israel and God as love (Neh 1:5). The love between King David and the LORD became the source of the special relationship between God and the House of David (1 Chr 17). The committed love of marriage expressed the model of relationship God desired to share with humanity (Hos 2:19–20).

Jesus made a distinction between love that was dependent on being loved back and love that was given unconditionally. "If you love those who love you, what credit is that to you? . . . But love your enemies, do good, and lend, expecting nothing in return" (Lk 6:32, 35). For the Christian, Jesus' self-offering on the cross was the most powerful image of love (1 Jn 3:16). The love of money was the basis for many kinds of evil (1 Tim 6:10; Heb 13:5). Saint Paul described the perfection of love in the beautiful thirteenth chapter of 1 Corinthians, a passage often read at Christian weddings.

LOVE OF GOD: The New Testament says simply, "God is love" (1 Jn 4:16). The Old Testament used a special word to describe the love of God: *hesed*. The full meaning of this word is difficult to capture in English but it means loyalty, mercy, devotion, protection of the poor, and loving-kindness. This is the way God loves us and the way we are supposed to love one another. "Love one another. Just as I have loved you, you also should love one another. By this everyone will know that you are my disciples, if you have love for one another" (Jn 13:34–35).

LUCIFER (loo´si-fuhr): The fallen angel who struggles against God, whom we also call Satan. Lucifer is Latin for "light bearer." Lucifer has been thought of as the angelic being, the beautiful "Day Star, son of Dawn" (Isa 14:12), who fell from grace, retaining his powers and intelligence. Catholic Tradition says that Lucifer was a prince of archangels who seduced his legions in rebellion. His sin was pride, hatred of humanity, and idolatry, as he desired to raise his throne "above the stars of God" and to make himself "like the Most High" (Isa 14:13–15). His crimes caused him to be "brought down to Sheol, to the depths of the Pit" (Isa 14:15). Lucifer and his legions exist within a state of hell (Isa 14:12; Rev 12:10); he is kept in "eternal chains in deepest darkness for the judgment . . . day" (Jude 1:6). See also **Satan.**

LUKE: A Gentile friend and coworker of Saint Paul's (Philem 1:24), a physician (Col 4:14), and an Evangelist. Luke did not know Jesus personally but found his faith in Christ from the witness and ministry of Saint Paul. Because some of the passages in Acts referred to "we," it is assumed that Luke ministered with Paul in Jerusalem (20:6—21:18) and Rome

(27:1). Luke also was a companion to Paul during the time of Paul's imprisonment (Philem 1:24; Col 4:14; 2 Tim 4:11).

Luke is traditionally considered to be the writer of the Gospel of Luke as well as the Book of Acts. Most Scripture scholars agree that Luke and Acts were written by the same person in Greece about AD 80–85, but these scholars can't confirm that it is the same Luke who traveled with Paul. Perhaps the author was a disciple of Luke's who named his work after the sainted companion of Paul. See also **Paul**.

LUST: A sin that denies the dignity and honor of the human person. Lust can refer to a sinful sexual desire (Mt 5:28) or a consuming longing for property, title, or pleasure (Ps 68:30; Mk 4:19; Mt 5:28). Lust is one of the seven capital (chief) sins that eat at the peace of the soul, pervert the heart, and damage one's proper relationships with one another and with God.

LXX: See **Septuagint**.

LYDIA (lid´ee-uh): A businesswoman, a seller of purple cloth, and the first European baptized into Christ. On the day Lydia embraced Christ, she had gathered with other women to honor the Sabbath with prayer. Paul and Silas approached them, and as Lydia listened to Paul's teachings, God "opened her heart" (Acts 16:14). She and her entire household—family and slaves—were baptized that day. Lydia then invited Paul and Silas to be guests in her home (Acts 16:13–15). She gave her resources, hospitality, and service to spread the Gospel of Jesus. Lydia's home became a house church and is remembered as the place where Europe's first Christian community gathered (Acts 16:40).

We don't know if "Lydia" was a personal name or a title Luke used to connect the woman to her hometown. She was from the Roman colony of Thyatira in a region that historians also call Lydia (Acts 16:14), which is modern-day Greece. See also **Philippi**.

M

MACCABEES (mak´uh-beez): A family whose real name was the Hasmoneons but became known after the most famous son, Judas Maccabeus. Maccabeus was probably his nickname, meaning "the hammer." The Maccabees became the political and religious leaders of the Judean people in the second and first centuries before Christ.

The Syrian warlord Antiochus Epiphanes persecuted the people, forbade the Torah, and murdered thousands of Jews (167 BC). Antiochus's "abomination of desolation" was his altar dedicated to Zeus in the holy Temple of Jerusalem. This blasphemy triggered the Maccabean War led by Mattathias Hasmon and his sons. After Mattathias died,

Judas took up the cause and became the leader of the revolt (1 Macc 1—2).

The Maccabees were victorious over the Seleucids (Greeks). 1 and 2 Maccabees—which are part of the deuterocanonical books—reveal the struggle and triumph of the Judean people over Antiochus. Their victory culminated in the celebration of Hanukkah (1 Macc 4:52–59). The books contain the story of the rededication of the Temple of Jerusalem, the practice of prayer for the dead, and the Jewish belief in resurrection (2 Macc 7:14, 12:40, 12:43). See also **Hasmoneans; Judas Maccabeus.**

MACEDONIA (mas´uh-doh´nee-uh): The northern part of the Greek peninsula. In New Testament times, Macedonia was a Roman province. Saint Paul preached throughout Macedonia (Acts 16:9–10).

MAGDALA (mag´duh-luh): A town in Galilee, northwest of Tiberias, a few miles outside Jerusalem. The Gospels note that one of the disciples known as Mary was from the area called Magdala (Mk 15:39). In Aramaic, *magdala* meant "tower." The area had a "tower of dyers," which could explain the name.

MAGI (may´j*i*): Mystics of the East who followed a new star that directed them to the birth of the infant king of Israel. The Magi were wise men, seers, and diviners of wisdom from Persia, Babylon, Syria, Arabia, or Egypt. They are mentioned only in the Gospel of Matthew (Mt 2:1–12). Their desire to seek the newborn Christ served as a proclamation that the new king they sought would bring people together from the whole world to form the family of God. See also **Epiphany.**

MAGIC: The art of divination, sorcery, charms, and spells, as well as speaking incantations. Magical readings were made through rods (Hos 4:12), cups (Gen 44:5), arrows, the consultation of teraphim—or household gods—the inspection of livers (Ezek 21:21), or the consultation of oracles (Mic 3:11). The Law of Moses forbade the use of magic (Deut 18:9–14).

In the New Testament, practitioners of magic included Simon Magus (Acts 8:9), Bar-jesus (Acts 13:6), a slave girl (Acts 16:16), and the notorious dealers in magical books at Ephesus (Acts 19:19).

MALACHI (mal´uh-k*i*): His Hebrew name meant "my messenger." The writer of the prophetic Book of Malachi remains unknown, although the writings are thought to be a compilation of several works edited together after the Babylonian Captivity.

The prophet proclaimed God's dissatisfaction with shallow worship and had harsh criticism for faithlessness. Malachi was the last book of the Old Testament; it proclaimed a coming messenger of God who would pass judgment on the good and the bad (Mal 3:1–5). It also proclaimed that the prophet Elijah would usher in the time of the Messiah (Mal 4:5–6). This idea became central to early Christian thought and connected Elijah with John the Baptist (Mt 17:10–13).

MAMMON (mam´uhn): A Chaldean and Syrian word meaning "blessings of wealth or riches" (Lk 16:13).

MANASSEH (muh-nas´uh): The thirteenth king of Judah, the only son of the noble Hezekiah. Manasseh (698–642 BC) had the longest reign of any king of the House of David, fifty-five years (2 Kings 21:1).

Manasseh made a career of desecrating his father's religious reforms. He returned Judah to the ways of the foreign nations, erected Asherah poles, rebuilt the altars to Baal, restored the high places, committed numerous murders, sacrificed children including his own son as a burnt offering, worshipped the hosts of heaven within the Temple of Jerusalem, practiced soothsaying and augury, and brought back many foreign practices that had been abolished. His was a reign of great shame, a time in which the Law was blatantly abused (2 Kings 21:1–18). The Assyrians took Manasseh captive. During captivity, Manasseh repented and was eventually released to return to Jerusalem. Upon his return, he destroyed the idols and restored proper worship in the Temple (2 Chr 33:10–17).

Manasseh was also the name of one of the sons of Joseph, Jacob's son. Manasseh and his brother, Ephraim, each received a share of their grandfather Jacob's blessing. Because of this, one of the Twelve Tribes of Israel is descended from and named after Manasseh. See also **Ephraim; Joseph of Egypt; King.**

MANGER: A type of stall or trough where animals were fed. The manger was located in the bottom floor of a home, carved into a wall, or situated within a cave. In the Gospel of Luke, the infant Jesus was laid in a manger at the time of his birth, for there was no room at the inn (Lk 2:7).

MANNA (man´uh): A foodstuff that the Hebrews gathered from the desert floor during the sojourn, after the Exodus from Egypt (Ex 16). The word *manna* meant "the allotment," or the gift from God. Manna was described as a little round piece of bread that the Hebrews prepared as their food. The people consumed manna on the day they gathered it. On the Sabbath, no manna was found, but on Fridays, a double portion appeared. When the Israelites arrived in the Promised Land, the LORD no longer supplied manna. At the first harvest of corn, the appearance of manna ceased (Josh 5:12).

The New Testament referred to Jesus as the true bread from heaven (Jn 6:48–51) and the "hidden manna" (Rev 2:17). See also **Bread; Exodus.**

MARANATHA (mair´uh-nath´uh): A proclamation of hope that meant "My Lord is coming" or "come Lord quickly."

MARDUK (mahr´dyook): A Chaldean thunder god whose name meant "son of the storm." Marduk—also called Bel—became the main god of Babylon. As the power of Babylon's military intensified in the Middle East, the Babylonians ordered that Marduk be worshipped as the universal and absolute god. During the Babylonian Captivity, the Israelite captives in Babylon were forced to worship Marduk and build temples and statues in his honor. The Book of Daniel told the story of brave Israelites who refused to worship Marduk. See also **Tiamat.**

MARK: See **John Mark.**

MARRIAGE: A covenant or a sacrament that God created to sustain love and life between a man and a woman (Gen 2:24; Mt 19:4–6). The purpose of marriage is to build bonds of love and unity between men and women, to have and nurture children, and to create family units that will be sources of God's blessings. The couple bonds with one another and with the community, which supports and blesses their sacramental commitment.

The Creation story in Genesis provides an image of God's gift of marriage. God created the woman Eve and the man Adam as partners for the journey of life (Gen 2:18–24). Without each other, they would have been lonely and unfulfilled.

Prophets used the symbol of the marriage union as an allegory for God's relationship with humanity (Isa 54:5; Hos 2:20). Jesus offered the wedding feast as a model for the Kingdom of Heaven, as a family affair (Mt 22:1–14). He also strengthened the status of marriage by condemning the practice of easy divorce (Mt 19:3–9). A New Testament allegory described Jesus as the wedding groom, heaven as the wedding banquet, and the Church as the bride of the Lamb (Eph 5:25–27; Rev 19:7–9). See also **Divorce; Wife.**

MARRIAGE FEAST: See **Wedding Feast.**

MARTHA OF BETHANY (beth´uh-nee)**:** A close friend and disciple of Jesus, along with her younger siblings, Mary and Lazarus. It was possible that Martha's parents had died, leaving her in charge of the household. She was always focused on the work that needed to be done. So Jesus said to Martha, "Martha, Martha, you are worried and distracted by many things; there is need of only one thing" (Lk 10:38–42).

Martha came to understand what Jesus meant. Jesus revealed his true identity and mission to Martha, told her that he was the "resurrection and the life," to which Martha responded, "I believe that you are the Messiah, the Son of God" (Jn 11:25–27). Jesus raised Martha's

brother, Lazarus, from the dead, the miracle that culminated Jesus' ministry in the Gospel of John. See also **Bethany; Lazarus; Mary of Bethany.**

MARY MAGDALENE (mag´duh-leen)**:** One of several female disciples who traveled with Jesus and who financially supported his ministry (Lk 8:1–3). Magdalene is not a last name; this Mary was from the small fishing village of Magdala in Galilee. Sometimes, she was called Mary of Magdala.

People sometimes confuse Mary Magdalene with the sinful woman in Luke 6, but she is not the same person. When Mary Magdalene met Jesus, seven demons possessed her (Lk 8:2), a critical spiritual and physical illness that infected her total person. Jesus completely healed Mary, and she, like so many others, was made a new creature. Jesus became her teacher and Lord (Jn 20:16).

Mary Magdalene followed Jesus to the end, walked with him on the road to Golgotha, and stood with the Sorrowful Mother and John the Beloved at the foot of the cross (Lk 24:20; John 19:25). In the Gospels of Matthew, Mark, and Luke, Mary and the other faithful women went to anoint Jesus' body early Easter morning but found an empty tomb. In the Gospel of John, Jesus appeared to Mary Magdalene before anyone else and sent her to tell the other disciples that he had risen (Jn 20:11–18). Her proclamation "I have seen the Lord!" became the first hallelujah of Easter (Jn 20:18). The Church fathers called her the apostle to the Apostles.

MARY OF BETHANY: (beth´uh-nee)**:** A close friend and disciple of Jesus, along with her older sister, Martha, and her brother, Lazarus. Mary of Bethany was remembered as a model disciple. At Passover, Lazarus, Martha, and Mary invited Jesus and the disciples to dinner in their home. As Martha busied herself with the demands of hospitality, Mary sat at Jesus' feet. Martha became irritated with Mary and demanded that Jesus tell her to help with the tasks at hand. Jesus affirmed Mary's desire to listen to the teacher, saying she had chosen the better way (Lk 10:38–42). This story of Martha and Mary of Bethany was offered to teach the disciples of Jesus to be aware of the glory of God and to balance life between prayer and works.

This Mary also took a pound of perfumed nard, poured the rich essence on the feet of Jesus, and dried his feet with

her hair. This rite symbolized faith, service, hospitality, and reverence in preparing Jesus for his passion and death to come (Jn 12:1–8). See also **Bethany; Lazarus; Martha of Bethany.**

MARY OF NAZARETH (naz´uh-rith): The mother of Jesus, the mother of God. Mary was a Jewish woman from Nazareth. At an early age, she was betrothed to Joseph of the House of David (Mt 1:16–18). The archangel Gabriel appeared to the Virgin Mary, called her favored by God, chosen to be the mother of the Messiah—Jesus, the Son of the Most High (Lk 1:26–38). Mary said, "Let it be with me according to your word" and offered herself as "the servant

of the Lord" (Lk 1:38).

Mary sought counsel from her cousin Elizabeth (Lk 1:40), married Joseph, and because of a decree by Caesar Augustus, journeyed to Bethlehem, where she gave birth to the Christ child (Lk 2:1). Shepherds, angels, and Magi from the East came to honor her son (Lk 2:8–18; Mt 2:1). When Mary and Joseph presented the child at the Temple, the prophets Anna and Simeon affirmed his mission as redeemer but warned Mary that she would become the Sorrowful Mother, suffering great sorrow as his mother (Lk 2:29–38). Mary is sometimes called the first disciple of Jesus because she followed him from the beginning and was the first to believe in his power, asking him to perform a miracle at the wedding feast of Cana (Jn 2:5).

Tradition teaches that Mary remained a virgin. Scripture presents Mary with an extended family: the brothers James, Joses, Judas, and Simon, and unnamed sisters of Jesus (Mk 6:3). These could have been Joseph's children from a previous wife or more likely cousins of Jesus. Jesus called his disciples his family and offered Mary to the community as its mother (Mt 12:46–50; Jn 19:27).

Mary watched Jesus suffer torture and be condemned to death, accused as a traitor by the Roman state. The Sorrowful Mother stood at the foot of the cross with Mary Magdalene, Mary Clopas, Johanna, Susanna, John the Beloved disciple, and Salome, the mother of James and John (Mt 27:56; Jn 19:26–27; Lk 24:20).

Scripture placed Mary of Nazareth with the frightened followers of Christ who gathered in fear of Rome, as the Holy Spirit descended in the form of tongues of fire on the first Pentecost of the Church (Acts 2:1–12). While not recorded in Scripture, at Mary's death, she was assumed into heaven, body and soul. She is a model of faith and discipleship for all. Across the ages, Mary has been held in reverence as the Virgin Mother of Christ, the Blessed Mother of Jesus, and Mother of the Church. See also **Annunciation.**

MARY THE MOTHER OF JOHN MARK:

This Mary's home was the place the Christians in Jerusalem gathered. Saint Peter fled to her for sanctuary after his release from prison (Acts 12:12). See also **John Mark.**

MARY THE WIFE OF CLOPAS

(kloh´puhs)**:** One of the Galilean disciples who followed Jesus throughout his ministry. In the Gospels, Mary Clopas is remembered as the other Mary (Mt 28:1). She may have also been the mother of James and John (Mt 27:56), but this is difficult to determine since Mary was such a common name, and the Gospels do not always distinguish among the different Marys.

Mary Clopas stood at the foot of the cross with Mary, the Sorrowful Mother, and Mary Magdalene. She may have been the Blessed Mother's sister (Jn 19:25). She was with Mary Magdalene and Joseph of Arimathea as they wrapped the dead body of Jesus in the shroud and laid it in the tomb (Mt 27:61). At dawn, she returned with her daughter Salome and Mary Magdalene to anoint the body of Jesus, found the empty tomb, and heard the angel announce that Jesus had been raised from the dead (Mk 16:1).

MASSORETIC SCRIPT

(mas´uhret´ik)**:** The Hebrew word *masorah* refers to the transmission and preservation of the Hebrew Scriptures. The Massorites were rabbis of AD ninth-century Palestine who translated the ancient Hebrew Scriptures—or the Old Testament—into modern Hebrew by adding vowels, grammar, and punctuation. Their translation, the Massoretic Script, is still used today.

MATRIARCH:

Word referring to an original mother of a group, who would become a "house." Matriarchs were female ancestors like Sarah (Gen 17:15), Rebekah (Gen 24), Rachel (Gen 29), and Leah (Gen 29). The matriarch Tamar bore Perez to Judah, and her house continued (Gen 38:25). Rahab was the matriarch of a family that survived in Israel (Josh 6:25). Deborah became a "mother in Israel" (Judg 5:7), and the honorable matriarch Ruth mothered a house whose descendant was King David (Ruth 4:11–22). See also **House; Patriarch.**

MATTATHIAS HASMON

(mat´uhthi´uhs haz´muhn)**:** A priest who, with his five sons, began a revolt against the Seleucid (Greek) occupation of Israel (167 BC). His sons were known as the Maccabees, and after Mattathias's death, they continued the revolt to a successful conclusion (1 Macc 2). Their descendants ruled Israel for several generations and were called the Hasmoneans. See also **Hasmoneans; Judas Maccabeus; Maccabees.**

MATTHEW

(math´yoo)**:** A tax collector in Capernaum. Matthew was also called Levi, son of Alphaeus (Mk 2:14). Tax collectors were hated in the occupied territories of Palestine. They collected funds, paid themselves, turned over the bulk of the monies to the Temple or Rome, and kept the rest for themselves. Matthew was sitting in his tax booth when Jesus said "Follow me" (Mt 9:9).

Matthew hosted a dinner during which Jesus, his disciples, other tax collectors, and people known as sinners broke bread together. The Pharisees asked the disciples why Jesus would eat with such people. Jesus said these were the people who needed him, that the sick needed a doctor, and these were the people for whom he came (Mt 9:10–13). Jesus said the tax collectors and the prostitutes were more righteous than the chief priests (Mt 21:31–32).

The Gospel attributed to Matthew was probably not written by this Apostle but by an unknown disciple in the city of Antioch around AD 75–80. See also **Apostle.**

MATTHIAS (muh-thi′uhs): Replaced Judas Iscariot as the twelfth Apostle. The Apostles prayed that Jesus would lead them in their choice for the ministry of apostleship, and Matthias was chosen by lots (Acts 1:15–26).

MEEKNESS: The virtue of humility, the opposite of the sin of pride. John the Baptist expressed the quality of meekness when he proclaimed he was unworthy to "untie the thong of [the] sandal" of the One who was to come (Jn 1:26–27). In the Beatitudes, Jesus taught that meekness was a primary value in the Reign of God. The meek would inherit the earth (Mt 5:5). The gentleness of the meek was a virtue bonded to a refusal to abuse power such as when Jesus refused to summon angels to help him in his Passion (Mt 26:53). Meekness is essential to the Christian life: "Clothe yourselves with compassion, kindness, humility, meekness, and patience" (Col 3:12).

MEGIDDO (mi-gid′doh): A city in the Plain of Esdraelon in northwestern Palestine. Megiddo was a strategic location for armies and trade routes coming north from Egypt or south from Damascus and Syria. Legend says more battles have been fought in Megiddo than any other place. On the Plain of Esdraelon, the great battlefield of Palestine, Deborah of Ephraim, judge and prophet, joined Barak to defeat the Canaanites by the waters of Megiddo (Judg 4—5). At Megiddo, King Josiah died at the hands of the Egyptians (2 Kings 23:29). Because of its history, Megiddo is used symbolically in apocalyptic literature. In the Book of Revelation, Armageddon—a name derived from Megiddo—is the site of the battle at the end of days, the final victory of Christ over the Antichrist (Rev 16:16). See also **War.**

MELCHIZEDEK (mel-kiz′uh-dek): The king of Salem and a "priest of God Most High" (Gen 14:18). Abraham met Melchizedek after battle with the kings of Elam and Sodom and Gomorrah. Lot had been taken prisoner of war, and Abraham returned him to safety. Melchizedek offered bread and wine in thanksgiving (Gen 14:18–24).

The early Christians valued the image of Melchizedek. He was a priest, yet not of the priestly class of Aaron. No father, mother, or genealogy is attributed to Melchizedek—like many early Christians. The priesthood of Jesus was understood in relation to the tradition of Melchizedek, who offered bread and wine to God (Heb 7). See also **Priest.**

MESHACH (mee′shak): Judean friend of the folk hero Daniel. During the Babylonian Captivity, Abednego, Shadrach, and Meshach refused to worship the gods of Nebuchadnezzar and were sentenced to die in a fiery furnace. God spared all three young men from the king's intended execution: the fires left them unharmed. The officials who threw them in the furnace did die from the heat (Dan 3). The story was written during the time of the Maccabean War in 167 BC to show the power of faith in the true God. See also **Abednego; Shadrach.**

MESOPOTAMIA (mes´uh-puh-tay´ mee-uh): Greek word meaning "land between the two rivers." Mesopotamia was an ancient center of civilization between the Tigris and Euphrates rivers, where the family of Abraham had its roots (Gen 11:16). Today, Mesopotamia is called Iran and Iraq.

MESSIAH (muh-si´uh): Hebrew word meaning "God's anointed one." Translated as "Christ" in Greek. The title applied to kings, high priests, patriarchs, or prophets whom God called for a special purpose. God promised David that his house, or descendants, would be an eternal dynasty, and the Jews believed the Messiah would come from the House of David (2 Sam 7:13–26). After the Babylonian Captivity, the people of Israel longed for a messiah who would reestablish Israel as a political power, offer himself as a suffering servant before God (Isa 53:11), and lead the people to freedom from all bondage. Many were expecting the messiah to be a warrior king—like David—which is why many did not recognize Jesus as the Messiah.

In the New Testament, Jesus was revealed as God's Messiah (Jn 1:41, 4:25–26). He was referred to as Christ or Messiah more than 380 times. See also **Anointing; Christ; Jesus Christ; Oil.**

METHUSELAH (mi-thoo´suh-luh): The son of Enoch, and the grandfather of Noah. Methuselah lived longer than any other biblical figure, a legendary 969 years (Gen 5:21–27). Methuselah was a figure of great wisdom and honor.

MICAH (mi´kuh): A prophet from Judah whose name meant "like God." Micah lived in the late eighth century BC as Assyria plundered Israel. Micah warned that idolatry and injustice had caused the suffering and that the truth was never welcome to those blinded by sin. Micah said that immoral sexual behavior, theft, and violence had left the people spiritually weak; all these things led to economic collapse and paved the way for war (Mic 1—2).

In 721 BC, the Assyrians destroyed Israel, the northern kingdom, and Micah blamed the destruction on political and religious leaders who "hate the good and love . . . evil" (Mic 3:1–4). He offered hope that healing would follow repentance (Mic 2:12–13). Micah prophesied that a time was coming when nations "beat their swords into plowshares, and their spears into pruning hooks; nation shall not lift up sword against nation, neither shall they learn war any more" (Mic 4:3–4). Micah prophesied that one day, a woman from Bethlehem would give birth to a royal shepherd who would bring peace to the earth (Mic 5:2–5). See also **Prophet.**

MICHAEL, THE ARCHANGEL: One of the three archangels mentioned in the Bible. Michael is Israel's angelic prince, invoked to offer strength and protection against attack (Dan 10:13, 12:1–2). In the New Testament, he is

said to have "contended with the devil" (Jude 9). And in Revelation, he is pictured as leading the triumph of good over the powers of evil (Rev 12:7–9).

MIDRASH (mid´rash): A Jewish literary teaching tool that ancient scribes and rabbis used to pass wisdom to the current generation. The Hebrew word meant "to inquire." Midrash was a type of writing intended to teach wisdom. A midrash was a commentary developed to interpret Scripture. There were two types of midrash: the chanting of the Law and stories; and commentary offering further insights about a biblical text. Midrash did not attempt to explore the literal sense of a story, but rather its moral and religious meaning.

MIDWIFE: One of the medical practitioners, usually a woman, who assisted with pregnancy, labor, and the birthing of babies. The Book of Exodus tells of Shiphrah and Puah, midwives who refused to cooperate when Pharaoh ordered the murder of all Hebrew male children at birth (Ex 1:15–21).

MILCOM (mil´kuhm): See **Molech.**

MILLSTONE: Stone used to grind food grains, beans, or corn into meal or flour. Individuals used small, hand-held grinding stones for this purpose. Households or communities had stationary millstones made with a rock foundation and a movable top stone that crushed foodstuffs. Lower millstones were chosen for their hardness; both the hand-held and stationary models worked in similar ways. The grain was pulverized into flour by the weight of rotating stone.

The millstone was used as a symbol of survival because its loss represented a lack of bread, one of the basic foods of biblical people. Laws were set in place

that made it unjust to claim a millstone as collateral for debt (Deut 24:6). Jesus once said metaphorically, "It would be better for you if a great millstone were hung around your neck and you were thrown into the sea" (Mk 9:42) rather than be a stumbling block for children to believe in him.

MIRIAM (mihr´ee-uhm): The sister of Moses and Aaron and a coleader of the Exodus. Miriam's name reflected *mara*, the sorrow and bitterness of the Egyptian slavery in which she was raised. When Pharaoh ordered the killing of every Hebrew baby boy (Ex 1:22), Miriam's mother placed Moses in a basket and released him on the waters of the Nile River. Pharaoh's daughter rescued him, and Miriam arranged for their mother to care for her infant brother (Ex 2:4–8). After the Israelites crossed the Red Sea on dry land, she gathered the women, grabbed her tambourine, and sang the song of liberty, the "horse and rider he has thrown into the sea" (Ex 15:21).

Miriam journeyed with her people throughout their sojourn in the desert and died in the wilderness of Zin at Kadesh before the Israelites entered the Promised Land (Num 20:1). She was revered as a prophet of the people (Mic 6:4). See also **Aaron; Moses.**

MITE: The least valuable coin in the time of Christ, a small bronze or copper coin. Sometimes translated in modern Bibles as "penny" (Lk 12:59, 21:2).

MOABITE (moh´uh-bit): The ancient enemy of the Israelite people. Moab was the land across the Jordan River, east of Israel (Num 22:1–4). The land was named for the patriarch Lot's eldest grandson, Moab, who was conceived through incest with his daughter (Gen 19:33–37). The judge Ehud (Judg

3:12–30), King Saul (1 Sam 14:47), and King David (2 Sam 8:2) all had conflicts with the Moabites.

Yet in Moab, Moses looked out over the height of Pisgah and saw the Promised Land. On the highest mountain of Moab, Mount Nebo, he died (Deut 34:5–6). Ruth was a Moabite woman (Ruth 1:4). These stories may have reflected a later attempt to heal the ancient alienation between Moab and Israel. See also **Ehud; Lot.**

MOLECH (moh´lek)**:** The Canaanite god of the abode of the dead, also known as Milcom. The religions of Molech were child sacrifice cults intended to ensure fertility, wealth, and the control of death by passing children through the fire (Lev 18:21).

MONEY: In the ancient world, jewelry, wire, and lumps of gold, silver, copper, and even lead were used as money. Solomon exchanged horses as the commodity of trade (1 Kings 10:28–29). One chariot could be bought for four horses. Precious metals were used as currency based upon their weight in shekels—a common unit of weight. One silver shekel equaled 8.25 grams of precious metal; 1 talent equaled 60 minas, or 3,600 shekels. Ancient texts identify that an ox was worth 1 gold shekel or two tons of grain.

Metal coinage did not come into wide use until the sixth century BC. The Persians (539 BC) and then the Greeks began a system of coinage. Later, Roman coinage was used to unify the authority of the empire. The Roman denarius, a large silver coin, was the usual pay for one day's labor (Mt 20:2). The widow's mite equaled the smallest coin used, the Greek lepton, valued less than a U.S. dime (Mk 14:42). See also **Wages; Weights and Measures.**

MONEY CHANGER: Money changers had offices at the city's gate or within the Temple complex. Money changers acted as bankers and were an essential part of Jewish life in Jesus' time. Money changers exchanged the Roman currency, which had images of false gods and emperors who claimed they were gods, for Jewish currency. Only Jewish currency was acceptable for paying the Temple tax and buying animals for sacrifice (Mt 22:21). However, in Jesus' time, money changers charged excessive fees for this exchange and probably shared some of the profits with the chief priests. Jesus drove these thieves from the Temple to cleanse his Father's house and return it to being a house of prayer (Mt 21:12–13; Mk 11:15; Lk 19:45–46).

MONOTHEISM: The belief in and worship of one, true God. The Israelites were unique in their monotheism; the other peoples in biblical times were polytheistic. That is, they believed in many gods and goddesses.

MORDECAI (mor´duh-ki)**:** The son of Jair, of the tribe of Benjamin, who was carried into the Babylonian Captivity. He was the famous uncle and guardian of the heroine Esther. See also **Esther.**

MORNING STAR: A name given to Christ that proclaimed him as the Light of the World, a symbol of royalty, and the sign of a new age (Num 24:17; 2 Pet 1:19; Rev 22:16).

MOSES (moh´zis)**:** The great liberator, teacher, and lawgiver of the Israelites. Moses is one of the key figures of the biblical story. He was the son of Levi and Jochebed, the brother of Aaron and Miriam (Ex 2:1–11).

speak for him to set the Israelites free (Ex 3–4). Because of this, Moses is considered Israel's first, and greatest, prophet.

Moses returned to Egypt with his brother, Aaron. With signs and wonders, God empowered Moses, Aaron, and their sister Miriam to set the people free, leading them out of slavery in Egypt, across the waters of the Red Sea, and into the desert (Ex 5—18). Moses received the Ten Commandments carved in stone on Mount Sinai and taught the people how to be faithful to the Covenant by following God's Law (Ex 19—23). After many trials and tests in the sojourn in the desert, Moses directed the Israelites into the Promised Land. The Book of Deuteronomy is written as Moses's last great speech, in which he again reminds the Israelites to embrace God's Law. He himself died before their conquest of Palestine (Deut 34).

In the New Testament, Moses continued to be a prominent figure. Christianity honored Moses as the forerunner of the Christ (Jn 1:17; Heb 3:5–6). At the Transfiguration of Jesus, Moses appeared along with Elijah (Mt 17:1–9). In John's Gospel, Jesus claimed that Moses prophesied about Jesus' coming (Jn 5:46). In the Letter to the Hebrews, Moses was a model of faith (Heb 11:23–28). See also **Aaron; Burning Bush; Covenant; Exodus; I AM; Miriam; Mount Sinai; Prophet.**

His life began in Egypt in a most precarious way. Pharaoh intended the infant Moses to drown in the Nile with the other Hebrew male infants he had ordered murdered. Moses's mother crafted a basket into which she placed the baby and released him on the river in hope of sparing his life. Pharaoh's own daughter saved the infant Moses. His Hebrew mother nourished him, and he grew to manhood in the court of Pharaoh (Ex 1:1—2:10).

After seeing an Israelite slave beaten, Moses killed the abuser and, to protect his own life, exiled himself to the deserts of Midian. There he married Zipporah, the daughter of the priest of Midian. One day, while Moses tended his flocks on Mount Horeb, the mountain of God, the angel of the LORD appeared to him in a burning bush. God called to Moses and said, "I am . . . the God of Abraham, . . . of Isaac, and . . . of Jacob" and told him to remove his sandals, for he stood on holy ground (Ex 3:6). God knew of the misery of the Israelites in Egypt and planned to deliver them from their slavery. He then revealed his name to Moses, "I AM WHO I AM" (Ex 3:14). God asked Moses to

MOTHER: The woman who gives birth, nourishes, and cares for children. In the Bible, a mother was a care provider, a source of intimacy, compassion, and understanding. While the father was esteemed as the protector and provider, the Bible teaches that respect and honor was also due to the mother (Ex 20:12; Mt 19:19). Although in biblical times, women often were not considered to be as important as men, some biblical mothers were honored for their courage and faith. Chief among these mothers was Mary of Nazareth, whom we honor as the mother of God and the mother of the Church.

While father is the primary image of God in the New Testament, there are motherly images of God in the Bible. In Isaiah, God said, "As a mother comforts her child, so I will comfort you" (Isa 66:13). Jesus described his longing to protect his people as a mother hen protects her chicks (Mt 23:37).

MOUNT ARARAT: See **Ararat, Mount.**

MOUNT GERIZIM: See **Gerizim, Mount.**

MOUNT HOREB: See **Horeb, Mount.**

MOUNT OF OLIVES: See **Olives, Mount of.**

MOUNT SINAI: See **Sinai, Mount.**

MOUNT ZION: See **Zion, Mount.**

MOURNING RITUAL: In the biblical world, certain rituals expressed grief over the death of a loved one or over a national disaster. The rituals included whipping and gashing the body (Jer 16:6), tearing clothes and wearing sackcloth (Gen 37:34), shaving the head (Job 1:20), going naked (Mic 1:8), and fasting. Friends offered food and a "cup of consolation" (Jer 16:7).

Laments were sung or proclaimed during mourning rituals as cries of despair marked by the wail of "alas" (Jer 22:18). The literary form of lament was developed to use in formal rituals of grief presided over by priests and singers who led the community in a plea to

God for mercy, as in the Book of Lamentations.

The Gospels recorded traces of several mourning rituals (Mt 9:23; Jn 11:19, 11:31–33). In the Beatitudes, Jesus taught, "Blessed are those who mourn, for they will be comforted" (Mt 5:4). See also **Lament.**

MURDER: The intentional killing of an innocent person; a sin condemned by God (Ex 20:13). The primal story against murder is Cain's killing of his brother, Abel (Gen 4:1–16). Yet the Old Testament did not completely prohibit killing. The Mosaic Law allowed for the death penalty for certain sins, as it was believed that murder and other serious sins caused an imbalance and that only the death of the culpable person could restore equilibrium: blood for blood (Ex 21:12–27; Lev 20; Deut 19:10–13). Accidental killing of another was not considered murder (Josh 20:3), nor was justified warfare in defense of life and property.

In the New Testament, Jesus preached a more challenging moral code, one based on unlimited mercy, love, and forgiveness. In the Sermon on the Mount, he spoke against harboring anger (Mt 5:21–26), against taking retaliation and returning "eye for eye" (Mt 5:38–42), and about having unconditional love for all, even for enemies (Mt 5:43–48). Jesus stopped the murder by stoning of an adulteress, a murder that would have been justified under the Law of Moses (Jn 8:1–11). See also **Cain and Abel.**

MUSIC: Art form enjoyed from ancient times. Rhythm and melody flowed from strings, flutes, trumpets, cymbals, harps, lyres, and drums (Ps 150). Music was part of public celebrations, used in liturgical life, and considered a form of prayer. It was played for entertainment, joy, and sadness. Music was played to acknowledge victory in war (Jdt 16:1) and to celebrate God's favor (Ex 15:20).

The first person Scripture identified as a musician was Jubal, who played lyre and pipes (Gen 4:21). King David was remembered as a musician and poet who surrounded himself with music. He danced and sang to the Lord with his people (2 Sam 6:5).

MYSTERY: Christians believe that God is always seeking to make God's self and God's love known to human beings. Yet God's purposes and designs are beyond human ability to understand fully. This is sometimes called mystery. The Incarnation is an example of one such mystery: that Jesus Christ can be both truly God and truly human is a clear teaching but beyond human ability to comprehend fully. The Bible also referred to another mystery, God's plan of salvation. The mystery of salvation was not fully understood until revealed in the life, death, and Resurrection of Jesus (Rom 16:25–27; Eph 3:1–6). The believer celebrates these mysteries of faith. Not only has God revealed the divine to humanity, God also invites us to participate in the mystery of God's manifestation.

MYTH: Stories passed down across the generations to teach lessons and offer insight into the mysteries of life, particularly about the nature of the spirit world and its relationship to the physical world. Many times, mythical stories are cosmic in their scope and are used to shape a culture or religion's fundamental beliefs. Many myths use symbol, allegory, meter, and rhyme; sometimes, they are ritualized or put to music. Mythic stories may sound like real events, but they are not meant to convey history or science. They teach spiritual, moral, and religious truth. See also **Myth in the Bible.**

MYTH IN THE BIBLE: Around 1000 BC, the Hebrews learned the art of writing and began to preserve their sacred history, beliefs, and ethical regulations for future generations. The writers of the Bible were inspired to use well-known myths and folk tales as a source for their work, but inspired by the Holy Spirit, they rewrote and edited these myths and stories. The writers changed the focus, the image of God, and the ethical outcomes in the myths to convey the religious and moral truth God wished to reveal.

Most people accept that the stories of the first eleven chapters of Genesis are mythic. They are sometimes called the primal history to distinguish them from natural history. They may have been somewhat based on, or in reaction to, the myths of other cultures. When Assyria occupied Israel (721 BC) and later, when the Israelites were slaves of Babylon (beginning in 586 BC), they heard Mesopotamian myths such as the epic escapades of the hero Gilgamesh. They heard the myths of Enkidu, the natural man who became the earthling, stories of the ancient serpent who stole the plant of life, as well as the Sumerian myths of Ianna and her sacred tree.

Unlike the Epic of Gilgamesh, the mythic stories of Genesis teach about an all-powerful Creator God who exists without any other gods. The mythic stories of Genesis also teach about human free will, about listening to the wisdom of God, and about the inevitable destruction sin causes. The lessons of Adam and Eve (Gen 1—3), Cain and Abel (Gen 4), Noah (Gen 5—9), and the Tower of Babel (Gen 11:1–9) all teach about a God who is the one and only all-powerful Creator, who wishes to be in loving relationship with God's creation. See also **Flood; Myth; Noah.**

N

NAHUM (nay´huhm): A prophet from Elkosh in southwestern Judah (Nah 1:1) who lived between 663 and 612 BC. The short book of his prophecies described visions of the destruction of Nineveh, divine anger against sin, and the judgment on Assyria for its abusive conquest and occupation of Israel. Nahum's vision became a source of strength and hope during later persecutions of the Judean people and offered the hope that God would restore Israel. See also **Prophet.**

NAOMI (nay-oh´mee): The elder widow in the Book of Ruth. Naomi's Israelite family left Bethlehem in famine and took refuge in Moab—the land of Israel's ancient enemy. Naomi's sons Mahlon and Chilion took the Moabite women Ruth and Orpah as their wives. In a tragic turn of fate, Naomi's husband and sons died, leaving Naomi alone with her beloved Moabite daughters-in-law (Ruth 1:1–5).

As a widow, Naomi had no way to support herself or these young women. In grief, she ordered the younger women to return to their people to spare them the march across the desert to Bethlehem. Weeping, Orpah turned back to Moab, but Ruth refused to leave Naomi. "Where you go, I will go; / where you lodge, I will lodge; / your people shall be my people, / and your God my God" (Ruth 1:16). The story of Ruth's faithfulness to the Jewish faith and to the family she married into encouraged religious tolerance. See also **Ruth.**

NAPHTALI (naf´tuh-l*i*): The second son of Bilhah and Jacob (Gen 30:7–8). Naphtali became a patriarch of one of the Twelve Tribes of Israel. The territory of Naphtali was bounded on the east by the Jordan River and the Sea of Galilee. Its northern boundary was the territory of Dan; its western boundary, Asher. The southern boundary was the land of Zebulun and Issachar.

The Canaanites constantly challenged the land of Naphtali. One descendant of note was Barak, the general who served with Deborah and defeated the armies of Sisera (Judg 4:6–10). The tribe thrived throughout Israelite history until the Assyrians conquered the territory of Naphtali and deported the people to Assyria (2 Kings 15:29). See also **Twelve Tribes.**

NATHAN (nay´thuhn): His name meant "gift from God." The prophet Nathan counseled King David in the Law of God and made David confront his murder of Uriah and his adultery with Bathsheba (2 Sam 12:1–15). Nathan prophesied the eternal dynasty of David. He also prophesied that the construction of a Temple was not David's to do, but rather his son's (2 Sam 7:1–17). Nathan was instrumental in working behind the scenes to see that Solomon was appointed to follow David as king (1 Kings 1).

Nathan was known as a chronicler of the royal histories and served through the reigns of David and Solomon (1 Chr 29:29; 2 Chr 9:29). His sons Zabad and Azariah served in the court of King Solomon (1 Kings 4:5). Nathan appeared in the genealogy of Jesus (Lk 3:31). See also **Bathsheba; David.**

NAZARENE, NAZOREAN (naz´uh-reen) (naz´uh-ree´uhn):
A title that identified a person living in the village of Nazareth in Galilee. Jesus was called a Nazarene (Mt 2:23). The followers of Christ were called "the sect of Nazarenes" (Acts 24:5).

NAZARETH (naz´uh-rith):
A small farming village in the hills of modern-day southern Lebanon, set between the Sea of Galilee on the east and Mount Tabor on the west. Joseph, Mary, and Jesus made their home in Nazareth of Galilee (Lk 2:39). Jesus began his ministry in the region of Galilee (Mt 4:13). As Jesus traveled from town to town, he returned to Nazareth. After an initially warm reception, the people threw him out of town (Lk 4:16–30), which led Jesus to make the famous statement, "No prophet is accepted in the prophet's hometown" (Lk 4:24).

The Roman and Jewish authorities distrusted Galileans, mocked them as troublemakers, and considered Galilee insignificant. Even Nathaniel asked, "Can anything good come out of Nazareth?" (Jn 1:46). See also **Galilee, Galilean.**

NAZIRITE (naz´uh-rit):
In the Hebrew tradition, a Nazirite was a person consecrated to God. The mother could dedicate her child while it was still in her womb. In pregnancy, she was to abstain from alcohol and unclean food and to leave the child's hair uncut (Judg 13:2–25).

Men or women could become Nazirites by taking vows and following some strict practices. Nazirites could not drink alcohol, vinegar, or grape juice. They weren't to eat grapes or raisins or anything from the grapevine, not even the seeds or skins. They were forbidden to cut their hair or shave. They were forbidden to touch the corpse of an animal or human. They were dedicated to prayer and fasting. These practices were designed to dedicate the Nazirite entirely to the service of God (Num 6).

Scripture identified three Nazirites: Samson (Judg 13:4–5), Samuel (1 Sam 1:11), and John the Baptist (Lk 1:15). Saint Paul, as well as other early Christians, apparently took similar temporary vows. When the time of their vows was finished, these Christians were required to remove their hair as part of the rites of purification (Acts 18:18, 21:23–26). See also **Hannah; John the Baptist; Samson.**

NEBUCHADNEZZAR (neb´uh-kuhd-nez´uhr):
A king of Babylon also known as Darius I (605–562 BC). The name Nebuchadnezzar meant "Nebu, preserve the offspring." He conquered Israel and Judah, destroyed the Temple and the holy city of Jerusalem, and finally took the Israelites into captivity in Babylon (2 Kings 25). As a symbol of his conquest, he tortured the Judean king, Zedekiah, putting out his eyes, killing his sons, and subjecting him to imprisonment for the duration of his life (2 Kings 25:6–7).

Nebuchadnezzar was also a central character in the hero stories of the Book of Daniel. After attempts to force Daniel and his friends to worship idols, the king was humiliated when God sentenced him to act like a deranged person

(Dan 4:28–33). When he recovered, Nebuchadnezzar finally acknowledged and Most High God. Nebuchadnezzar died in 562 BC at the age of eighty-four after reigning as king for forty-three years. As predicted by the prophets (Jer 27:7), the Babylonian Empire fell to Cyrus the Persian in 538 BC. See also **Babylonian Captivity; Exile.**

NEEDLE'S EYE: Jesus used this hyperbole, or exaggeration, to teach the difficulties of being attached to material things. "It is easier for a camel to go through the eye of a needle than for someone who is rich to enter the kingdom of God" (Mk 10:25). Some people say the needle's eye may have been a narrow gate in the city wall, but no evidence supports this.

NEHEMIAH (nee'huh-mi'uh): His name meant "Yahweh comforts." Nehemiah (446–413 BC) was a cupbearer to the Persian king in Susa. Upon hearing of the condition of the Temple of Jerusalem, he wept, prayed, fasted, repented, and asked God to hear his prayer. He approached the king and asked permission to rebuild the land of his father's graves. The king granted permission and funds for Nehemiah to rebuild the walls of Jerusalem (Neh 1:1—2:10).

Nehemiah faced opposition in the restoration but ended the quest in victory as governor of the city. Under his leadership, the walls were rebuilt and the population thrived (Neh 11—12). Nehemiah rebuilt not only walls but also the people's identity. This was accomplished through the public reading of the Torah (Neh 8:1–8), tithing, honoring the Sabbath, and most controversially, calling the Israelite men to divorce their Gentile wives (Neh 13). The Book of Nehemiah portrays Nehemiah as working in tandem with the scribe Ezra,

but it is questionable whether they really lived at the same time. See also **Cyrus of Persia; Ezra.**

NEPHILIM (nef'uh-lim): The legendary giants of Palestine who lived on earth before the Flood. The Nephilim were the children of the sons of gods, or fallen angels who raped human women (Gen 6:4). In the mythic accounts of Genesis, the Nephilim were killed in the great Flood and remembered as the spirits of Sheol, the land of the dead (Job 26:4; Isa 14:9).

NERO (nihr'oh): Roman emperor who reigned (AD 54–68) during the writing of Mark's Gospel. Nero (AD 37–68) was the son of Claudius's fourth wife, Agrippina. Nero was a cruel tyrant. When a fire broke out in Rome (AD 64), he blamed it on the Christians and executed many believers, probably including Saint Peter and Saint Paul. The land cleared by the fire permitted Nero to build a new palace, called the gold house.

The effeminate Nero was remembered for his public brutality and sexual perversions. He murdered his own mother and his wives, and then called himself a god. When the Britons, Gauls, and Spanish revolted against Roman rule, Nero fled the Eternal City of Rome and killed himself. Revelation 13:1–18 identifies the beast as 666, which is probably an acronym and numeric spelling for Nero. See also **Beast; Caesar.**

NICODEMUS (nik'uh-dee'muhs): A Pharisee and a leader among the Jews. Nicodemus's encounter with Jesus in the Gospel of John provided the setting for Jesus to explain God's plan of salvation and the nature of Christian Baptism. Jesus proclaimed these well-known words to Nicodemus, "For God so loved the world that he gave his only Son, so that everyone who believes in him may not perish but may have eternal life" (Jn 3:16).

Nicodemus followed Jesus to the end. He joined Joseph of Arimathea in the burial of the Lord. Nicodemus contributed the "mixture of myrrh and aloes, weighing about a hundred pounds" (Jn 19:39) to prepare the body of the Lord for eternal rest.

NINEVEH (nin´uh-vuh): The Assyrian capital city on the shore of the east bank of the Tigris River. In the eighth century BC, Nineveh was a great urban center spanning thirty miles. For hundreds of years, Nineveh was considered the most powerful city in the world before falling to the combined forces of Babylon and the Medes in 612 BC.

The destruction of Nineveh and the fall of the empire was foretold in the writings of Nahum and other prophets (Nah 2). In the story of Jonah, the reluctant prophet, Jonah is sent to Nineveh to call the Ninevites to repentance. See also **Jonah.**

NOAH (noh´uh): Noah's story was set in the primal history of the first chapters of Genesis. Like the other stories in the first eleven chapters, it is mythic in nature. Noah was the grandson of Methuselah, born after the death of Adam. It was a time when sin had corrupted the world with depravity and violence. God looked at creation with regret and decided to "make an end of all flesh" (Gen 6:13) with a planetwide flood. Noah was righteous, so God chose him and his family to repopulate the earth. God gave Noah the exact directions to make an ark and told him to fill the boat with everything needed to survive: men, women, food, and animals. Noah listened to the word of God and obeyed (Gen 6:9—7:10).

When Noah, his family, and the animals were safely inside the ark, the rains raged for forty days and forty nights. When the waters subsided, the rainbow of the covenant between God and humanity filled the sky as a sign of God's glory and the promise of life (Gen 8—9). Noah and his family survived because they had faith in God and God's word (Gen 6:8–9). See also **Ararat; Flood; Myth in the Bible.**

NOD: Place-name meaning "exile," "wandering," "unrest," given to the land east of Eden to which Cain fled after he murdered his brother Abel (Gen 4:16).

NOMAD: One of a traveling people who follow herds and flocks in search of grazing lands. The nomads move across their territory according to the season, the feeding grounds, and water supplies. They live in tents and usually travel in tribal groups. The patriarchs of Genesis were nomads who traveled in response to God's command (Gen 11:31—12:1–9).

NUMBERS: In the English language, numbers simply represent quantities, but not so in the world of the Bible. In Hebrew and other ancient languages, some numbers had symbolic meanings. The following numbers had special meanings: 3, 4, 6, 7, and 12.

The number *3* and its multiple *9* communicated balance, completeness, union, and life force. There are three states of existence: heaven, earth, and hell. There were three times for prayer: dusk, dawn, and noon. Three-year-old animals were worthy for the rite of sacrifice (1 Sam 1:24). For three days and three nights, Jonah prayed in the belly of the fish before he was vomited up on the shore (Jon 2:1–10). Jesus was resurrected after three days. There are three Persons in the Trinity: Father, Son, and Holy Spirit. The legendary people in justice all lived for multiples of *3:* Adam lived 933 years, Seth 912 years, and Methuselah 969 years (Gen 5:27).

The number *4* and its multiple *40* represented balanced forces, the right number, and the right amount of time to complete healing or new creation. There were four winds (Jer 49:36), four directions, and four living creatures that stood before the face of God (Rev 4:6). The Flood raged forty days and forty nights (Gen 7:12). The Israelites ate manna and wandered in the desert forty years before they reached the Promised Land (Ex 16:35). Both King David and King Solomon reigned forty years (2 Sam 5:4; 2 Chr 9:30). Jesus fasted in the desert forty days and forty nights to prepare for his mission (Lk 4:2). For forty days after the Resurrection, Christ appeared to the disciples before ascending into heaven (Acts 1:3).

The number *6* and its multiple *600* represented human weakness and evil because it was one less than the perfect seven. The number six was ominous, suggesting danger and doom. Noah was 600 years old when the Flood overtook the earth (Gen 7:6). Pharaoh's 600 chariots couldn't prevent the Exodus (Ex 14:6–7). The boy David faced the six-cubit-tall giant Goliath, whose javelin weighed 600 shekels (1 Sam 17:4–7). There are six things the Lord hates (Prov

6:16). Daniel was in the lions' den for six days (Dan 14:31). The number of the beast in Revelation was 666 (Rev 13:18).

The number *7* represented perfection and completeness as seen in seven days of Creation, the seventh day of Sabbath, the seven stars and seven lampstands placed in visions of God (Rev 1:20). Every seventh year, the land was to lie fallow to renew itself and debts were to be forgiven in the Jubilee (Lev 25). Jesus sent seventy disciples to proclaim the Good News (Lk 10:1–17). Jesus commanded Saint Peter to forgive seventy-seven times (Mt 18:21–22).

The number *12* equaled the whole people, the life force, and completion. A boy became a man at age twelve (Lk 2:42). Jacob was the patriarch of the Twelve Tribes of Israel (Gen 35:22–26). Armies were victorious in battle with the defeat of 12,000 men, or the deployment of 12,000 soldiers, or 12,000 of the heavenly community (Josh 8:25; Judg 7:2; Rev 7:5–8). Jesus chose twelve special disciples as Apostles. After Jesus multiplied the loaves and fish, twelve basketsful of food were left over (Jn 6:13). The Kingdom of Heaven had twelve thrones for the twelve Apostles, who would judge the Twelve Tribes of Israel (Mt 19:28).

O

OATH: A solemn commitment or vow. In the Bible, people usually made oaths in the name of God or with God as witness (Deut 6:13). Sometimes, oaths called for God's curse if one broke a promise (Ruth 1:16–17). Because oaths were made before God, breaking an oath was seen as a most serious offense against God and a person's honor. See also **Vow.**

OBADIAH (oh´buh-di´uh)**:** His name meant "servant of the LORD." Obadiah was a Judean prophet who was a contemporary of Jeremiah and Ezekiel. His prophecies are contained in the shortest book in the Old Testament, the Book of Obadiah. He preached against Edom for its cruelty against Judah. He also preached that injustice produces injustice: "As you have done, it shall be done to you; / your deeds shall return on your own head" (Ob 15). See also **Prophet.**

OBEDIENCE: In the Old Testament, the Hebrew word for obedience meant primarily "listening" or "hearing." An obedient person heard God's word and followed it (Ex 15:26). To be obedient was simply to align oneself with God's will.

This was especially seen in the New Testament. Jesus was completely obedient to God's will, even if it meant his death (Phil 2:8). Such perfect obedience was necessary to restore humanity's full relationship to God. Obedience to God brought salvation, the common good, and health and happiness. Obedience to parents, government, and even religious leaders was good, but only as long as these authorities reflected the will of God (Mt 28:20; Eph 6:1; Heb 13:17).

OIL: A precious commodity with many uses in the Bible. Olive oil was made by beating and draining the liquid from ripe olives. Lower-grade oil was obtained by pressing the beaten flesh of the fruit a second time. Oil was used for anointings, for healing salves mixed with balm, and for perfumes prepared with spices, cinnamon, and myrrh. It was also used in cleaning and preserving leather.

Olive oil was a food staple used in baking bread, as a garnish, and as a cooking agent. Oil was used as a household fuel. Oil was used to consecrate sacred persons, objects, and places. The rite of pouring oil formalized the role of a messiah or "anointed one": a priest, prophet, or king. See also **Anointing; Messiah; Olive.**

OLD TESTAMENT: The books of the Hebrew Scriptures that contain the religious beliefs and history of the Jewish people. From the beginning of the Church, Christians have recognized these books as the inspired word of God. Ultimately, the Jewish canon became incorporated into the Christian Scriptures as the Old Testament. The titles Ancient Covenant or Old Testament were used early in the history of the Christian Church, coined by the early fathers Tertullian (AD 160–230) and Origen (AD 185–254).

While respecting the Jewish interpretation of the Old Testament, Christians understand the Old Testament differently than do Jews. In the Old Testament,

Christians see prophecies and symbols that point to Jesus as the promised Messiah. Christians believe that the Old Covenant has now been extended to all people of every race and nation in a New Covenant through Jesus Christ. The Law of Moses is fulfilled and seen in its true purpose because of Jesus' moral teaching and the theology of Saint Paul.

The Roman Catholic canon considers sacred the forty-six books of the Septuagint. Since the Reformation, the Protestant canon of the Old Testament has used a different collection of the Hebrew Scriptures, so their Bible contains thirty-nine Old Testament books. See also **Canon; Deuterocanonical Books; Septuagint.**

OLIVE: A tree and its fruit common in the lands of the Bible. Olive trees grow throughout the Mediterranean area, including Palestine. Olives and olive oil were an important part of the Israelite diet. See also **Oil.**

OLIVES, MOUNT OF: Ancient site east of Jerusalem where David fought with his beloved son Absalom (2 Sam 15:30). The Mount of Olives—also called Mount Olivet—is most sacred to the followers of Christ. The Gospels recall that after days of teaching in the Temple, Jesus spent the nights on the Mount of Olives (Lk 21:37). From the village of Bethphage, at the Mount of Olives, Jesus borrowed a donkey for his triumphal entry into Jerusalem (Mt 21:1). After Jesus' Last Supper with his disciples, he retired to the garden of Gethsemane at the Mount of Olives to pray and prepare for his Passion to come (Mk 14:32–42). From the Mount of Olives, Jesus ascended into heaven (Acts 1:12).

OMEGA: See **Alpha and Omega.**

OMRI (om´ rī)**:** The sixth king of the northern kingdom, Israel (876–869 BC). While only a short section of the Bible is devoted to Omri (1 Kings 16:21–28), we know from other sources that in the history of the Middle East, Omri was politically significant. He united Samaria, healed tribal wars, created alliances with his neighbors, and was popular among the foreigners. He built a capital city in Samaria, cementing the northern kingdom's independent identity. In Assyrian documents, the word for all Israelite kings, as well as for the land of Israel, became *Omri*. King Omri brought stability, prosperity, and peace to Samaria and was hailed in Assyria as a statesman for 100 years after his death.

The Law of God, however, does not measure political and financial success as a sign of ethics and morality. Omri "did more evil than all who were before him" (1 Kings 16:25). Omri's idolatry, betrayal of the Covenant, and romance with foreign gods was cause for his condemnation and set the stage for the even greater idolatry and evil of Omri's son, Ahab, and the infamous Jezebel.

ONAN (oh´ nuhn)**:** His Hebrew name meant "power." Onan was the son of the patriarch Judah and his Canaanite wife, Shua. When Onan's older brother died, it was Onan's duty to take his brother's childless wife as his own and have children with her. Onan refused to impregnate Tamar; every time they had sexual intercourse, he spilled his semen on the ground (Gen 38:8). This was displeasing in the sight of the God and because of this, Onan died. He refused the God of life and deprived Tamar of her right to be a mother in Israel (Gen 38:1–10). See also **Levirate Marriage.**

ONESIMUS (oh-nes´uh-muhs): See **Philemon.**

ORACLE (or´uh-kuhl): A message from a god. In the Old Testament, diviners and soothsayers of other nations were consulted for a message or direction from the gods of the foreign nations. The prophets of Yahweh also delivered oracles, particularly as warnings to other nations (Isa 13:1, 14:28).

ORAL TRADITION: In the ancient world, storytellers preserved the sacred wisdom, parables, regulations, and rules of life revealed to the ancestors and passed down across the ages. By telling these stories around campfires and at religious festivals, the sacred wisdom was passed from one generation to the next, until later scribes wrote it down. Many of the stories and teachings in both the Old and New Testaments were passed on by oral tradition for a generation or more before they were written down.

ORIGINAL SIN: In the beginning, God created in goodness all that is. The serpent stole into the sacred garden of Eden and seduced the humans to eat from the Tree of the Knowledge of Good and Evil. Adam and Eve entered into an idolatrous relationship with the serpent, because they trusted the serpent rather than God (Gen 3). This mythic story taught about the first sin that caused humanity to fall from grace and fractured humans' relationships with God, other human beings, and all of creation. Original grace and holiness were lost as a result of the disobedience that marred human nature and confused our understanding of God's will for life.

The Church refers to this first wound as original sin. No one born on earth is personally responsible for this original fault, yet we are all affected by its infection. This wound of the soul is passed on to the generations as an inclination toward sin and an alienation from God.

Throughout the Bible's story, God reached out to humanity, offered covenants, and sent judges, saints, priests, prophets, and kings to lead humanity to repentance and return to grace. God's son Jesus Christ, the "new Adam," was the ultimate gift. Jesus offered his life, teachings, death, and Resurrection to fully reconcile us to the love of God. Christ redeemed humanity, healed this alienation, broke the bonds of original sin, and offered himself as the New Covenant with God (1 Cor 15:21–22). Through Baptism, we are united with Christ, and original sin is washed away. See also **Eden; Fall; Redemption; Tree of the Knowledge of Good and Evil.**

ORPHAN: A child without parents or, in the Bible, a child whose father had died. A mother alone was not capable of caring for herself or her child without a patron, because women had no rights in most places in the ancient world. An orphan was born into poverty and destitution, without a patron or the means to survive. The Law of Moses provided for the care of orphans (Deut 24:17–22). Jesus promised not to leave his followers orphaned as he gave them an intimate relationship with his Father (Jn 14:18; Jas 1:27). See also **Justice.**

OTHNIEL (oth´nee-uhl)**:** The first judge of Israel. After entering the land of Canaan, the Israelites fell into the ways of the nations and worshipped the Baals and the Asherahs. As a result of their idolatry, they were occupied for eight years by Aram under King Cushan-rishathaim. God called Othniel into service of the Covenant. Othniel defeated the Arameans because the "spirit of the LORD came upon him" (Judg 3:10). He served Israel as judge for forty years. Sadly, at Othniel's death, Israel returned to the practices of the Baals (Judg 3:7–11). See also **Judge.**

P

PALESTINE: In the time of Jesus, an occupied territory of Rome. Named for the Philistine peoples who had inhabited the land of Canaan for millennia, Palestine was divided into three general areas: Galilee was to the north, Judah to the south, and the central lands of Samaria in between. The capital and religious heart of Palestine was the city of Jerusalem with the reconstructed Temple of David. See also **Canaan, Canaanite.**

PALM: A tree with a long, slender trunk and with branches and leaves clustered at the top. The palm has been cultivated in the Middle East for millenia. In Mesopotamia and the Middle East, the palm symbolized fertility, abundance, wisdom, and sexuality.

In the Hebrew culture, the palm was considered a sign of survival, security, rest, and oasis (Num 24:6, 33:9). Carved palms covered with gold leaf were used to decorate the Temple of

David (1 Kings 6:29). Ancient Jericho was known as "the city of palm trees" (2 Chr 28:15). Palms were used in celebrations (Neh 8:15) and as a sign of peace (1 Macc 13:37), as well as a sign of victory in war (1 Macc 13:51). The hero Maccabeus was welcomed with the swaying of palms (2 Macc 10:7). The palm was the symbol of Jesus' triumphal entry into Jerusalem and is used today during the Passion liturgies of Palm Sunday to begin the celebration of Holy Week.

PAMPHYLIA (pam-fil´ee-uh)**:** An eighty-mile-long area on the coast of the Mediterranean Sea in southern Asia Minor. Paul, John Mark, and Barnabas ministered in the area (Acts 13:13). A Roman road connected Pamphylia's main port of Attalia with Perga. Paul and Barnabas left for Antioch from Attalia (Acts 14:24–26).

PAPYRUS (puh-pi´ruhs)**:** Water plant that grew along shallow waters at the banks of rivers in the countries bordering the eastern Mediterranean. Papyrus was especially prolific along the delta of the Nile and was processed in the making of paper, medicine, clothing fabrics, rope, and even foodstuffs. Many books of the Bible were first written on papyrus paper.

PARABLE: A story that uses symbolism and allegory as a teaching tool. An honored tradition among the Judean peoples, telling parables was used to pass on the wisdom of the ancestors to the next generation (Ps 78:2–4). A well-crafted parable could uncover injustice, lead to repentance, and bring about change (Judg 9:7–21; 2 Sam 12:1–15; 14:2–24).

Jesus is the best-remembered storyteller in the Scriptures. With parables, he changed hearts, healed souls, and

The Parables of Jesus

Parable Name	Mark	Matthew	Luke
The Barren Fig Tree			13:6–9
The Dishonest Manager			16:1–13
Feasting and the Bridegroom	2:19–20	9:14–15	5:34–35
The Fig Tree	13:28–31	24:32–35	21:29–33
The Fishnet		13:47–50	
Good and Faithful Servants		24:45–51	12:42–46
The Good Samaritan			10:25–37
The Great Banquet			14:16–24
The Household Servants	13:34–37		
The Laborers in the Vineyard		20:1–16	
The Lamp	4:21	5:15	8:16–18
The Lost Coin			15:8–10
The Lost Sheep		18:12–14	15:1–7
Marriage of the King's Son		22:1–14	14:16
The Master of the House		13:51–52	
The Mustard Seed	4:30–32	13:31–32	13:18–19
New Cloth	2:21	9:16	5:36
New Wine	2:22	9:17	5:37–39
The Persistent Friend at Midnight			11:5–8
The Pharisee and the Tax Collector			18:9–14
The Prodigal Son			15:11–32
The Rejected Stone	12:10–11	21:42–46	20:17–19
The Rich Fool			12:13–31
The Rich Man and Lazarus			16:19–31
The Seed and the Harvest	4:26–29		
The Sheep and the Goats		25:31–46	
The Sower and Soils	4:1–9	13:3–23	8:4–8
The Talents		25:14–30	19:11–27
The Talents and the Servants			19:12–27
The Ten Virgins		25:1–13	
The Thief at Night		24:43–44	12:39–40
The Treasure and Pearl		13:44–46	
The Two Debtors			7:40–45
Two Sons		21:28–32	
The Unmerciful Servant		18:23–35	
Watchful Slaves			12:35–48
The Wedding Banquet		22:1–14	14:15–24
The Wheat and the Weeds		13: 28–31, 36–43	
The Wicked Tenants	12:1–9	21:33–41	22:9–16
The Widow and the Judge			18:1–18
The Wise and Foolish Builders		7:24–27	6:46–49
The Worthless Salt	9:50	5:13	14:34–35
Yeast		13:33	13:20–21

proclaimed the Reign of God. Jesus gathered the multitudes with tales that taught timeless spiritual and ethical truths. His parables used cultural symbols that were understood in the context of the world in which he lived. See chart **The Parables of Jesus**.

PARACLETE (pair´uh-kleet): A Greek name for the Holy Spirit meaning "advocate" or "spirit of truth." The word indicates that the Holy Spirit is like a divine attorney who helps us defend our faith and protects us from evil (Jn 14:16–17; 1 Jn 2:1). See also **Holy Spirit; Spirit.**

PAROUSIA (puh-roo´zhee-uh): A Greek term for "the coming of the Lord" (Mt 24:15–28, 36–44; 1 Cor 15:23). The ultimate place and time of peace and justice proclaimed by the prophets, the Lord's Day (Isa 11:1–9). The Parousia is the place and time of the coming of the Kingdom of God when the apocalyptic chaos and unjust powers of the world are judged and submit to the authority of God. It is a time when Eden, Jerusalem, and the Reign of God will be established anew (2 Pet 3:10–13; Rev 21:1—22:5). The ultimate hope of believers, it is the time when "the coming of the Lord is near" (Jas 5:7–8; Mt 24:29–31; 1 Thess 3:13). See also **Day of Judgment; Lord's Day.**

PASCHAL LAMB (pas´kuhl): The sacrificial lamb shared at the Seder of Passover on the night the Hebrews escaped from Egypt (Ex 12:3–11). The image represents the suffering servant of God who was chosen to carry the burden of self-sacrifice for the people (Isa 42:1–4, 49:1–7). Jesus is the Paschal Lamb of God who, in his self-sacrifice on the cross, "takes away the sins of the world" (Jn 1:29, 19:31–37). Jesus provided, offered, and was the sacrifice of

redemption for humanity (Mt 26:26–30; Lk 22:14–20; Mk 14:22–25). The blood of his sacrifice was offered for the salvation of humanity (Rev 5:6–10). See also **Passover.**

PASSION: The suffering and death of Jesus (Lk 22:39—23:47; Mt 26:36—27:50; Mk 14:32—15:37; Jn 18:1—19:30).

PASSOVER: On the night before the Exodus from Egypt, the Hebrews sacrificed a lamb, smeared its blood on their doorposts, prepared unleavened bread, bitter herbs, and the wine of blessing, and shared the sacred Seder meal as family. They wore their belts and kept their sandals on their feet and staffs in hand.

That night, the Lord passed over the houses of Egypt, and in all the houses not marked with the blood of the lamb, the firstborn children and animals died. Pharaoh sent the Israelites away. They crossed the Red Sea and became a free people. Moses directed the Israelites to memorialize the Passover, never to forget that God called them out of bondage into freedom (Ex 12:1–28).

The Passover festival with its Seder meal and its Paschal Lamb memorialized the creation of a new people, a society of justice based on a sacred trust between Yahweh and Israel. Passover honors a God who heard the cries of his people and responded with miraculous power to free them from a terrible oppressor.

Jesus gathered his disciples together on Passover to celebrate the Seder and offer them the bread of life (Mt 26:17–30; Mk 14:12–26; Lk 22:7–23; 1 Cor 10:1, 11:23–26). On that same night, Jesus was arrested and sentenced to die as a common criminal. On Good Friday, Jesus died on the cross and "passed over" into the Reign of God. He is the ultimate Paschal Lamb; no other sacrifice is now needed. The death and Resurrection of Christ are the new Passover within Christianity that is celebrated in the Mass and anticipates the final Passover of the Church in the glory of the Kingdom of God. See also **Bread; Eucharist; Exodus; Last Supper; Paschal Lamb; Pilgrimage; Seder; Unleavened Bread.**

PATMOS (pat´muhs): An island in the Aegean Sea used in the Roman Empire as a place of exile (Rev 1:9). Around AD 95, John, the writer of the Book of Revelation, was banished to the isle of Patmos in the persecution of the Christians by the Roman emperor Domitian.

PATRIARCH: The father and spiritual leader of a tribe, clan, and tradition. Abraham, Isaac, and Jacob (Heb 7:4; Josh 14:1; Acts 7:8–9) were the patriarchs of the Israelite people (Acts 2:29). In the Christian tradition, the Twelve Apostles, the Church fathers, and certain bishops in the Eastern Catholic Churches are considered patriarchs. See also **Abraham; Isaac; Jacob; Joseph of Egypt; Matriarch.**

PAUL: The Apostle to the Gentiles, also known as Saul. Born in AD 35, Saul was a first-century Hellenistic Jew of the tribe of Benjamin, a Pharisee dedicated to the Law of Moses (Phil 3:3–6). Saul was also a Roman citizen from Tarsus of Cilicia in Asia Minor (Acts 21:39). He was a tentmaker by trade (Acts 18:3). Before his conversion to Christianity, Saul was a committed enemy of the Christian people (Acts 8:1–3; 1 Cor 15:9). Saul became better known by the Roman version of his name, Paul, which was used exclusively after his conversion (Acts 9:1-19).

Paul became a dedicated Christian missionary as a result of a call from Christ. Experiencing a conversion of faith, he held a deep conviction that the crucified Jesus was the Messiah and that Paul was commissioned to proclaim the Gospel to the Gentiles until the Lord returned (Acts 9:1–19; Gal 1:11–17). Together with Barnabas, Silas, John Mark, Priscilla, Aquila, and many other early Christian evangelizers, Paul journeyed throughout the Middle East and Eastern Europe, starting Christian communities. The stories of his travels are told in the second half of the Acts of the Apostles.

Paul's vocation was filled with conflict and grace. Some early Christians felt that to become Christian, a Gentile first had to accept all the Jewish laws and traditions. Paul strongly disagreed with that. He knew the Law of Moses was only a step in God's plan. This position put him in conflict with both Jews and some Christians. He was hated, beaten, whipped, and imprisoned (Acts 16:22–24; 2 Cor 11:23–28). His missionary work was marked by accusations of blasphemy and beatings as well as with miraculous interventions by angels and the hand of God (Acts 27:23). The Acts of the Apostles ends with Paul under house arrest awaiting a hearing with the emperor, but almost without doubt,

Paul suffered martyrdom and was decapitated in the persecutions of Rome in AD 62. See also **Barnabus; Conversion; Luke; Pauline Letters.**

PAULINE LETTERS: Saint Paul was a prolific letter writer who used letters to stay in touch with the Christian communities he helped to start. The New Testament contains thirteen letters written by Saint Paul or by disciples who wrote in his name. These Pauline letters offer advice, pastoral encouragement, teaching, and community news to the early Christian communities. Romans, 1 Thessalonians, Galatians, 1 and 2 Corinthians, Philemon, and Philippians, are the letters clearly written by Saint Paul. Ephesians, 2 Thessalonians, Colossians, 1 and 2 Timothy, and Titus are letters probably written by unknown Christian writers and attributed to this great saint who spread the Gospel to the Gentiles and gave his life for Christ. See also **Paul.**

PEACE: Hebrew word for "peace," *shalom,* is a blessing of God that provides wholeness, balance, completeness, health, and happiness (Lev 26:6). Peace was used as a greeting and a blessing at departure (Judg 6: 23; Jn 20:19–21). Peace also means the absence of hostilities and war (Josh 10:1–4; Rev 6:4).

Peace is a prayer for truth, blessing, health, welfare, and the good life in righteousness (Isa 32:17–18; Rom 12:18). Peace is a gift offered from the grace of the Holy Spirit (Gal 5:22–23). The Messiah was prophesied to be the Prince of Peace (Isa 9:6). Jesus taught love of enemies and peace among people (Mt 5:38–48). He called the peacemakers the blessed "children of God" (Mt 5:9). The Apostles called the Christian mission "preaching peace" (Acts 10:36), and they proclaimed "the gospel of peace" (Eph 6:15). God's blessings at the end of the age will offer peace (Ezek 34:25–31, 37:26).

PENTATEUCH (pen´tuh-took)**:** Greek word that refers to the first five books of the Old Testament—Genesis, Exodus, Leviticus, Numbers, and Deuteronomy, known equally as the Law and the Torah. The Pentateuch is filled with inspired stories of people of faith and the teachings, laws, and history of the Chosen People of Israel. It is God's covenant of love, heralding justice and the promise of the coming of the Messiah.

Traditionally, the writing of the Pentateuch was attributed to Moses, the great Lawgiver and teacher of the Hebrew people. In reality, however, many writers over hundreds of years contributed to the Pentateuch. The final editors were priests and historians who, after the Babylonian Captivity, compiled the sacred writings of salvation history to unify and rebuild the Jewish people. See also **Chronicler; Deuteronomist; Priestly Tradition.**

PENTECOST: The feast of Pentecost was an Israelite agricultural celebration, originally held seven weeks after the wheat harvest began. It was a thanksgiving to God for the gifts of the harvest. Pentecost was also known as the Feast of Weeks, celebrated fifty days after the Passover (Deut 16:9–12).

In the Christian tradition, on the Feast of Pentecost, after Christ had ascended into the heavens, the Holy Spirit descended in the form of tongues of fire that rested on the heads of the Apostles and other disciples (Acts 2:1–4). Pentecost is often called the birthday of the Church. Through the grace and manifestation of the gifts of the Holy Spirit, on that very day the Apostles went out in confidence, preached to the Jews gathered in Jerusalem to celebrate Pentecost, and baptized 3,000 new believers to form the first Christian community in Jerusalem (Acts 2:5-42). From there, the Gospel spread throughout the earth. See also **Pilgrimage.**

PERSIA: Nation evolved from a tribe of Aryan Medes who settled east of the Persian Gulf. Ancient Sumer became Babylon and was renamed Persia after the conquest of Cyrus in 530 BC (2 Chr 36:20). Although Persia's borders have fluctuated over time, modern-day Iran and Iraq encompass most of the land of Persia. At the height of its power, Persia controlled territory from India to Greece.

Cyrus the Persian became a hero to the Judean people when he subdued Babylon and permitted the Judean slaves to return to Jerusalem to rebuild (2 Chr 36:22–23). See also **Babylonian Captivity.**

PETER: See **Simon Peter.**

PHARAOH (fair´oh)**:** The Egyptian title for the king of Egypt. During the time of the patriarchs, Pharaohs were rulers of a mighty land. Numerous Pharaohs were listed in Scripture, but two of the most memorable were the Hyksos Pharaoh, who gave Joseph, the son of Jacob, authority over the land of Egypt (Gen 41:45), and the Pharaoh of the Exodus—thought to be Rameses II (1279–1212 BC)—who continually refused Moses's request to let the Israelites go free (Ex 7:14). See also **Exodus; Joseph of Egypt; Moses.**

PHARISEE (fair´uh-see)**:** A member of a Jewish religious group formed during the persecutions of Antiochus Epiphanes (167 BC). Also called the Hasidim, the Pharisees were strict observers of the Law of Moses and joined in the revolt of the Maccabees when Antiochus forbade the practice of their religion and murdered the Judean people. The Hasidim separated themselves to preserve the Law for future generations. Their descendants were the Pharisees.

The Pharisees were rabbis, scribes, and doctors of the Law of Moses who worked among the people to teach the fullness of Torah, the prophets, and the traditions of the Jewish faith. The Pharisees believed in angels, demons (Mt 9:34, 12:24), guardian spirits, signs and omens (Mt 12:38), last judgment, eternal life, the soul, and resurrection (Acts 23:6–9). Their opponents were the Sadducees, who believed only in the authority of the Pentateuch, ignored the prophets and their demand for justice, and did not believe in life after death.

Jesus and the Pharisees battled back and forth in of the Gospels in verbal duels (Mt 19:3–9). The debate was not over the worthiness of the Law of God, but rather a question of authority and mercy (Jn 7:45–52; Mt 9:11–13). There were Pharisees whom Jesus considered honorable. Jesus called Bartholomew (also called Nathanael)—who was a Pharisee and doctor of the Law—to be an Apostle (Mt 10:3). Jesus also made enemies among the Pharisees (Mt 12:14; Jn 11:46–53). Saul of Tarsus, who became known as Saint Paul, was proud to profess that he was a Pharisee (Acts 23:6; 26:4–5). See also **Sadducee; Scribe.**

PHILEMON (fi-lee´muhn): An early Christian convert, Philemon was a Colossian slaveowner to whom Saint Paul wrote a letter. The letter asked Philemon to accept the escaped slave Onesimus back as a brother in Christ. Philemon was a patron of a community and on occasion hosted Paul in his home (Philem verse 2, 22).

PHILIP, THE APOSTLE: One of the Twelve Apostles (Mt 10:3; Mk 3:18; Lk 6:14). Philip grew up in the Galilean town of Bethsaida on the coast of the Sea of Galilee and worked in the fishing trade with Peter and Andrew.

Philip was in Bethsaida when a multitude gathered to hear Jesus. Jesus asked Philip where they could "buy bread for these people to eat." Overwhelmed, Philip said the cost of that much bread would exceed "six months' wages" and then witnessed Jesus feed 5,000 with just a few fish and five loaves of bread (Jn 6:1–14; Lk 9:10).

Philip asked Jesus to satisfy the desire of his heart, "Lord, show us the Father" (Jn 14:8). And Jesus said to Philip, "Whoever has seen me has seen the Father. . . . I am in the Father and the Father is in me" (Jn 14:9, 11). Philip followed Jesus from the beginning and saw him ascend to heaven. Philip was among the disciples who received the Holy Spirit on Pentecost (Acts 1:13). See also **Apostle.**

PHILIP, THE EVANGELIST: As the Good News spread, the Apostles asked the disciples to choose seven good men "full of the Spirit and of wisdom" (Acts 6:3) to serve the needs of the Christian community. Philip was among the first on whom the Apostles laid hands and ordained to Holy Orders, to the rank of deacon of the Church (Acts 6:1–7).

The Jerusalem Church was under persecution. The Deacon Stephen had been murdered for Christ, and many of the disciples were scattered throughout the countryside. Philip went to Samaria, where he preached the "good news about the kingdom of God and the name of Jesus Christ" (Acts 8:12). The ministry of Philip caused such joy in the city that many were baptized, including Simon Magus, who converted from practicing magic and repented at the hands of Saint Peter (Acts 8:1–24). Philip opened the Scriptures to the Ethiopian eunuch and baptized him (Acts 8:26-40).

Philip's mission took him to Caesarea, seventy miles north of Jerusalem on the Mediterranean coast. At the time, Caesarea was the headquarters of Pontius Pilate, the Roman governor of Judea. There Philip lived and ministered with his wife and four daughters (Acts 8:40). See also **Ethiopian Eunuch.**

PHILIPPI (fi-lip´i): A town in northern Greece founded in the fourth century BC. Philippi was taken over by the Romans along with Macedonia in 168–167 BC. In 42 BC, Marc Antony and Octavian (Caesar Augustus) defeated Brutus and Cassius west of Philippi. Marc Antony settled veterans of this battle in the city of Philippi, resulting in the town becoming strongly Roman influenced.

In AD 50–51, Saint Paul and Silas brought the faith to Philippi through the conversion of a woman named Lydia, a woman of faith and "worshiper of God" from the city of Thyatira (Acts 16:14). Lydia's home became a "house church" and is remembered as the place where Europe's first Christian community gathered (Acts 16:40).

The community of Philippi thrived from the missionary efforts of Paul, Silas, Timothy, and Lydia. Paul referred to saints, bishops, and deacons within the community of Philippi (Phil 1:1–2). Paul wrote a letter to the church in Philippi in AD 61, a few years before his death. See also **Lydia.**

PHILISTINE (fi-lis´teen): A member of the sea people of Philistia, a southern Canaanite coastal plain of Palestine, who overtook Lebanon and the Jordan valley, as well as Crete and other Mediterranean islands. The Philistines—meaning "wanderers or strangers"—had inhabited Palestine since the twelfth century BC. They were part of the Aegean and Greek migration that took place in the thirteenth century BC. The Philistines became an enemy of Israel (Judg 15:11; 1 Sam 13:15–22). The hostilities didn't cease until the time of King Hezekiah (715–687 BC)(2 Kings 18:7–8).

PHOEBE (fee´bee): A Gentile Christian much admired by Saint Paul. When Paul introduced Phoebe to the community, he described her as "our sister" (Rom 16:1). Not only did this suggest Paul's care for her as a member of the family of Christ, but "sister" also meant a coworker in service of the Gospel. That Paul also called Phoebe a deacon and benefactor of the church of Cenchreae further supports this view. This identified her as one who used her status and social influence to provide care for the sick and economic support for the poor. Paul was indebted to Phoebe for her gracious service and praised her as a woman who provided hospitality, service, and care not only to Paul personally but also to the Church (Rom 16:1–2).

PIETY: A gift of the Holy Spirit that means reverence and respect for the things of God. Those called to pass on the faith are asked to do so in a manner that honors piety. Piety empowers both the individual and the community to express faith, hope, reverence, and fear of the Lord (Isa 11:1–3; 1 Tim 4:6–16).

PILGRIMAGE: A trip to a shrine or holy place as part of a religious observance. Once the Temple was built, Israelites commonly pilgrimaged to Jerusalem to celebrate major religious festivals. The most important feasts for pilgrimages were Passover, Pentecost, and the Feast of Tabernacles. Jesus and his disciples were on pilgrimage to Jerusalem for the Passover at the time of his death. See also **Passover; Pentecost; Tabernacles, Feast of.**

PLAGUE: Painful affliction or disease, severe calamity, or even the judgment of God (1 Kings 8:37–40). God sent a series of ten miraculous plagues that forced the Egyptian Pharaoh to release the Israelites from bondage (Ex 6:14—12:32). See chart **The Ten Plagues of Egypt.** See also **Exodus.**

POETRY: A writing style characterized by the use of allegory, symbolism, meter, and rhyme. The literary forms of songs, proverbs, and prophetic statements most commonly use poetry. Poetry uses metered patterns to offer a feeling of movement, emphasize strong emotion, present riddles, and offer variations on the same thought or theme.

Hebrew poetry was characterized by two-part sentences. The second part of the sentence emphasized, added variations to, or completed the thought in the first part of the sentence. This type of poetry was particularly found in the wisdom books of the Old Testament. You will know you are reading poetry in the Bible when the second line of the

The Ten Plagues of Egypt

	Plague	Reference
1	Waters of the Nile River turned into blood	Ex 7:14–25
2	Swarms of frogs	Ex 8:1–15
3	Swarms of gnats	Ex 8:16–19
4	Swarms of flies	Ex 8:20–32
5	Disease and death of Egyptian livestock	Ex 9:1–7
6	Festering boils on humans and animals	Ex 9:8–12
7	Destructive thunder, lightning, and hail	Ex 9:13–35
8	Destructive swarms of locusts	Ex 10:1–20
9	Darkness for three days	Ex 10:21–29
10	The death of the firstborn of humans and of beasts	Ex 12:29–32

verses are slightly indented from the first lines. See also **Wisdom Literature.**

PONTIUS PILATE (pon´shuhs pi´luht)**:** The Roman prefect, or governor, of Judea, who served throughout the ministry of John the Baptist and Jesus of Nazareth and during the formation of the early Christian Church from AD 26 to 36 (Lk 3:1). Pilate's headquarters were at Caesarea, but on high holy days he had to go to Jerusalem to keep order.

Pilate was a typical Roman ruler: pleasure-loving, organized, self-important, and corrupt. He hated the Judean people due to their constant revolts and continued religious rebellions, and he executed them at will (Lk 13:1). Pilate's wife received a warning in a dream about Jesus of Nazareth, and she asked Pilate to have nothing to do with him. Regardless, Pilate handed Jesus over for crucifixion and released his body for burial in the tomb (Jn 18:28—19:16). In AD 36, Pilate was banished to Vi-

enne in Gaul for an unwarranted mass slaughter of Samaritans. In Vienne, according to tradition, he committed suicide.

POTIPHAR (pot´uh-fuhr): The captain of the Egyptian guard during the time of the Pharaoh of the Exodus. The Ishmaelites traded Joseph to Potiphar as a bond servant after Joseph's brothers abused and sold him into slavery. Joseph found favor with Potiphar and became the steward of his estate, in charge of all he had. Potiphar's adulterous wife desired Joseph. When Joseph rejected her advance, she lied and accused Joseph of inappropriate sexual advances. Potiphar had Joseph imprisoned for years due to her false accusations (Gen 39:1–23). See also **Joseph of Egypt.**

POTTER'S FIELD: The parcel of land purchased with the money Judas Iscariot had been paid for his betrayal of Jesus of Nazareth. After Jesus' arrest, Judas threw the bounty fee at the priests' feet and went out and hanged himself on a tree. The priests collected this blood money and purchased a field in which to bury foreigners, criminals, and destitute persons (Mt 27:3–9). Potter's Field, which came to be known as the "Field of Blood," was on the site of the ancient place where children were sacrificed to the Baals of Molech (Acts 1:16–20).

POVERTY: In a just society, the beggar, the suffering, the leper, the widow, the orphan, the alienated, the foreign refugee in the land, and the poverty-stricken were to be cared for (Ex 23:10–12; Deut 15:11). The justice of Hebrew spirituality insisted that on the seventh year, debts needed to be forgiven and the slate of indebtedness erased to permit people to be liberated from the cycle of liability (Lev 19:10, 25:39–54).

The Law of Moses provided for the poor (Deut 14:28–29). The *anawim*, or "God's little ones," were precious. The heart of Jesus reached out to those who were infirm or physically challenged. These people were most often forced into poverty (Lk 16:19–31). See also **Justice.**

PRAETORIAN GUARD (pri-tor´ee-uhn): An elite unit of the Roman army. Service in the Praetorian Guard was desired for its prestige, good salary, and choice duty as bodyguards for the Caesars and other rulers of high station, such as Pontius Pilate. The Passion of Jesus began at the headquarters of the Praetorian Guard (Mt 27:27). There, Jesus was scourged, crowned with thorns, dressed in royal purple, and handed a scepter in mock kingship rites. Intended to humiliate Jesus, this display emphasized for believers Jesus' divine kingship.

PRAYER: Prayer is communion, a bonding of oneself—spirit and soul—with the Creator and saintly heavenly beings for the sake of protection, guidance, and thanksgiving. Although worship is reserved for God, prayer can be shared with one's ancestors of faith, the angels, and saints, as well as the Creator and Lord. Prayer offers praise, asks for aid, and seeks direction in life.

In prayer, one opens one's being in sincere reverence (Heb 10:22). Jesus said, "Ask, and it will be given you" (Mt 7:7). Christians pray in the name of Christ Jesus (Eph 5:20). Prayer can be a private, social, family, or community sharing (Mt 6:5–6; Jas 5:14). The public prayer of the Church is the Eucharistic Liturgy in which Christ is offered as the Word of prayer made flesh. See also **Blessing.**

PRESENTATION OF CHRIST: Joseph and Mary presented the infant Christ in the Temple for blessing and dedication according to the Law of

Moses (Lk 2:22–39). See also **Anna; Simeon.**

PRIEST: One who offers sacrifice to God on behalf of the people. The first priestly man in the Hebrew tradition was Melchizedek of Salem. With Abraham, he offered bread and wine and was a "priest of God Most High" (Gen 14:18). As part of the Sinai Covenant, God instituted an order of priests that began with Aaron and his sons. Since they were of the tribe of Levi, the Levites became known as the priestly class. As the Israelites settled Palestine, they built local temples at which the priests led the community in prayer and offered the required animal sacrifices.

Once the Temple was built in Jerusalem, religious observances became centered there. All local temples were destroyed, and the priests were all moved to Jerusalem, where they assisted with worship and sacrifice in the Temple. The high priest was the chief priest and led all the major religious rituals in the Temple.

In the early Church, the role of priests took time to evolve. The first Christians gathered in people's homes to celebrate the Eucharist. An elder in the community often led these gatherings. These elders were also called presbyters. The presbyters became known as priests, and their role evolved as taking their authority from the local bishop to lead the community in the sacrifice of the Mass and the other sacraments. While priests today do not offer animal sacrifice, they continue to stand between God and humanity in the sacrifice of the Mass. See also **Aaron; High Priest; Holy Orders; Levi, Levite; Melchizedek.**

PRIESTLY TRADITION: A particular theological tradition present in the Old Testament. The priestly tradition is the work of priestly scribes who hoped to restore the memory of the divided kingdoms of Israel and Judah and form them into a new people united in covenant relationship with the God of their ancestors. As these scribes compiled and edited Genesis through Numbers, they hoped to restore focus on the Sinai Covenant. The priestly scribes had survived the Babylonian Captivity, and they hoped to heal their people from the idolatry that led to their downfall. They proclaimed the Law and the Holy One of Israel and Judah as the Creator of all, the Lord God of Hosts.

The work of the priestly scribes is evident in their blending of the sacred names from northern Israel and southern Judah into a unified title for the Holy. Whenever the unspeakable name Yahweh was intended, the scribes used the honorable title *Adonai* with the generic *El* and called the Holy One "Adonai Yahweh Elohim." In English, this translates as "LORD God." Scholars refer to the work of these priestly scribes as the "P" Tradition. See also **Chronicler; Deuteronomist; Pentateuch.**

PRISCILLA AND AQUILA (prisil′uh) (ak′wi-luh): Also called Prisca, Priscilla and her husband, Aquila (Acts 18:2), were tentmakers from Corinth who worked with Saint Paul (Rom 16:3; 2 Tim 4:19). In AD 50, Priscilla and Aquila fled Rome when Claudius Caesar commanded all Jews and Christians to leave. After meeting Paul, Aquila and Priscilla traveled with him to Ephesus, where they ministered in the Gospel of Christ (Acts 18:18–26). They are a testimony that married couples as well as single people were active as evangelists in the early Church.

PRODIGAL SON: A parable Jesus taught about the profound love the Father has for his children. Two sons are in the story, the honorable, yet resentful,

PROPHECY: The proclamation of the will of God toward justice. Scriptural prophecy did not claim to foretell the future; rather, it was a warning offered in hope that the faithful would change the path of destruction they were headed for because of sin. Prophecy challenged those who betrayed God's steadfast love and divine mercy (Isa 3:9).

The prophets taught that sin destroys people, nations, and future happiness (Amos 8:2). Apocalyptic prophecy was an announcement of wrath, the warning against the reality of sin's destructive nature (Isa 3:11). Prophecy identified the logical outcome of the situations people created by sinful choices. Prophecy called for a change of heart—within individuals and society—so that the future would be in accordance with the Creator's will of love, mercy, and justice (Hos 2:16-22).

son and the abhorrent and ungrateful son. The point of the story is that the father, who personifies God, unconditionally loves and forgives both sons. The elements of this parable teach the *hesed,* or faithful, love of God, who loves humanity without limit (Lk 15:11–32). See also **Love of God.**

PROMISED LAND: Abraham and his descendants, the Hebrew people, were called from the land of Ur into the Promised Land. Called Canaan, this was the land God promised to the children of Abraham (Gen 11:31—12:7). The Promised Land was situated between the Red Sea and the Jordan River, with Egypt to the south and Lebanon and Syria to the north. This land was later known as Palestine. Today, it is part of Israel. For most of Israel's history, the Judean people have had to pray, dream, work, and fight for the land that God promised to their ancestors (Num 13:1–3, 25–33). See also **Exodus.**

PROPHET: Someone called by God to speak for God to others. The Bible mentions many prophets, both men and women. Seventeen prophets had books in the Bible named after them. The prophecies of other prophets such as Moses, Deborah, Nathan, Elijah, Elisha, and Anna were recorded in other books. Isaiah, Jeremiah, and Ezekiel are called the major prophets because so much of their prophecies were written down.

The message of the writing prophets fell into two major themes. Before the Assyrian conquest (721 BC) and Babylonian Captivity (586 BC), the prophets' message was generally one of warning. They called the rulers and the people to stop their worship of other gods, to live justly, and to care for the poor as called for by the Law of Moses. During and after the Babylonian Captivity, the prophets' message turned to themes of comfort and hope. They spoke of God's love and God's not abandoning them—

that if the people repented of their sin, they would find joy and freedom again.

The life of a prophet wasn't easy. The rulers in power did not necessarily want to hear their call to reform. So prophets were ridiculed, thrown into wells, chased, beaten, and killed. The Gospels presented Jesus as the ultimate prophet. As the Son of God, he spoke God's truth with a power and authority like no other prophet, past or future. See also **Elijah; Elisha; Ezekiel; Hosea; Isaiah; Jeremiah; Joel; Micah; Moses; Nahum; Obadiah; Vision.**

PROSTITUTE: A person who degrades the gift of sexuality for money. In Bible times, prostitutes were often from the lower class, were objects of scorn, and were considered unworthy (Lev 21:7). The Scriptures condemned prostitution as part of a cycle of injustice and social sin. Some prostitutes' own families sold them into bondage (Lev 19:29). Some had been captured as the booty of war and turned into objects of lust by their captors (Amos 7:17).

Temple prostitutes, or harlots, led idolatrous fertility rituals (Deut 23:17–18). These women were practitioners of the fertility cults, the rites of the Baals, which blended sexuality and power (Judg 8:33). The prophets condemned these rites and ritual practices as religious betrayal (Jer 5:7). Babylon and Rome were called the Great Whore, another word for prostitute (Rev 17:1–5). See also **Whore.**

PROVERB: A short saying that teaches a basic moral or spiritual truth or life lesson (Prov 1:1–6). Proverbs are often created to be witty and easy to remember. The Book of Proverbs is a collection of poems and proverbs representing the wisdom from generations of Israel's history.

PSALMS (sahmz)**:** A collection of poetic song lyrics written to honor God. These hymns were written across the ages by various authors. They were dedicated to God and sung to praise the Lord's mercy, compassion, steadfast love, and faithfulness (Ps 36:7).

Often attributed to kings David and Solomon and other anonymous poets, the Psalms were intended to be sung, proclaimed, and prayed. They celebrated and thanked God for blessings (Ps 47), lamented and petitioned God in time of need (Ps 38), and praised God for wisdom and the wonders God has worked (Ps 113, 114). Some were written as if a single person were praying (Ps 23). Some Psalms were community prayers (Ps 132). See also **Worship.**

PSALTER (sawl´tuhr)**:** A book used in liturgy and prayer that is a collection of psalms.

PURIM (pyoo´rim)**:** This holy day finds it roots in Persia (486–465 BC) in the story of Queen Esther and her cousin and patron, the faithful Mordecai, both of whom successfully averted a plot to kill all Judeans in the land (Esth 9:18–32). Today, Jewish families honor Purim with fasting and prayers for Jews throughout the world. After fasting, the family and friends gather to chant or read the story of Esther in its entirety. It's a festive theatrical event in which the costumed people ritually mock the evil Haman when his name is heard. See also **Esther.**

PURITY CODES: Regulations developed to protect the population and religious rituals from defilements. The purity codes forbade infractions of social codes, such as eating with strangers (Gen 43:32) or inappropriate interaction with the lower classes, such as socializing with shepherds (Gen 46:34).

An infraction of the code could also refer to a religious impurity such as the sacrificing of unclean animals in worship or committing idolatry (Mt 24:15), sinful behaviors, or a blasphemy.

Q

"Q" SOURCE: A collection of ancient documents of the teachings of Jesus, shared among the early followers of Christianity. Scholars believe that the Evangelists Matthew and Luke used this collection, also called the Sayings of Jesus, in creating their Gospels. The collection is called the "Q," or Quelle, source. *Quelle* is a German word meaning "source" or "spring." See also **Synoptic Gospels.**

QUEEN: In the Scriptures, a Middle Eastern queen functioned as the consort of the king. It was an honorary position that, with few exceptions, held little personal power or authority. Her role was to support her husband as his unquestioning, loyal subject. The queen was the property of the king and very likely the primary wife in his harem. Her influence was increased with the birth of a son who could become the king's heir. An honorable queen was faithful to her religious commitments and was subject to the king's authority. A shameful queen was one who practiced idolatrous religions, attempted to go beyond the rules of patriarchal power, or asserted authority. See also **Bathsheba; Esther; Jezebel.**

QUEEN OF HEAVEN: A title used for the mother high goddess worshiped in Egypt and by some Israelites in the time of Jeremiah (Jer 7:18, 44:17–19). Many goddess images merged in the queen of heaven—Ishtar, Asherah, Artemis, and Cybele. The Queen of Heaven was the power of fertility, war, nature, and healing. Jeremiah strongly condemned worship of the Queen of Heaven as idolatry (Jer 44:18–30). See also **Asherah; Ishtar.**

QUMRAN (koom´rahn): A site near the northwestern coast of the Dead Sea, eight miles south of the ancient city of Jericho. A Judean sect, thought to be the Essenes, built a desert community here that thrived from the second century BC to the Roman destruction of Jerusalem in AD 70. Qumran preserved a collection of writings known today as the Dead Sea Scrolls. These scrolls are considered the most profound scriptural archeological find of the twentieth century. They have been a remarkable source for understanding the world of the New Testament. See also **Dead Sea Scrolls.**

R

RABBI, RABBOUNI (rab´*i*) (ra-b*oo*´n*i*): An honored teacher in the Judean tradition. The word can be translated as "master," "teacher," or "most great one." The rabbi is equipped to judge cases of Judean law and offer spiritual guidance.

In the New Testament, Jesus was addressed with the title rabbi (Mk 9:5), as well as the Aramaic rabbouni, or teacher (Jn 20:16).

RACHEL: The daughter of Laban and the beloved wife of Jacob. Jacob served his future father-in-law for seven years to marry the beautiful Rachel, but Laban substituted Rachel's older sister, Leah, in the wedding rite. So Jacob worked another seven years for the bride price of Rachel (Gen 29:16–28). When Rachel left Haran, she stole the teraphim, or household gods, thus claiming her clan inheritance (Gen 31:34, 35). Rachel, Leah, and their slaves, Bilhah and Zilpah, gave birth to Jacob's twelve sons, whose names came to represent the Twelve Tribes of Israel (Gen 35:22–26). Rachel gave birth to Joseph, died in labor with Benjamin, and was buried near Bethlehem (Gen 35:18–20).

In the early years of the child Jesus, Herod slaughtered the children of Bethlehem in an attempt to eliminate the prophesied infant Messiah. Matthew's community lamented that horrible grief as "Rachel weeping for her children" (Mt 2:18). See also **Bilhah; Dowry; Jacob; Leah; Twelve Tribes; Zilpah.**

RAHAB (ray´hab)**:** The first Canaanite to convert to the worship of Yahweh. As the Israelites entered the Promised Land, the first spies to enter Canaan felt like "grasshoppers" and shook in fear before the cannibalistic giants of Canaan (Num 13:32–33). When Joshua sent spies into Canaan, they met the harlot Rahab beside the legendary walls of Jericho.

She risked her own life to protect them. Rahab offered the invaders a safe place to stay, made the men vow to protect her family in the conquest to come, and then set the men free. They gave her a crimson tie with which to mark her window. Like the Passover lamb's blood painted on the doors in Egypt, the crimson mark spared those in the house from death (Josh 2). Rahab was a woman of *hesed* (faithful) love whose descendants included Jeremiah, Huldah, King David, and Jesus of Nazareth (Mt 1:5). See also **Jericho.**

RAINBOW: The bow in the clouds of heaven, a reflection and refraction of sunlight through the rain, causes a magnificent display of color. The rainbow is the ancient sign of the covenant between God and humanity and a sign of God's glory and the promise of life (Gen 9:12–17; Rev 10:1).

RAMESES (ram´uh-seez)**:** The best part of the land of Egypt that Pharaoh granted to Joseph to give to his father, Jacob, and his brothers (Gen 47:11). Four hundred years later, the Hebrew people were enslaved in this same land where they were once welcomed. This city, which the Egyptians called the House of Rameses, is named after Pharaoh Rameses II (1279–1212 BC). See also **Exodus; Joseph of Egypt; Moses.**

REBECCA: See **Rebekah.**

REBEKAH (ri-bek´uh)**:** A matriarch of Israel. Rebekah was the daughter of Bethuel. She was wife of the patriarch Isaac, who was the son of Abraham and Sarah. Rebekah's brother was Laban of Haran. Her story helps us understand the ways in which families bonded through marriage rites in the ancient world of the Torah.

Abraham sent his slave to Haran to seek an appropriate bride for Isaac from among his own clan in Haran. The servant prayed for a sign, and an angel led him to a spring of water where Rebekah offered him a drink and watered his camels. It was a sign he had anticipated.

The servant approached Laban and Bethuel with Abraham's marriage deal, showered the family with rich gifts as a bride price, closed the contract to which Rebekah agreed, and blessed her (Gen 24:49–60). Rebekah journeyed to Canaan, where she married Isaac (Gen 24:60–67) and gave birth to twin sons, Jacob and Esau. She became the mother-in-law of the matriarchs Rachel and Leah, who, with their slavewomen Bilhah and Zilpah, mothered the men who became the patriarchs of the Twelve Tribes of Israel. See also **Esau; Isaac; Jacob.**

RECONCILIATION: The sacrament of healing and new birth. The essence of this sacrament is God's unconditional love for humans (Gal 4:7). God created us to live in perfect relationship with God and to care for others in perfect love (Mk 12:28–34). When we fail, miss the mark, break our commitment to love, ignore justice, and fall into sin, it fractures our relationship with God and other people. God longs for us to heal those relationships. Jesus offered his life, death, and Resurrection as the means of grace to reconcile ourselves with God and with others.

Jesus, through the action of the priest, invites us to release the past, be forgiven, and reject sin (Jn 8:11). Jesus bestowed

on the Apostles and the Church the power to forgive and to liberate souls from the burden of sin through the sacrament of Penance and Reconciliation (Jn 20:23; 2 Cor 14—6:2). See also **Repentance; Sacrament.**

REDACTION CRITICISM: See **Exegesis.**

REDEEMER: A word used to honor a human political leader, as well as a spiritual title for the Messiah and for God (Ps 19:14). A redeemer was one who saved the people from bondage. Moses was a redeemer who established freedom and justice by leading the people out of the slavery of Egypt (Ex 3:1–15).

The future redeemer, prophesied across the ages, would be a messiah and savior who would offer himself as the suffering servant of the Lord and lead the people from slavery—both political and spiritual (Isa 52:13—53:12, 59:20). The New Testament proclaimed Jesus as that Redeemer, the suffering servant of God (Jn 19:36–37; Gal 4:4-5). He was the High Priest of the Most High who provided, offered, and was sacrificed for the redemption of humanity (Acts 3:13–26). See also **Redemption; Salvation.**

REDEMPTION: Freedom from slavery, bondage, captivity, and domination. The word *redemption* implied that a person's redeemer had paid all debts and released that individual from the bond of slavery or paid the required ransom for a captive to be released (Lev 25:39–54). This liberation included rescue from war; from attack, powers, ignorance, and limitation; and from sickness and death (Neh 5:1–13; Isa 61:1–2).

The New Testament presented the life, teaching, death, and Resurrection of Jesus Christ, as well as his gift of the Church, as the means of redemption.

His death on the cross has paid in full all debt for sin (1 Cor 6:20). Christ's blood is the ransom for sin, the gift of reconciliation, the redemption and atonement that heals the relationship between God and humanity (Gal 4:4–7). See also **Atonement; Blood of Christ; Jesus Christ; Original Sin; Redeemer.**

RED SEA: The body of water that divides the Middle East from Africa and flows into the Indian Ocean. In this age, the Red Sea is connected to the Mediterranean Sea by the Suez Canal at the Sinai Peninsula. In the Exodus from Egypt, the Israelites escaped from the bondage of Pharaoh by crossing the marsh lands of the Nile delta's Bitter Lakes region, north of the Gulf of Suez, called the Sea of Reeds, or Yam Suph (Ex 13:18), which is most likely a description of the area rather than a proper name. As an infant, Moses was saved in an ark or basket made with reeds, or suph (Ex 2:3–5), and his people were redeemed from bondage by crossing the Red Sea on dry ground (Ex 14:15–31). See also **Exodus.**

REHOBOAM (ree´huh-boh´uhm): The fourth and last king of the united kingdom (922–915 BC). Rehoboam was also the first king of the southern kingdom of Judah. He was the son of King Solomon and Naamah, the Ammonite princess (1 Kings 12:21–24). When the northern tribes revolted because of the taxation and hard service mandated by Solomon (1 Kings 12:3–4), they appointed Jeroboam as their king—leaving Rehoboam as king only of the southern kingdom.

Rehoboam was a king much hated by his own people. He was remembered for building high places for the worship of foreign gods. His idolatry and injustice became the fodder for the civil war led by Jeroboam (2 Chr 10:1–9). Re-

hoboam was remembered as a fool "lacking in sense," whose political policies "drove the people to revolt" (Sir 47:23–25). See also **Jeroboam of Israel; Judah, Judea; King; Samaria.**

REIGN OF GOD: See **Kingdom of God.**

REMNANT: The leftover ones, or the small percentage of the whole. In the Scriptures, the most essential meaning of *remnant* refers to a small portion of the population from Israel and Judah who escaped death in the Babylonian Captivity and chose to return to Jerusalem to begin the challenge of reconstruction (Isa 10:20–22, 11:10–16).

The remnant were the loyal few who held firm to their faith and commitment to mission. The remnant, like yeast, spread throughout the community, leading all to a life-giving relationship and a renewed faith in God. Jesus used the concept in his parable of the woman baking bread, implying that the faithful remnant's presence in the world would bring about the Reign of God (Mt 13:33).

REPENTANCE: When we miss the mark and fall short of the Creator's plan for our happiness, when we have disobeyed God's law, this break in our covenant relationship is called sin. The path to healing begins with repentance—the intention to change and be made new. Repentance is a commitment to sin no more, to change our lives, and to offer restitution (Deut 5:32–33). To be repentant is to accept God's invitation to start over, to change our mind and heart, to be reconciled with God.

Repentance invites us to be free, to submit our souls before God, and to ask to be liberated from the guilt and broken relationships our sin caused. John the Baptist called for the repentance of sins (Lk 3:3–14). Jesus Christ provides the path to reconciliation (2 Cor 5:18–19). See also **Conscience; Reconciliation.**

RESURRECTION: The belief that the dead will be raised to eternal life. This belief was not part of the biblical tradition until late in the Old Testament. Only in the writings of the last two centuries BC were there indications of a belief in life after death (Dan 12:1–3; 2 Macc 12:44; Wis 5:15).

This belief changed dramatically in the New Testament. In fact, it is safe to say that the central event that holds the whole New Testament together is Christ's Resurrection from the dead (1 Cor 15:12–34). The Bible holds Jesus up as the model for human destiny. Just has he has been raised, so all who die believing in him shall also be raised to glorious and eternal life (1 Cor 15:20–23). We do not know what a resurrected body will be like, but it will be glorious and immortal (1 Cor 15:35–58). See also **Death; Easter; Immortality; Resurrection of Christ.**

RESURRECTION OF CHRIST: After Jesus was crucified, Joseph of Arimathea, a member of the Sanhedrin, secured Jesus' body from Pontius Pilate and laid it in his own tomb (Jn 19:38–42). There the body of Jesus remained until dawn on that first Easter Sunday morning.

The disciple, Mary Magdalene, and some other women gathered at the tomb intending to anoint the body of Jesus (Mk 16:1–8). Mary Magdalene approached the tomb and discovered the stone had been removed. She was the first to witness the Resurrection and announce to the disciples that Christ had risen (Jn 20:1–18).

Christ spent forty days between the day of his Resurrection and his Ascension into heaven. During that time, he visited the disciples and Apostles. He promised to come again (Lk 24:13–53). See also **Ascension; Jesus Christ; Resurrection.**

REUBEN (roo´bin): A patriarch of the Twelve Tribes of Israel. Reuben was the eldest son of Jacob and Leah (Gen 29:32). Reuben saved Joseph from being killed when his other ten brothers planned to murder Joseph (Gen 37:21–22). Reuben's reputation in Scripture was marred because he seduced Bilhah, his father's concubine, thus shaming Jacob (Gen 35:22). Jacob never forgot that offense and, as he lay dying, refused to bless Reuben (Gen 49:4). See also **Twelve Tribes.**

REVELATION: The act or process by which God reveals God's self and God's plan to humanity. Revelation is a gift, a mystery of the divine presence breaking into human history. Revelation can be experienced in many ways. God is revealed to us through our human reason and through the natural world as we contemplate the mysteries of life. God touches us through prayer, through visitations from angels, through the prophets, saints, and wisdom teachers (LK 1:26–38, 2:29–38).

The ultimate Revelation of God is Jesus Christ. "If you know me, you will know my Father also" (Jn 14:7). "He is the image of the invisible God" (Col

1:15). Everything God wants us to know for our salvation has been revealed through Jesus Christ. This Revelation is also known as the Apostolic Tradition, handed down from the original Apostles through their successors, the pope and bishops. The writings of the New Testament also record much of this Revelation. Thus, through the Scriptures and sacred Tradition, we come to know God's Revelation to all humanity. See **Apostolic Tradition; Tradition.**

RIGHTEOUS: Following the law of God, honoring justice, and embracing compassion as a way of life (Prov 4:18).

ROMAN CENTURION: See **Centurion.**

ROMAN RELIGION: The Romans were highly superstitious. They were afraid of offending any of the gods, so they worshiped them all. When the Romans conquered a people, they honored that people's gods and incorporated them into Roman religion. This provided spiritual and political unity among diverse populations. Several of the emperors were deified and proclaimed as gods. All subjects of the empire were mandated to honor the divinity of the emperor and his ancestors.

Judeans, as an occupied people, refused to honor idols (Ex 34:17). The followers of Christ also embraced only the God of Israel (1 Thess 1:9). Rome considered both Jews and Christians aberrant atheists—unbelievers of the gods—and a threat to the unity of the state. Sporadically, over the first three hundred years of Christianity, the Romans persecuted thousands of Jews and Christians, killing them in theatrical displays, gladiatorial shows, and beast fights to honor the gods of Rome and entertain the population. See also **Caesar.**

ROME: The city that Western civilization considered the center of the world for almost one thousand years. At the height of its power, the military of Rome had conquered territory from Spain to the Euphrates River, and from Scotland to Romania. The tools Rome used to control its captives were cruelty, power, order, terror, organization, and religion.

Rome considered itself religiously and politically tolerant and spread its power by building up its conquered territories. The Romans built amphitheaters, sewers, aqueducts, temples, and roads. They built 200 million miles of road throughout the empire. These roads brought eastern cults, barbarian rebellions, new ideas, and Christian missionaries to the city as early as AD 50. Rome was the marketplace of the world, buying and selling produce, oil, spices, fish sauce, wine, and wheat.

Peter, the first Bishop of Rome and first Pope, ministered in the city with John Mark. In Rome, Paul wrote several letters (Acts 28:23–30). Rome was the site of Peter and Paul's martyrdom, which was the first official persecution of the Church, and eventually the home of the faith. Rome was the capital of the empire until Constantine built Constantinople in modern-day Turkey in AD 330.

RUTH: The story of Ruth honored loyalty, love, and racial diversity. Ruth was a foreign woman, a Moabite, one of the ancient enemies of Israel. The Israelites considered Moabite women untrustworthy idolaters who led men astray. Ruth shattered the stereotype and was offered as a model of faith and compassion.

The Judean family of Naomi and Elimelech and their sons, Mahlon and Chilion, left Judah as refugees in the midst of a famine. Both sons married Moabite women; Ruth married Mahlon, and Orpah married Chilion. When all three men died, the women soon became impoverished widows, and Naomi planned to make the journey home to Judah alone.

Ruth's faith in God and her love for the aged Naomi were profound. Ruth refused to leave Naomi, whether it meant life or death. Ruth said, "Your people shall be my people, / and your God my God" (Ruth 1:16). She cherished the old woman as her own mother, gleaned food for her, and committed herself to face an unknown future by Naomi's side. With Naomi's guidance, Ruth married Boaz of Bethlehem, gave birth to Obed, and made Naomi the child's nurse (Ruth 4:16). Obed became the father of Jesse, who was the father of King David. Ruth became a matriarch in the family tree leading to Jesus of Nazareth (Ruth 4:1–18; Mt 1:5–16). See also **Boaz; Naomi.**

S

SABBATH: Time of rest. The Sabbath was the seventh day of the week, the day that God ceased the work of Creation (Gen 2:2). God called the Hebrew people to keep the Sabbath holy, to put aside all labor and obligations (Ex 16:23). Today, the Jewish people honor the Sabbath as a day of prayer, relaxation, and family bonding. Sabbath services in synagogues and temples honor the sacredness of the day. The Jewish Sabbath begins at sunset on Friday night and continues to sunset on Saturday night.

Catholic Christians honor the Sabbath by gathering as the Church on the Lord's Day, or Sunday, to celebrate the Eucharist. From Saturday night's evening Mass until Sunday night's evening liturgy, the Church gathers to proclaim the word, celebrate the Eucharist, and build the community of Christ. See also **Lord's Day.**

SABBATICAL YEAR: The seventh year, when all slaves were released, the land was left to rest, and debts were forgiven (Deut 15:1–18). See also **Jubilee.**

SACRAMENT: Words and actions that signify a spiritual reality. For example, in Baptism, the words and the immersion in water signify the spiritual reality that a person dies to sin and is reborn as a child of God. Jesus was the original sacrament of God. All his words and actions signified the reality of the Kingdom of God (Jn 14:6; Mt 1:23). The Church is the secondary sacrament; it is the sign of Christ's continued presence in the world through the power of the Holy Spirit.

The seven sacraments of the Catholic Church are rooted in Jesus' words and actions, through which Christ himself pours out his life to us (Acts 8:17). He passed on these awesome sacramental gifts through the ministry of his Apostles. The power of those original events continues today through the sacramental life of the Church. The sacraments impart sanctifying grace, enliven our ability to receive Christ's unconditional love, and fill us with the gifts of the Holy Spirit—the tools with which to build and heal the world. See also **Anointing of the Sick; Baptism, Sacrament of; Confession; Confirmation; Eucharist; Holy Orders; Reconciliation.**

SACRIFICE: To make holy; a rite offered to God on behalf of the people, presided over by a priest who leads and represents the community in adoration, repentance, gratitude, and honor (Heb 2:17). In the Old Testament, a sacrifice was needed as an atonement, a healing rite to restore holiness, cleanse the people from infractions of the Law, and reconcile their covenant relationship with God (Ps 51:1–17).

Like Native American peoples, the ancient Israelite communities honored the life force of an animal taken for the sustenance of the tribe by offering it to God. The taking of life was marked by careful, painless, swift slaughter and cleanliness in butchering. Portions of the meat were holocaust, or burnt offering, and some were gifted to the priests and the people as food offerings (Ex 29:26–28). The animal products were used for clothing, blankets, and parchment. Special celebrations called for the sacrifice of a lamb: Sabbath, the feast of the New Moon, Trumpets, Tabernacles, Pentecost, and Passover, as well as lesser feast days (Num 28—29; Lev 23).

Christians honor the sacrifice of Jesus on the cross as the ultimate atonement, healing, and final restitution between God and humanity. In sacred liturgy, Christians offer Jesus to God as the worthy and perfect sacrifice of thanksgiving for the gifts of salvation he offered with his life, teachings, death, and Resurrection. Christ is honored as the high priest who gave his all to God—offered his very self as the lamb of sacrifice for salvation (Heb 2:17). The Crucifixion of Jesus was made holy by his divine nature, his intention to offer himself as reconciliation, and is eternally made present in the celebration of the Eucharistic liturgy. Jesus offered the cup and said, "Drink from it, all of you; for this is my blood of the covenant, which is poured out for many for the forgiveness of sins" (Mt 26:27–28). See also **Altar; Blood; Jesus Christ; Lamb; Levi, Levite.**

SADDUCEE (sad´joo-see)**:** A member of a group of political religious priests who served in the Temple in Jerusalem during the time of Christ. The Sadducees stood in opposition to the scribes and Pharisees. These priests revered the Torah but denied the value of the prophets and many of the religious traditions of the Law of Moses. They were politically and religiously liberal and were in partnership with the Roman authorities. They did not believe in angels, final judgment, or resurrection of the dead (Mk 12:18–27). John the Baptist called both the Pharisees and Sadducees a "brood of vipers" (Mt 3:7). Like John, Jesus took issue with both groups, calling them an "evil and adulterous generation" (Mt 16:4).

The Sadducees, under the leadership of the high priests Annas and Caiaphas, suppressed the people, collected the Temple tax, and used the Temple courtyards for commercial gain. Sadducees were politically associated with the Herodian kings and benefited financially from their support of the Roman warlords. For this reason, Jesus staged a rebellion with a bullwhip in the Temple square (Jn 2:13–16). Together with members of the Sanhedrin, the Roman rulers were the authorities who crucified Jesus (Jn 18:13, 24). Their power remained intact until the Romans destroyed the Temple and Jerusalem in AD 70. See also **Pharisee.**

SALOME (suh-loh´mee)**:** The daughter of Herodias and Herod Philip. The historian Josephus recorded her name as Salome. Her mother, Herodias, illicitly married Philip's brother, Herod Antipas. John the Baptist vehemently condemned the adultery.

At the birthday party of Antipas, the princess Salome was exhibited as a harlot in a public arena at a banquet in front of the king's "courtiers and officers and for the leaders of Galilee" (Mk 6:21). In payment for the dance, Antipas offered Salome any wish. The girl, prodded by her mother, demanded the head of John the Baptist presented on a platter. John

was beheaded that night (Mt 14:1–12) in the fortress of Machaerus. See also **Herod the Great.**

SALT: A mineral used to season and prepare foods and as fuel to fire earthen ovens. Salt was an element of hospitality, relationship, cleansing, preserving, and destroying (Ezek 16:4; Judg 9:45). Jesus compared the disciples to salt, an image of discipleship as a fire that would spread across the earth. Jesus said, "You are the salt of the earth . . . the light of the world" (Mt 5:13–14).

SALVATION: The Hebrew concept of salvation meant freedom from bondage and the reception of mercy and forgiveness of debt. Salvation meant being freed from slavery and rescued from imprisonment. The quintessential salvation was the Exodus, in which Moses led the Hebrew people out of the slavery of Egypt on the first Passover night (Ex 15).

The Christian concept of salvation honors the Jewish beliefs and affirms that salvation includes both life on earth and life in heaven after death. Jesus personifies salvation and saves us from the enemy. He is the divine Lamb of God, who takes away the sin of the world. Jesus offers himself as the Redeemer for the salvation of humanity (Heb 2:5–18). See **Atonement; Blood of Christ; Redeemer.**

SAMARIA (suh-mair´ee-uh): The name of both the capital city and the central hill country of Palestine (1 Kings 16:24). The reign of Solomon, followed by the reign of his son Rehoboam, fueled the fracture that led ten of the Twelve Tribes north to Israel, leaving two tribes in Judah. The separation of the nation was permanent (1 Kings 11:31). Samaria was part of the northern kingdom of Israel and became the cult center for the worship of Baal and the palace of Ahab and Jezebel (1 Kings 16:29–31).

In 721 BC, the Assyrians destroyed the northern kingdom and deported or killed much of the population. The survivors who stayed behind lived with their Assyrian conquerors, and the population blended into an interracial, interreligious group known as the Samaritans. For centuries, these people were the subject of mockery and racial discrimination from the southern kingdom.

In the time of Jesus, the ethnic hatred between the Jews and the Samaritans centered on which historic site was appropriate for worship. After and during many conquests, Samaria had bound itself to five different god systems and worshipped on Mount Gerizim, where the Samaritan temple drew pilgrimages rivaling those to Jerusalem (2 Kings 24—41). The tribes that who settled the southern kingdom of Judah, considered the Temple in Jerusalem the true place of worship (Jn 4:19–20). See also **Ahab; Jezebel; Samaritan Woman.**

SAMARITAN WOMAN: Jesus was in Samaria, at the village of Sychar, near the well of Jacob, when he met an unnamed woman and asked her for water. The woman knew that Jesus could not accept food or drink from her. She was a Samaritan and a woman, and he was a Jew. Jesus offered her the waters of "eternal life" (Jn 4:14). The Samaritan woman was the first person to whom Jesus revealed that he was the Messiah. The woman put down her water jar and became a disciple. During the Lenten season, the story of the Samaritan woman's encounter with the Christ is read during rites that prepare adults for Christian Initiation and reception into the Catholic Church at Easter. See also **Samaria.**

SAMSON: A mighty son of the tribe of Dan and the twelfth and final judge of Israel mentioned in the Book of Judges, who served for twenty years. An angel revealed Samson's coming birth, telling his mother he would be a Nazirite who would deliver Israel from the Philistines (Judg 13:2–5).

Samson violated every Nazirite vow. He had an inordinate passion for women, used prostitutes, had multiple marriage partners, drank alcohol, and lusted for power. He ate grapes, touched dead bodies, and even ate honey from the dead body of a lion (Judg 14:1–16).

His wondrous feats were legendary. The tribal hero devastated Philistine cities and fields. When the spirit of the Lord rushed on him, he tore a roaring lion apart with his bare hands. He single-handedly slew 1,000 Philistines with a jawbone of an ass (Judg 15).

Samson foolishly revealed to Delilah, his Philistine lover, that the source of his power was in his uncut hair. When his hair was severed, his strength left. He was bound, his eyes were burned out, and he was imprisoned in a Philistine work camp. As Samson's hair grew back, however, his heart repented and his strength returned. As the most powerful political, military, and religious Philistine leaders gathered for the heathen rites of the god Dagon, Samson stood between the pillars of their temple and pulled the edifice down on the crowd. He died in the destruction along with 3,000 Philistines (Judg 16). See also **Delilah; Judge; Nazirite.**

SAMUEL: The last judge and a prophet of Israel, a priest and son of Hannah and Elkanah. Hannah consecrated Samuel as a Nazirite when he was a child. As a boy, messages from the Lord flooded his soul (1 Sam 1:20–22).

Samuel was the spiritual leader of the people during the years the Philistines overtook Shiloh and captured the ark of the Covenant, placing it in the temple of the god Dagon (1 Sam 5:1–7). Samuel stayed faithful through the years that the Philistines oppressed Israel. After the chaos of the Philistine warfare, the ark was returned to Israel, and the land eventually returned to peace. Samuel served as judge, seer, and prophet of the Lord for many years.

When the Hebrew people first came to Samuel asking for a king, he refused because he did not want Israel to be like the other nations (1 Sam 8:4–6). After prayer, Samuel came to understand that God would accept a king. God wanted a king who would protect the needy and be in union with the Law of God (1 Sam 9:15–16). Samuel anointed Saul as the first king of Israel (1 Sam 10:1–8). When Saul turned out to be lacking faith in God, Samuel anointed David king, and the prophet felt he had fulfilled his mission (1 Sam 16:11–13). See also **David; Hannah; Judge; Saul of the Hebrews.**

SANHEDRIN (san-hee´druhn): An assembly of rabbis, doctors of the law, chief priests, religious leaders, and elders who functioned as the council of Jerusalem in the time of Christ (Mt 5:22). Some leaders of the Sanhedrin were opposed to the teachings of Jesus and ultimately condemned Jesus as a blasphemer (Mt 26:59).

Not all members of the Sanhedrin were against Jesus. Joseph of Arimathea was a member of the Sanhedrin and a secret follower of Christ who asked Pontius Pilate for the body of Jesus and then buried it in his own tomb (Mk 15:43). Rabbi Gamaliel was a highly revered Pharisee who taught against the Temple state of the Sadducees. He served as a leader of the Sanhedrin high council during the reigns of the Roman emperors Tiberius, Caligula, and Claudius (Acts 5:34–41). Saint Paul was his student (Acts 22:3).

SARAH: The matriarch of the Hebrew people. Sarai was her given name in the House of Terah in Mesopotamia. Her clan was a nomadic group who followed their flocks to the village of Haran, where Abram, her husband, encountered God. The elderly couple was asked to travel to a new land, Canaan (Gen 11:27–32).

Abram and Sarai were promised a covenant relationship with the LORD God. God promised that old Abram and barren Sarai would give birth to a great nation, receive the land of Canaan, and become a blessing to the whole earth (Gen 12:1–7). Abram and Sarai traveled to Canaan and waited for the promises of God to become reality. As a sign of God's covenant with them, God renamed them Abraham and Sarah (Gen 17:5, 15).

Although Sarah was quite old and barren, God promised she would bear a son to Abraham. Sarah laughed when she heard this, but she did bear a son and named him Isaac, which meant "the laughter of God." Isaac's son was Jacob, the father of the Twelve Tribes of Israel. Christians consider themselves adopted children of Abraham and Sarah, heirs to the promise of the covenant through Jesus (Rom 9:6–8). See also **Abraham; Barren; Covenant; Isaac.**

SATAN: His name meant "the adversary." In the Bible, Christians identify Satan as the serpent who tempted and seduced humanity in the garden of Eden (Gen 3) and the devil who tempted Jesus in the desert (Mt 4:1–11). In the Old Testament, Satan's identity is murky. In the Book of Job, he was described as an accuser, part of God's court (Job 1:6–12). He was also identified as a prince among angels who rebelled against heaven and rejected God (Isa 14:12). In the New Testament, he was more clearly identified as a powerful agent of evil fighting against God (1 Thess 2:18), as instrumental in Jesus' death (Lk 22:3), as tempting people to sin (1 Cor 7:5), and as being called the devil (Rev 12:9). See also **Beelzebub; Demon; Exorcism; Lucifer.**

SAUL: See **Paul.**

SAUL OF THE HEBREWS: A man from the tribe of Benjamin whom Samuel anointed as the first king of Israel (1020–1000 BC). Saul was a military king who committed his life to freeing the Israelites from the plunder of Israel's enemies (1 Sam 14:47–48). Saul was married to Ahinoam, the daughter of Ahimaaz (1 Sam 14:50).

Saul's stellar career as a warrior came into question when he failed to follow Samuel's orders. He refused to kill an enemy, King Agag, and failed to offer

Agag's best animals as holocaust, or burnt offering, to God. The prophet Samuel was outraged and deposed Saul as monarch (1 Sam 15:22–23).

Samuel anointed David as the next king. After David's victory over the Philistine giant, Goliath, Saul gave David his daughter Michal as a wife. When it was obvious that David was growing in popularity, Saul tried to kill him. The situation was complicated when Saul's son, Jonathan, became David's best friend. David, fearing Saul, exiled himself to Ramah (1 Sam 16—20).

Saul was a great warrior who was not completely removed from the ways of the foreign nations. He sought counsel from the soothsayer of Endor, yet feared Samuel, the prophet of the Lord (1 Sam 28:3–20). When the Philistines won the victory at Mount Gilboa, he killed himself by falling on his own sword. The Philistines cut off his head and hung it on the wall of Beth-shan in the temple of Dagon at Ashdod (1 Sam 31:1–10). See also **David; Jonathan; Samuel.**

SAVIOR: A benefactor who forgave debts, provided benefit, and protected one from the enemy (Neh 9:27). A savior was a liberator, a redeemer who freed one from the perils of life and from the Sheol of death. In Hebrew, the name Jesus is Yeshua or Joshua, which means "God saves" (Mt 1:21).

Jesus was called the Savior of the world, the Redeemer, the Shepherd, and guardian of souls (Jn 4:42; Lk 1:68–69). He was called Lord both as a title of respect and as a divine honor, and his ministry was seen to offer salvation (Acts 2:34–36; Mt 8:25). Christ has claimed the victory over death (1 Cor 15:54–57). Those who have faith, who have the Savior, have won victory (1 Jn 5:4). See also **Jesus Christ.**

SCAPEGOAT: Modern term referring to an innocent person taking the blame for something he or she has not done. The word's ancient meaning was the same but further connected to a ritual of forgiveness that pleaded for mercy before God (Isa 42:21–25). On the Day of Atonement, the high priest symbolically placed the sins of the people on a goat and then abandoned the goat in the desert as a sacrifice for sin. See also **Atonement; Azazel.**

SCOURGING: A form of ritualized shaming and torture. The victim was flogged or whipped with rods, reeds, ropes, or leather whips. The Hebrew Law forbade a flogging to exceed forty lashes (Deut 25:1–3). The beating was limited to thirty-nine lashes; however, this could also be used as a future threat, suggesting the victim was still owed one more lash (2 Cor 11:24). The Romans used scourging as punishment and a death penalty. Their scourgings could be so severe that the victim died from loss of blood. As was Roman policy, Jesus was scourged before his Crucifixion to intensify suffering and inflict shame.

SCRIBE: A person who was a trained copyist. Professional letter writers, scribes also copied books and sometimes worked in government offices as secretaries. The scribe prepared decrees in the name of officials. Baruch was the official scribe of the prophet Jeremiah (Jer 36:4). Ezra the scribe was a scholar of the Law of Moses (Ezra 7:6).

In the time of Jesus, the scribes had affiliated themselves with the Pharisees and the doctors of the Law and were experts in the interpretation of tradition (Lk 20:27–39). Scribes were well connected at court, in the Temple, and in business circles (Acts 4:5–6). See also **Pharisee.**

SCRIPTURE: See **Bible.**

SCRIPTURE STUDY: See **Exegesis.**

SEA OF REEDS: See **Red Sea.**

SECOND COMING: See **Day of Judgment; Parousia.**

SEDER (say´duhr): The yearly celebration meal that honors the Jewish Passover. The Seder includes special foods, readings, symbols, and rites honoring the night the Israelites were freed from the bondage of Egypt. The Seder and its Paschal lamb memorialized the sacred trust between Yahweh and Jewish people throughout the world (Ex 12:5). See also **Exodus; Passover.**

SEMITIC: The ancient language, culture, and various racial groups that make up the Middle East all have a common Semitic ancestry. The Hebrew, Aramaic, Arabic, and Akkadian languages, as well as the lost Hyksos language of Egypt, all have a Semitic source or root.

SEPPHORIS (sef´uh-ris): In the time of Christ, Herod Antipas hosted the reconstruction of Sepphoris a few miles from Nazareth. Its recent discovery has changed many assumptions about life in Nazareth. Sepphoris was a thriving and sophisticated urban center. This view challenges the long-held idea that Jesus grew up in a completely isolated peasant environment.

SEPTUAGINT (sep´too-uh-jihnt): The ancient Greek canon of the Hebrew Scriptures. The Septuagint included the forty-six books of the Old Testament. It is often referred to by the Roman numerals LXX—which means seventy—in honor of the legendary seventy rabbis who translated the Hebrew text into Greek in supposedly seventy days. See also **Deuterocanonical Books; Hellenism; Old Testament.**

SEPULCHRE (sep´uhl-kuhr): A tomb made from rock or a cave. A sepulchre was a type of mausoleum, an aboveground grave. Sometimes, sepulchres were cut into the walls of natural caves and sealed with large gravestones (Mt 27:66).

SERAPHIM (ser´uh-fim): A choir of seraphs; a race of heavenly angelic beings; guardians of the throne of the

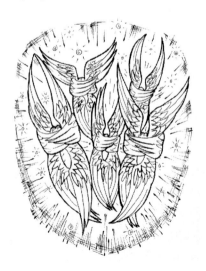

Most High. In a vision, the prophet Isaiah encountered the creatures as they adored the LORD God in the heavenly temple (Isa 6:1–3). Seraphim are mysterious and powerful messengers, guardians, and advocates for humanity who have been encountered across the ages. They have been experienced as fiery beings, messengers of the Holy One. See also **Angel; Archangel; Cherub, Cherubim.**

SERMON ON THE MOUNT: See **Beatitudes.**

SERPENT: As part of its natural life cycle, the serpent sheds its skin. Primitive people thought that in its molting, the serpent controlled new life. Ancient Middle Eastern peoples thought of serpents and trees as symbols of the life force. In the Eden story, the serpent tempted Eve to eat from the Tree of the Knowledge of Good and Evil and promised that she would not die (Gen 3:1–20).

Although Western medicine still uses the image of a serpent coiled around a staff as an image of healing, to most of us the image of a serpent does not represent the divine. For the ancient Middle Eastern world, however, the image of the serpent represented power and divine presence. The serpent Rahab or the Sumerian goddess Tiamat, who was the ancient serpent of chaos in Semitic myth, attested to the common image of the serpent as a religious power (Isa 51:9). In the time of Moses, even the power of Yahweh was imaged as a serpent (Ex 7:8–13).

Later generations viewed the image of the dragon and the serpent as satanic and evil (Rev 12:17). See also **Tiamat; Viper.**

SHADRACH (shad´rak): The three faithful friends of Daniel—Abednego,

Shadrach, and Meshach—refused to worship the golden idols that King Nebuchadnezzar of Babylon erected on the Plain of Dura. The king went into a rage so intense that his face became distorted, and he condemned the three friends to die in the fiery furnace. Miraculously, the young men remained unharmed by the flames, and the king learned a lesson on the power of the true God (Dan 3:12–23). See also **Abednego; Meshach.**

SHALOM (shah-lohm´): See **Peace.**

SHAME: See **Honor and Shame.**

SHAMGAR (sham´gahr): The third judge of Israel. Shamgar served alongside Ehud during the eighty years of peace. Shamgar was the son of Anath, who converted to the Hebrew God. His story was connected to Deborah and Jael. He was remembered as a victorious warrior who personally defeated 600 Philistines and stopped caravans of foreigners from crossing into Israelite territory (Judg 3:31). See also **Judge.**

SHEBA, QUEEN OF: Scripture identified Sheba as the "queen of the South" who traveled from Ethiopia to Judah to hear the wisdom of Solomon (Mt 12:42). King Solomon filled the queen's every desire and answered her questions, and she gifted him with gold and fine woods for crafting lyres and harps, as well as with precious stones. She honored him by saying, "Happy are your wives!" (1 Kings 10:1–13). The Ethiopians honor her as the mother of Solomon's son, Menelik. The official title of Haile Selassie I, King of Ethiopia (1892–1975) was the "Lion of Judah." Many African peoples honor him as the last living member of the House of David. See also **Solomon.**

SHECHEM (shek´uhm)**:** One of the most ancient cities of the world, Shechem was the shrine center of central Israel in the heart of Samaria. Abraham received his call from God in Shechem, and there he built the first Hebrew altar in the land of Canaan (Gen 12:6–7). In Shechem, Jacob brought his people to the very site where his ancestors Abraham and Sarah had entered the Promised Land and where Jacob made a covenant with the Lord (Josh 24:1–25).

Sadly, the people of Shechem were a source of shame and sadness between the clans of Jacob and the indigenous Canaanites. The Hivite prince named Shechem either raped or seduced Dinah, the daughter of Jacob and Leah, which resulted in an alienation that lasted for centuries (Gen 33:18—34:13). However, Shechem became a place of refuge where the bones of Joseph were buried (Josh 20:1–7, 24:32). In Shechem, at the well of Jacob, for the first time Jesus revealed his identity as the Messiah to a Samaritan woman (Jn 4:4–26). See also **Dinah.**

SHEKEL (shek´uhl)**:** A word meaning "a slice of metal"—silver, gold, brass, or iron. The shekel was used as a unit of value, as a type of money (1 Chr 21:25). Eventually, a shekel referred to a large silver coin from Tyre.

SHEM: A son of Noah, a brother of Ham and Japheth, who survived the great Flood in the ark (Gen 5:32). Abraham was a descendant of Shem (Gen 12:26).

SHEMA ISRAEL (shee´muh iz´ray-uhl)**:** The prayer known as the "shema Israel" has been said by observant Jews three times a day for thousands of years to honor the unity of God. In essence, it calls the faithful across the centuries to "Hear, O Israel: the LORD [Yahweh] is our God [Elohim], the LORD alone" (Deut 6:4). It leads the faithful to love the Lord with a whole heart, mind, and soul, and to love others as one loves oneself (Deut 6:5, 11:13–21). Jesus used the shema to summarize the Law and the faith of Moses into the two great commandments (Mt 22:36–40).

SHEOL (shee´ohl)**:** The place of the dead. In ancient times, the Israelite peoples rejected the concept of resurrection and eternal life as a way to reject the suppression of their slave masters in Egypt and the Egyptian concept of the eternal journey of the souls of the elite.

Over time, the Hebrews began to see Sheol as a place of the dead, as a state of existence, not a state of oblivion (Gen 37:34–36). Still, Sheol was a place of despair, not a paradise for the dead (Deut 32:22). It was a place of waiting, cleansing, and potential release (Job 14:13–15), the shadowy place of the dead, a place where God "brings low" but "also exalts" (1 Sam 2:7).

Redemption was possible even from the depths of Sheol, for God heard the cries of those who longed for release (Ps 139:8). The prophet Ezekiel offered visions of the resurrection of the dead from Sheol. The honorable slain, who rested in the earth, reclaimed their bodies and their lives in the presence of God (Ezek 37:3–14). Later generations of Jews believed that their prayers could change the status of the dead, that the compassion of the living could aid their departed loved ones, and that souls could be freed from Sheol (2 Macc 12:39–45). See also **Descent into Hell; Hell.**

SHEPHERD: One who cares for the flock. In Bible times, the shepherd led the animals to pasture; fed, nurtured, provided water, and kept the flock together; sought the strays; protected the group from predators; and brought the sheep home to the fold.

Shepherds were at the very bottom of the Israelite social world. They were considered untouchable, unclean, and not worthy of honor (Gen 46:34). Yet the image of the shepherd in Judeo-Christian spirituality is one of compassion and care, in terms of both human and divine leadership. The LORD God was imaged as a shepherd (Num 27:16–17; Ps 23:1). Kings of nations and humble shepherds honored the Nativity of Christ at his birth (Lk 2:15–20). Jesus was called the Good Shepherd who was willing to lay down his life for his sheep (Jn 10:11).

SHILOH (shi′loh): A shrine center in central Israel. After the Israelites entered the Holy Land, the tabernacle was set up in Shiloh. There it remained until the Philistines confiscated the ark of the Covenant (Josh 18:1–10). The Feast of Shiloh was an honored time of sacrifice and worship. The festival included clan rites in which the family pilgrimaged to the shrine center of Shiloh to worship (Judg 21:19).

SILAS (si′luhs): A Roman citizen, a loyal Christian, and a leader in the early Church (1 Thess 1:1). Silas was also known in the letters of Paul and 1 Peter by his Latin name, Silvanus. Silas was a prophet in Jerusalem, an associate of Judas Barsabbas who joined Paul and Barnabas to take the teachings of the Council of Jerusalem to the Church in Antioch (Acts 15:22–32). Silas evangelized Asia Minor, Macedonia, and Achaia with Saint Paul (Acts 15:40–41).

SILOAM (si-loh′uhm): Village in a valley southeast of Jerusalem. Siloam was the site of one of Jesus' most profound miracles. After healing the blind man Bartimaeus, Jesus sent him to wash in the pool of Siloam (Jn 9:1–7).

SIMEON (sim′ee-uhn): His name meant "he who hears." In the Old Testament, Simeon was the son of Jacob and Leah and a patriarch of one of the Twelve Tribes of Israel. Simeon and his brother Levi avenged the rape of their sister Dinah, even after a marriage was arranged with Shechem. Jacob cursed their anger, called them cruel, and cut them both from his blessings (Gen 34:30, 49:5–7).

The New Testament prophet Simeon spent his life in prayer and anticipation of the coming of the Messiah. He was present the day Joseph and Mary presented Jesus in the Temple, dedicating him to the Lord according to the Law of Moses. Simeon blessed the child and foretold the suffering that both Jesus and Mary were destined to experience (Lk 2:22–39). See also **Anna; Presentation of Christ.**

SIMON MAGUS (may′guhs): Simon Magus practiced magic in Samaria, where he heard Philip preaching the good news of Jesus Christ (Acts: 8:12). The ministry of Philip caused such joy in the city that many—including Simon—were baptized. When Peter and John came to Samaria, they offered the Baptism of the Holy Spirit and laid hands on the converts, who received the Holy Spirit.

When Simon Magus saw the manifestation of the Spirit as the Apostle laid hands on the people, he offered money to buy the power. Peter recognized that Simon's conversion was not heartfelt and demanded that he repent from his intention to manipulate the Spirit of God for profit. He told Simon to ask God for forgiveness. Simon became frightened, repented, and begged Peter for prayer (Acts 8:9–24).

SIMON PETER: The Galilean fisherman chosen by Jesus of Nazareth as the leader of the Apostles. Simon Peter, son of Jonah, grew up along the west coast of the Sea of Galilee in the fishing village of Bethsaida, with his brother Andrew (Jn 1:40–42). Jesus changed Simon, a Judean name meaning "one who hears," to Peter, which meant "rock" (Mt 16:17–18). Jesus healed Peter's mother–in–law (Mt 8:14–17). Peter's wife accompanied him on his missionary journeys, and it is possible that the Evangelist Mark was his son (1 Cor 9:5; 1 Pet 5:13).

Peter is a model of faith, brokenness, and reconciliation. Saint Peter proclaimed that Jesus was the Messiah, the faith on which the Church of Christ was built (Mk 8:29). During the trial, persecution, and Crucifixion of Jesus, Peter failed in faith by denying that he knew Jesus (Mt 26:74), but then later he repented and recommitted his life to Christ. When Mary Magdalene proclaimed that Jesus had risen, Peter believed her and ran to the tomb (Jn 20:1–9). Jesus appeared to Peter and the Apostles after his Resurrection and commissioned Peter to "feed my sheep," or the fold of the Church, until the day he died (Jn 21:15–19). Peter was the first Bishop of Rome and is considered the first Pope of the Catholic Church. Peter loved Jesus and worked to spread the Gospel. In the end, Peter gave his life as a martyr for Christ. He was crucified like Jesus, but upside-down as a gift of humility. See also **Apostle.**

SIMON THE CYRENE (si-ree′nee): Simon was from Libya in North Africa. He was in Jerusalem with his sons, Rufus and Alexandria, when the Romans forced him to help Jesus carry his cross (Mk 15:21).

SIMON THE ZEALOT: Simon was an Apostle of Jesus. His title is translated "the Canaanite" or the "Zealot" and suggests that he had been an insurgent who worked to defeat the Roman Empire (Lk 6:15). See also **Apostle.**

SIN: A Hebrew word translated into English as *sin* literally means "missing the mark." Sin is falling short of God's will for human life. In the Old Testament, sin was seen primarily as disobeying the Mosaic Law, especially breaking one of the Ten Commandments. In the New Testament, Jesus elaborated to say it wasn't just the physical actions that were sinful; the evil that was in hearts was also sin (Mt 5:22, 5:28, 15:18–19)

In the Bible, as strange as it sounds to modern ears, the word *sin* actually implied hope. If an action were condemned

as sinful, then the person could repent, change the situation, and be made new. We can resist and reject evil (Gen 4:7). Pain, despair, and sinful situations are not the will of God. In a world that believed in the powers of fate controlled by gods and powers of earth, sin was a word that inferred the possibility of healing, repentance, and change. God created humanity and offered free will.

God desires our love and free choice and longs for us to choose to live in a covenant relationship of justice and compassion. Sin breaks relationships and is the opposite of God's hope and vision for how we were created to live together. The Bible teaches that God forgives our sin; Jesus emphasized that we must also be willing to forgive the sins of others (Ps 103:12; Mt 12:31; Lk 6:37).

SINAI (s*i*´n*i*): The desert and mountain region east of Egypt and south of Canaan. In the wilderness of Sinai, the Israelites wandered with Moses for forty years. On Mount Sinai—which in the north was known as Mount Horeb—Moses received the stones on which the Ten Commandments were carved (Ex 19:20). See also **Exodus; Sinai, Mount.**

SINAI, MOUNT (s*i*´n*i*): A very sacred site in the Bible. At Mount Sinai—also called Mount Horeb in the northern tradition—God revealed himself to Moses from within the burning bush (Ex 3). On Sinai, Moses received the Law (Ex 19—23). From Sinai, God called to Moses from within the cloud (Ex 24:16) and revealed the divine nature to be "merciful and gracious, / slow to anger, / and abounding in steadfast love and faithfulness" (Ex 34:6). The actual location of Mount Sinai is debated. See also **Horeb, Mount; Sinai.**

SISERA (sis´uh-ruh): See **Barak; Deborah.**

SLAUGHTER OF THE HOLY INNOCENTS: A story told only in the Gospel of Matthew that emphasized the similarity between the infancy of Moses and that of Jesus. Mary and the vulnerable infant Jesus were safely in Joseph's care when Herod, the puppet ruler of Rome, heard rumors of the birth of a messiah. He ordered the death of all male children younger than two years of age to spare himself future threats to his power. The soldiers obeyed. Joseph, warned by an angel in a dream, fled with the Holy Family to Egypt and protected the child from death (Mt 2:7–18).

SLAVERY: The possession and suppression of human beings. Slavery was an accepted practice throughout the cultures of the ancient world. The Hebrews enforced limits on slavery, and the Law ordered Jubilee and periods of release (Lev 25:39–46).

In the time of Jesus, slavery was the prime source of the economy of the Roman Empire. Of the entire population, 75 percent was slave class. The system of slavery was such a common part of the Greco-Roman culture that even the New Testament had no direct prohibition against it. Scripture taught, however, that the blood of Christ had liberated humanity from all bondage and paid for its redemption with the blood of Jesus (Eph 1:7; Rev 1:5). In Christ, there could exist neither slave nor free (Gal 3:28). The early Church condemned the slave/master relationship. Christians were to see one another as brothers and sisters in Christ (Philem 16).

SODOM AND GOMORRAH (sod´uhm) (guh-mor´uh): The location of these legendary cities has been lost to history, but there is archeological evidence of ruins of urban centers to the east and south of the Dead Sea. It has been suggested that these are the lost cities of the plain—Sodom and Gomorrah (Gen 19:28).

Sodom and Gomorrah had legendary reputations for wickedness, sexual perversion, and lack of hospitality; so much so that these conditions brought divine punishment upon the population. Only Lot and his family escaped the fiery end (19:1–29). Sodom and Gomorrah were used as warnings of God's judgment against evil (Deut 29:23; Mt 10:15). The word *Sodom* has become associated with sexual perversity (sodomy).

SOLOMON: The third king of the united kingdom of Israel, the son of King David and Bathsheba (975–922 BC). Solomon was the second child of the royal couple; the first son died in infancy. Solomon's reign was noted for his building campaigns, which included the Temple of the LORD built to honor his father, David (1 Cor 22:11). The Chronicler praised Solomon for his wisdom (2 Chr 1:1–13).

Solomon honored his father's dream of a centralized government for Israel. He strengthened the army and made trade alliances with the surrounding nations. He collected 700 wives and 300 concubines. These women functioned as trade bonds with their fathers and ensured that peace and trade flourished. To soothe his political allegiances and the whims of the women in his harem, Solomon permitted his harem to continue the worship of their gods and joined them in their exotic rites (1 Kings 11:1–8). Solomon's reign was marked by a constant tension between his idolatry and his faithfulness to the God of Israel. Solomon provided hospitality to a variety of foreign nobles; the most interesting was the legendary Queen of Sheba. See also **Bathsheba; David; King; Sheba, Queen of.**

SON OF GOD: Title given to Jesus to identify his special relationship to God. The voice from heaven identified Jesus as the Son of God, as did those people who recognized that in Christ, God was in their midst (Mk 1:11, 15:39).

SON OF MAN: An ancient Hebrew divine title, Bar Nasa, that refers to God's chosen messiah and the coming of the Day of the Lord. The Son of Man will be announced by signs in the heavens and will come at the end times to bring on the Reign of God (Mt 24:30). The Ancient One or the Ancient of Days, both names for God, commissioned this divine warrior to conquer death and defeat the ancient dragon. God gives the Son of Man authority, leadership, and glory. All people and nations will serve him, and his reign will be eternal (Dan 7:9–14). All four Gospels depict Jesus referring to himself as the Son of Man, usually in connection to his Passion and death (Mk 13:26).

SORCERY: The dark craft of divination, condemned in the Scriptures as idolatry (Lev 19:26). Sorcery was listed in relation to the rites of Molech, abortion, child sacrifice, soothsaying, and augury. The practice of sorcery included an abuse of power, tarnished the free will, and set up a system in which the future was presumed set. This fate-based practice stood in contrast to a creation-based understanding of destiny. See also **Divination; Witch.**

SOURCE CRITICISM: See **Exegesis.**

SPIRIT: The wind of God's breath—*ruah* in Hebrew; the creative aspect of God; the mysterious breath of the presence of the Holy (Gen 1:2, 2:7); the essence of human life (Acts 7:59). The Old Testament did not talk about the Holy Spirit, but there were references to the Spirit of God. God promised to bring Israel back from the death of exile by the power of his Spirit (Ezek 37:1–12). Jesus promised to send the "Spirit of Truth"—the Holy Spirit—to be with his disciples after he returned to his Father (Jn 14:15–17). See also **Holy Spirit; Paraclete.**

STEADFAST LOVE: A biblical phrase describing the love story of God's covenant relationship with humanity (Deut 7:9). In Hebrew, steadfast love is translated as *hesed*, a very revered word meaning God's unconditional, total, unchanging, eternal love (Ps 136). Beginning with Creation, God has loved humanity into existence and continued to reveal God's self to human hearts. Even though human sinfulness wounds our relationship with God, others, and ourselves, God continues to reach out to us in covenant love (Ps 61). In Jesus, the New Covenant, love took on flesh and offered himself for our salvation (Lk 22:20). Jesus was the incarnation of this divine, total, steadfast love (Jn 15:9–17).

SUFFERING: The reality of suffering is a mystery, and the Bible gives us different glimpses into the reality of that mystery. In the Creation story, suffering was the result of the sin of our first parents (Gen 3:16–19). Throughout much of the Old Testament and even in the time of Jesus, suffering was seen as God's punishment for sin (Jn 9:1–2). The Book of Job struggled with whether punishment was really the cause of suffering, since Job was a just man, innocent of any serious sin. In the end, the book concluded that human beings could neither comprehend the complexity of the created order nor the mysteries of suffering, but it offered the compassion of God's love as the ultimate outcome experienced by the just (Job 38—41).

The New Testament began to see suffering from a very different perspective. Jesus affirmed that suffering from disease or physical challenge was not punishment for personal sin or retribution from the failings of a previous life (Jn 9:1–4). Not only that, Jesus accepted the reality of suffering for the sake of the Kingdom of God and asked the disciples to take up their cross (Mk 8:34–35). The first Letter of Peter goes on to suggest that faith is purified through suffering (Mk 1:6–7) and that people are blessed when suffering for doing what is right, because Jesus himself suffered for the same reasons (Mk 3:13–18, 4:12–19).

SUFFERING SERVANT: The prophets revealed that the people of Israel were God's suffering servant who endured the pain of alienation and grief across history. Yet the prophets also proclaimed that one to come, the promised one of God, would suffer as a result of his compassion for humanity. He was to be Emmanuel—God with us. The suffering servant of Yahweh would be one with the people and would be one who knew suffering. He would bear our sufferings and bring us redemption (Isa 52:13—53:12).

SUKKOTH (suhk´uhth): See **Tabernacle.**

SUSANNA (*soo*-zan´uh): Name of two women in Scripture. In the Book of Daniel, Susanna was a beautiful and honorable woman in a time in which a woman's word was meaningless and a man's was law. Two elders falsely accused her of adultery. They wished to take sexual advantage of her and condemned her to death. She proclaimed her innocence to God, and as she was dragged to execution, Daniel became her advocate. Daniel interviewed the men and revealed their lie. Because of this, he was remembered as an advocate for women's rights, a revolutionary for justice (Dan 13).

The New Testament listed a woman called Susanna as a follower of Jesus. She was remembered with Mary Magdalene; Joanna Chuza, the wife of Herod's steward; and other women cured of evil spirits (Luke 8:2–3).

SYNAGOGUE (sin´uh-gog): In the Jewish tradition, a synagogue was a gathering place—a place to pray to God, study Torah, socialize, and serve the community. There were no sacrifices in a synagogue. Sacrifice was reserved for the Temple.

It is unclear how synagogues began in ancient Israel, but they were already established by Jesus' time (Mt 4:23; Mk 1:21). Possibly, synagogues were started in the Jewish Diaspora as a place to gather and preserve Jewish heritage. After the Romans destroyed the Temple of Jerusalem in AD 70, synagogues became the rabbinical center for teaching and worship. See also **Worship.**

SYNOPTIC GOSPELS: The Gospels of Mark, Matthew, and Luke are called synoptic—a word meaning "seen together"—because they appear to have had a similar source. Mark was written first. Luke and Matthew used Mark, as well as the Quelle source, the Sayings of Jesus, to compile their Gospels. John is a unique Gospel and is based on a different community's stories about Jesus. See also **"Q" Source.**

SYRIA (sihr´ee-uh): The name of a region or country that surrounded the city of Damascus. Syria's boundaries changed over time, but it was generally the region beyond the Euphrates and Tigris rivers in Mesopotamia. Eventually, the whole area was subject to the rule of Damascus. In the time of Christ, the Romans claimed Syria and saw it as part of Palestine.

SYROPHOENICIAN WOMAN

(si´roh-fi-nish´uhn): An unnamed woman of Canaan. The Evangelist Mark used the story of the Syrophoenician woman to show Jesus' requirement for repentance as well as his heartfelt compassion for the suffering. Jesus had traveled to the Phoenician cities of Tyre and Sidon. The cities were remembered for their blatant idolatry and for the idolatrous Queen Jezebel of Sidon, priestess of the Baals, who was eaten by dogs (1 Kings 16:31–34).

The unnamed Syrophoenician woman begged Jesus to heal her daughter of the demon that possessed her. Jesus told the woman that he was sent only to Israel. She knelt and begged for help. The history of Israel's idolatry is woven within the woman's words with Jesus. He said to her that he couldn't take the food of Israel and throw it to the dogs; that is, to people whose history was infused with idolatry. Her response to him was a form of repentance and humility: "Sir, even the dogs under the table eat the children's crumbs." Jesus remarked on the strength of her faith and assured her that her daughter was freed and well (Mk 7:24–30).

T

TABERNACLE

(tab´uhr-nak´uhl): A portable, tentlike structure in which the Israelites kept the ark of the Covenant, the Altar of Incense, and the table for the Bread of Presence (Heb 9:1–5). Detailed directions for its construction are in the Book of Exodus (Ex 26:1–37). The tabernacle had an inner curtained room in which the ark of the Covenant was kept. The design of the tabernacle was exactly the same as that described for Solomon's Temple. In Catholic churches today, the sacred receptacle that reserves the Blessed

Sacrament is called a tabernacle in honor of the ancient Israelite tradition. See also **Tent of Meeting.**

TABERNACLES, FEAST OF

(tab´uhr-nak´uhlz): This ancient Hebrew feast was celebrated each year in autumn at the gathering of the grain harvests on the fifteenth through the twenty-second days of the seventh month (Lev 23:33–36; Deut 16:13–17). The feast recalled the desert wandering, when the Israelites were tent dwellers. They called their tents "booths" or "tabernacles"—which is why the feast is called Tabernacles, or Booths, or the Festival of the Harvest, or in Hebrew, *Sukkoth* (Ex 23:16).

Matthew's Gospel connects the Transfiguration of Jesus with the Feast of Tabernacles. After witnessing the manifestation of Moses and Elijah, Saint Peter wanted to honor the prophets and Jesus by preparing tents or tabernacles (Mt 17:3–4). See also **Pilgrimage.**

TABITHA

(tab´i-thuh): Her name meant "gazelle." Tabitha, a highly regarded Christian woman from Joppa, was known for her generous works of charity. The Jews called her Tabitha, and the Greeks, Dorcas. When she died unexpectedly, Peter healed and brought her back to life (Acts 9:36–42).

TAMAR OF THE HOUSE OF DAVID

(tay´mahr): The beautiful, kind, moral daughter of King David. Her maternal line is unclear. She is identified as the daughter of David's

163

wife Maacah (2 Sam 3:3, 13:1) and in another source as the child of an unnamed concubine (1 Chr 3:9).

Tamar was betrayed by her cousin Jonadab, who assisted her brother Amnon in plotting her rape. After violating Tamar, Amnon threw her out of the house and had the servant bolt the door. When Tamar told her brother Absalom of the defilement, he compassionately comforted Tamar, took her into his home, and in revenge executed Amnon for the rape of his sister (2 Sam 13:1–29).

TAMAR OF THE HOUSE OF JUDAH (tay´mahr):
Tamar had lost two husbands to untimely deaths, leaving her childless (Gen 38:6–10). According to the Levirate marriage law, Tamar had the right to marry Shelah—the third son of Judah—as soon as he matured. Judah hid Shelah, for according to the superstition of the day, a woman who had lost two husbands was thought to be under a curse. Judah also sent Tamar away in shame to live among her people. Tamar, however, knew her rights, and she resorted to trickery to make Judah get her pregnant, to secure an offspring from the House of Judah (Gen 38:12–19). She is listed in the genealogy of Jesus. See also **Levirate Marriage.**

TARSUS (tahr´suhs):
A city of Cilicia that stood on the banks of the Cydnus River near the Mediterranean coast in the southeastern section of Asia Minor. Tarsus was an urban center where Saint Paul was raised (Acts 21:39).

TEKOA (tuh-koh´uh):
A settlement in the hill country on the edge of the Judean wilderness about ten to twelve miles south of Jerusalem. A wise woman from Tekoa counseled David with a wisdom parable (2 Sam 14:1–20).

TEMPLE:
In the ancient Middle East of Egypt, Greece, and Rome, a temple functioned as the house of the gods. Unlike today, temples were not buildings in which the community gathered for worship and prayer. The people believed the gods lived in the temple in the form of a graven image or cult statue before which priests offered food, clothing, and incense and performed sacrifices.

The temple was the center of both religious and national identity. Ancient war plans included the destruction of the enemy's temple as a symbol of victory over a people and their god. The construction or restoration of a temple equated the return of the presence of the deity, its power and protection.

Israelite cultural practices connected to temples were similar to those of the Middle East, but the Israelites came to understand that God could not be contained in a temple: "The earth is the LORD's and all that is in it" (Ps 24:1). King David dreamed of building the God of Israel a sacred temple that would serve as a sanctuary and symbol of the nation (2 Sam 7:1–7). He was not able to fulfill that promise to God, but his son Solomon did.

Solomon built the First Temple in honor of his father, David (1 Kings 6). The Temple became the house of God, the central place of the worship of Yahweh, the symbol of the Judean people, and the earthly image of God's heavenly reign. Solomon's Temple was magnificent and functioned both as a political testament to the power of the monarchy (Ps 68:29) and as a symbol of the presence of Yahweh (Ps 65:4). Unfortunately, Nebuchadnezzar completely destroyed the First Temple before the Babylonian Captivity in 586 BC (Dan 1:1, 2; Jer 27:19, 40:1).

The destruction of the First Temple of Jerusalem utterly devastated the self-identity of the Israelites. The Temple site was in ruins for more than seventy years, during which time the humiliated survivors who weren't exiled offered sacrifice in its courtyard. When Cyrus the Persian conquered the Babylonian Empire in 538 BC, he received a divine mandate from "the LORD, the God of heaven" (Ezra 1:2) to allow the Israelites in Babylon to return to rebuild the Temple. He ordered the Babylonians to pay restitution, returned the sacred vessels Nebuchadnezzar had stolen, and provided cedars from Lebanon for reconstruction (Ezra 1:7, 3:7). The Second Temple was rebuilt on the ruin of the first under the direction of Zerubbabel, the leader of the exiles freed by Cyrus (Ezra 4:1–3).

In the Greek period, the Second Temple was desecrated when the Syrian warlord Antiochus erected an altar to Zeus (167 BC), triggering the Maccabean War. The Second Temple's cleansing and rededication brought healing from this shame (1 Macc 4:39–53) and is the source of the Feast of Hanukkah.

Herod the Great (37 BC–4 BC) built the Third Temple in an attempt to elevate his status among his people and to memorialize his name. It was a magnificent building, built to be like Solomon's Temple. Jesus used the Third Temple as a symbol of his own Passion and Resurrection (Jn 2:19). At the moment of his death, the sanctuary curtain of the Temple ripped in half (Mk 15:38). Ultimately, the Roman general Titus destroyed the Third Temple of Jerusalem in AD 70

when he put down a Jewish revolt and took the sacred vessels and the Temple treasury as booty.

Today, the ruin of the Temple of Jerusalem stands next to the Islamic shrine called the Dome of the Rock. Jews from all over the world travel to Jerusalem to write their prayers on slips of paper and place them within the crevices of the stones. The ruin of the Temple is known as the Wailing Wall. See also **Wailing Wall; Worship.**

TEMPTATION: In English, a word referring to seduction and enticement toward evil. The Greek word for *temptation* includes the idea of a testing, training, and preparation for strength. The Bible speaks about temptation in both these ways and explains that the test does not come from God but rather from human desires (Jas 1:13–15). The Gospels portrayed Jesus' temptation in the desert by the devil as an ordeal in preparation for his mission and taught us how to resist the lure of sin (Lk 4:1–13).

Jesus taught the disciples to ask God to help with their inclination toward sin. Jesus prayed that God would "not bring us to the time of trial, / but rescue us from the evil one" (Mt 6:13). With God's grace, evil can be mastered (Gen 4:7). Scripture teaches that turning our will to God and enduring temptations without giving in to evil will produce blessings (Jas 1:12).

TEN COMMANDMENTS: Sometimes called the Decalogue, the Ten Commandments summarize the Law of God contained in the Pentateuch, or Torah (Ex 20:2–27). When the Israelites were slaves in Egypt, they had no Law. God led the children of Israel out of slavery and Moses to the heights of Mount Sinai, where he received the Law that would protect the Israelites' freedom (Ex 13—19).

To be in Covenant relationship with Yahweh, the Israelites had to live in proper relationship with God and each other. The various laws scattered throughout the Pentateuch gave specific directions on how to build a society of justice and live as the people of God. The Ten Commandments were meant to be an easy-to-remember summary of all those various laws, one commandment for each finger on a human hand. Today, the Ten Commandments continue to provide Jews, Christians, and Muslims with moral direction. See chart **The Ten Commandments.** See also **Commandment.**

The Ten Commandments

Commandment	Meaning	Reference
I am the LORD your God . . . you shall have no other gods before me.	Love and obey God before all else and let nothing have greater importance in your life.	Ex 20:2–6; Deut 5:6–10
You shall not make wrongful use of the name of the LORD your God.	Honor the name of God. Be reverent in speech.	Ex 20:7; Deut 5:11
Observe the Sabbath day and keep it holy.	Honor the Lord's Day with worship, prayer, and rest. The Sabbath is marked as a day of remembrance.	Ex 20:8–11; Deut 5:12–15
Honor your father and your mother.	Honor your parents, listen to them, and care for them when they are elderly.	Ex 20:12; Deut 5:16
You shall not murder.	Choose life and do not murder.	Ex 20:13; Deut 5:17
Neither shall you commit adultery.	Choose chastity and loyalty. Honor marriage vows to protect the family.	Ex 20:14; Deut 5:18
Neither shall you steal.	Choose justice. Don't steal. Build security and confidence in one another.	Ex 20:15; Deut 5:19
Neither shall you bear false witness against your neighbor.	Choose honesty. Do not lie. Build trust and faith among people. Make your word and witness honorable.	Ex 20:16; Deut 5:20
Neither shall you covet your neighbor's wife. Neither shall you desire your neighbor's house.	Don't covet or entertain fantasies of being with another's spouse. Choose purity of mind. Reject jealousy.	Ex 20:17; Deut 5:21
Neither shall you desire your neighbor's . . . . male or female slave, or ox, or donkey, or anything that belongs to your neighbor.	Choose freedom from greed. Don't envy another's property or good fortune. Prevent sin by not entertaining jealous thoughts that might lead to stealing another's property.	Ex 20:17; Deut 5:21

TENT OF MEETING: A special tent that Moses directed to be set up where he and others could meet with God (Ex 33:7–11). This tent existed before the tabernacle was built; once the tabernacle was finished, the tent then functioned as the Tent of Meeting (Ex 40:2). See also **Tabernacle.**

TERAPHIM (ter´uh-fim): Household idols and images of ancestors considered sacred by ancient peoples of the Middle East. Teraphim represented the tribe's blessings and were a symbol of inheritance. The household idols could be small enough for Rachel to sit upon (Gen 31:34–35) or large enough for Michal to place in a bed as a decoy for David (1 Sam 19:13). The teraphim could function as ritual objects used by priests in liturgies (Hosea 3:4) or as fortune-telling tools (Ezek 21:21). After the time of Josiah (640–609 BC), the teraphim were condemned as idols (2 Kings 23:24).

TESTAMENT: Another word for a covenant, a solemn vow and contract in which God is witness. A testament or covenant is a binding oath that usually calls for a commitment to a new way of life. Jesus called the sacrifice of his blood the New Covenant or new testament of God's love (Lk 22:20).

The two major divisions of the sacred Scripture were called testaments. The Old Testament was the salvation history that focused on the original, or Old, Covenant relationship of the people of Israel with God. The New Testament focused on the New Covenant that God made with the whole human race through Jesus Christ.

TETRARCH (tet´rahrk): In its original meaning, a ruler over one-fourth of a larger region or kingdom. In New Testament times, the tetrarchs ruled the provinces of Judea (Lk 3:1). Herod the Great and Phasael, the sons of Herod Antipater, were the first tetrarchs in Palestine.

TEXTUAL CRITICISM. See **Exegesis.**

THADDAEUS JUDE (thad´ee-uhs): See **Jude.**

THANKSGIVING: Giving thanks to God is an important biblical theme. Throughout the Scriptures are various songs and prayers of thanksgiving for God's marvelous wonders, often expressed as praising and blessing God: the song of Moses and Miriam (Ex 15:1–21), the prayer of Hannah (1 Sam 2:1–10), various psalms (Ps 21, 30, 40, 149), the song of the three young men in the furnace (Dan 3:52–90), and Mary's Magnificat (Lk 1:46–55), to name a few. Thanksgiving offers to God one's life, hopes, and dreams in acknowledgment of the gifts with which one has been blessed (Jdt 15:14; Phil 4:6; 1 Tim 4:4).

The Greek word for thanksgiving, *eucharist*, has become the name of the central worship in the Catholic Church. Jesus is the gift of God, offered by God and to God as our great thanksgiving. We celebrate the Eucharist as our response to Christ's command to remember his sacrifice (Lk 22:19). In the Eucharist, we express our thanks to God, just as Jesus did at the Last Supper (Lk 22:17–20).

THEATER: The world of theater and the world of religious practice had a common source, that of ritual. The societies in the ancient world were performance cultures. The majority of the population could not read. Scribes did the writing, and reading was considered a mystical art. The theater developed as a way of instilling values and teaching traditions. It was a core influence in the Greek and Roman world that Jesus and the early Christians knew.

The Jewish people and early Christians banned the theater because of its connection to idolatrous religious rites; but the Romans loved it. The Romans used the theater to entertain, teach, and evoke loyalty to the state and as the basis for religious rites. The public loved dramas, comedies, and the circus.

Crucifixion was organized as a public performance intended to assure adherence to policy and the authority of the Roman state. Pontius Pilate delivered Jesus to Roman soldiers, who ritualized the walk to Golgotha as a type of spectacle. They costumed Jesus in a purple cloak, crowned him with thorns, proclaimed him King of the Jews, and knelt before him in mock homage (Mt 27:27–31).

THEOCRACY (thee-ok´ruh-see): A form of government in which the religious leaders and governmental authorities are closely connected or even are one and the same. A people's religious commitment binds them together in a theocracy. The term *theocratic model* means that the rule is God's (1 Sam 8:5).

THEOPHANY (thee-of´uh-nee): A term from the field of religious studies that refers to an experience of God that alters human life. A theophany is God's breaking into the human dimension so the individual's and the community's understanding of God is deepened or changed. There are many theophanies in Scripture: manifestations of God (Ex 3:2–16), a visit from an angel (Lk 1:22–26), a prophetic utterance (Isa 40:3–5), the voice of God, Christ, or other heavenly being (Acts 9:40; Lk 24:23), or visions (Acts 11:5; Rev 1:1–20).

THEOPHILUS (thee-of´uh-luhs): His Greek name meant "lover of God." The Gospel of Luke and the Acts of the Apostles were addressed to Theophilus, or Lover (Lk 1:3; Acts 1:1). Theophilus could have been an individual; equally possibly, the term might have been used generically to appeal to Greek-speaking Gentiles called "Lovers of God," or "God Fearers," who believed in the God of Israel.

THESSALONICA (thes´uh-luh-ni´kuh): A capital city of Macedonia situated on the Thermaic Gulf on the Aegean Sea. Thessalonica was a prosperous city that supported a large urban population, had a Roman forum, a Jewish synagogue, a stadium, a gymnasium, a temple to Serapis, a temple to Julius Caesar, and a large sacred area that offered evidence of cults to many gods and goddesses. Saint Paul, with Silas, preached in the synagogue of Thessalonica and was driven out of the city (Acts 17:1–9). He wrote to the Christian community in his epistle we call the First Letter to the Thessalonians.

THOMAS: An Apostle of Jesus also known as Didymus—Greek for "the Twin" (Jn 11:16). Thomas encouraged the other disciples to follow Jesus, even if it meant their death (Jn 11:16), yet he doubted that Jesus had been resurrected. Thomas said to the other Apostles, "Unless I see . . . and put my finger in the mark of the nails and my hand in his side, I will not believe" (Jn 20:25). A week later, Jesus appeared to Thomas and invited him to examine the wounds of his hands and side. Thomas replied, "My Lord and my God!" (Jn 20:28).

At the time of the writing of the Gospel of John (AD 90–110), the emperor Domitian erected a temple to himself in John's city of Ephesus. Under pain of death, citizens were required to offer sacrifice to Domitian while saying the words, "My Lord and God." The martyrs died rather than commit this blasphemy, but some terrified souls performed the rite. Like Thomas, they regretted their lack of faith and longed for reconciliation with the Christian community. Jesus' words to Thomas gave them peace. If Jesus could forgive an Apostle who believed only when he saw the resurrected Christ, then they, too, could be forgiven. See also **Deification.**

TIAMAT (tee-ah´maht): The great mother goddess of Sumerian and Semitic myths; the saltwater ocean goddess who rivaled Marduk for power. The Babylonian creation myths taught that from Tiamat's body, the gods created heaven and earth. The Bible's Creation stories may partially be a response to the Tiamat myth. In Hebrew, *tehom*—a root of Tiamat—referred to the chaos of the abyss, the "deep waters" mentioned in Genesis 1:2. See also **Marduk; Serpent.**

TIBERIAS (ti-bihr´ee-uhs): A city on the western shore of the Sea of Galilee. Herod Antipas founded Tiberias in AD 18 to replace Sepphoris as his administrative and banking headquarters. Herod named the city in honor of the Roman emperor Tiberius. Hot springs nearby made the site appealing to the wealthy, but traditional Jews considered the site unclean, as it was built on an ancient cemetery site on the trade route between Syria and Egypt. Tiberias had an extensive fishing trade; the Sea of Galilee and the surrounding area on its western shore became known as Tiberias (Jn 6:1).

TIGLATH-PILESER III (tig´lath-pi-lee´zuhr): An Assyrian king who conquered, reorganized, and restored the Assyrian Empire from the northern Sinai Peninsula in Egypt to the farthest reaches of the Middle East. In 729 BC, Tiglath-Pileser conquered all of Babylon. Tiglath-Pileser is remembered as the warlord Pul, who accepted rich bribes from the kings of Israel and Judah. This tribute permitted the kings to continue to rule for a time, while Tiglath-Pileser remained in charge. After three years of vicious battle in the north, he exiled the leaders of the northern kingdom of Israel to Assyria (2 Kings 17:5–6).

TIGRIS RIVER (ti´gris): The great rivers Tigris and Euphrates are the two major waterways that flow through Mesopotamia (modern-day Iraq) and empty into the Persian Gulf. Their source is in the mountains of Armenia. The Tigris flows for 1,146 miles and runs through Assyria and Armenia. The Tigris is one of the rivers of Eden (Gen 2:14) that flows east toward Assyria.

TIMOTHY: An early Christian disciple from Derbe of Lystra south of Iconium in central Asia Minor. Timothy was raised as a Gentile and led to Christ by his mother Eunice and his grandmother Lois, who were Jewish converts to Christianity. Lois and her daughter Eunice were friends of Saint Paul and considered models of virtue, learned in the Scripture and dedicated to their faith in Christ (Acts 16:1–2; 2 Tim 1:5).

After Paul had Timothy circumcised, the young man served as Paul's missionary companion. Timothy traveled from town to town as a messenger for the Apostles and elders of Jerusalem (Acts 16:3–4). Timothy was Paul's helper and beloved child in the Lord (1 Cor 4:17). He is listed in numerous letters as well as in the Acts of the Apostles. Timothy worked with Silas and possibly Titus.

An unknown Christian writer who attributed his work to the great Saint Paul wrote the two letters addressed to Timothy.

TITHE: To give one-tenth of one's income or resources to certain causes. Often, a conquering king demanded a tithe from the people he ruled (1 Macc 10:31). Sacred tithes were given as gifts or payment for blessings, visions, and religious services. The first incidence of tithing occurred when Abraham offered the king and priest Melchizedek a tithe (Gen 14:20). The Law of Moses required a tithe of the Israelites to be eaten in the Temple and every third year given to the priests, resident aliens, orphans, and widows (Deut 14:22–29). After the Israelite refugees returned from their exile in Babylon, they instituted a Temple tax, or tithe, to support the priests and the Temple rites (Neh 10:37–38).

Many Christians continue the practice of tithing in support of their churches and for charitable work.

TITUS (ti´tuhs): Gentile embraced by Saint Paul as a fellow worker in Christ. After Paul's first missionary journey, Paul traveled with Barnabas and a Greek named Titus to attend the Council of Jerusalem. Paul defended Titus to the Apostles in Jerusalem as the model of an uncircumcised, yet faith-filled, Christian (Gal 2:1–10). Titus worked in the missions with Paul, then traveled to Crete and Dalmatia and served as a loyal servant of the Gospel of Christ (2 Tim 4:10; Titus 1:4–5).

Titus was much loved in the community and upheld as a man of joy and consolation (2 Cor 7:13). Like Paul himself, Titus was honored for his passionate support of the mission of Christ and love of the Church (2 Cor 8:16–23). The Letter to Titus is most likely written in Paul's name by his disciples.

TOBIT (toh´bit): A story recalling the sadness of the Judean people after the Assyrian destruction of the northern kingdom of Israel (721 BC). Although the Book of Tobit was written in later centuries (200 BC), the story of Tobit and his family reflected God's faithfulness after the Assyrian invasion scattered God's people.

In this fictional short story, Tobit remained loyal to Yahweh and the Law of Moses, even though his tribe had strayed from the faith. Tobit was a compassionate man who offered food, clothing, and a ministry of burial of the dead. Sadly, an infection from bird droppings that fell into Tobit's eyes blinded him. As the story progressed, Tobit sent his son, Tobias, on a journey to find himself a wife. Aided by the archangel Raphael, Tobias found Sarah, a woman cursed by the demon Asmodeus, who had killed her seven previous husbands on their wedding nights. Raphael taught Tobias how to free Sarah through an exorcism rite and how to heal Tobit's blindness. Tobias and Sarah married, and Tobit was healed from his blindness when Tobias and Sarah returned home. This wisdom tale offered faith in crisis and hope in times of grief.

TOMB: A place of burial. In the Bible, tombs were often caves or openings carved in rocky cliffs or hills where families honored their dead. People prepared for their deaths by preparing a tomb in the place where their ancestors had been buried. Jacob bought a tomb for Rachel and set up a pillar at her grave (Gen 35:20). Joseph buried his father, Jacob, in the tomb that he had prepared for himself in Canaan and where he had buried Rachel (Gen 50:5). Jesus of Nazareth was killed in Jerusalem miles from his family burial area.

Joseph of Arimathea, a respected member of the Sanhedrin, donated his own tomb for the burial of Jesus. Joseph bought a linen shroud to wrap the body of Jesus and laid him in the tomb. He then laid a stone against the door (Mt 27:59–60). On the first Easter morning, the female disciples of Jesus found the tomb empty and were told by angels that he had risen (Lk 24:1–12).

TORAH (toh´ruh)**: See Law of Moses; Pentateuch.**

TRADITION: This word (from Latin, meaning "to hand on") refers to the process of "handing down" the Gospel. Tradition—sometimes called the Apostolic Tradition—began with the oral communication of the Gospel by the Apostles, was written down in the Scriptures, and is handed down and lived out in the life of the Church. It is interpret-

ed by the Magisterium (the bishop of the Church in the union with the Pope) under the guidance of the Holy Spirit. See also **Inerrancy; Revelation.**

TRANSFIGURATION: The event in the synoptic gospels of Luke, Matthew, and Mark in which Jesus' divine glory is briefly revealed. This scene foreshadowed Jesus' Resurrection. Peter, James, and John witnessed Jesus interacting with Moses and Elijah. Moses symbolically connected Jesus to the Exodus and Law; Elijah connected Jesus to the prophets and their prophecies of the coming Son of God (Mt 17:1–13; Mk 9:2–13; Lk 9:28–36).

TRANSJORDAN: The land east of the Jordan River.

TREE OF LIFE: In the Creation story (Gen 2—3), the tree God placed in the garden of Eden that offered wisdom, health, nutrition, and the life-giving re-

lationship with God. Adam and Eve were welcome to eat from this tree of fertility and eternal life as a free gift from the God of Creation. The symbolism of sacred trees was well known in the religious mythology of the Middle East. All the gods had sacred gardens with sacred trees. This explained the meaning of the Asherah, or the sacred trees or poles that stood beside the shrines of the goddess and her Baal.

The Book of Proverbs taught that finding wisdom was like finding the tree of life (Prov 3:13–18) and that "the fruit of the righteous is a tree of life" (Prov 11:30).

TREE OF THE KNOWLEDGE OF GOOD AND EVIL: The tree in the garden of Eden from which God forbade Adam and Eve to eat. It offered no wisdom but only knowledge. Although later in the Bible, knowledge represented a good, in the Torah, the first five books of the Bible, it represented defilement and lost innocence.

The Tree of the Knowledge of Good and Evil symbolized the lie that a choice could be good and evil at once. The fruit of the tree symbolized the lie that idolatry produced the good of peaceful relationships with the enemy who eventually attacked and controlled Israel. The fruit of this tree was poison; it caused death and alienation from the covenant of God and one another. The Tree of Knowledge of Good and Evil was a trap to be avoided. See also **Eden; Original Sin.**

TRINITY: The word *trinity* is not found in the Bible but is used to describe a biblical concept of the reality of one God in three Persons: Father, Son, and Holy Spirit. The concept of Trinity is expressed in the New Testament as a formula (Mt 28:19; 2 Cor 13:13). The

Bible itself does not have a complete doctrine of the Trinity, but the doctrine is part of the Apostolic Tradition and was clarified and taught by several of the early Church councils. The Scriptures have much to say, however, about each of the three Persons of the Trinity.

The first Person of the Trinity is understood as the Father Creator, the ultimate loving giver of life, the guardian of the abandoned, the "Father of orphans and protector of widows" (Ps 68:5–6).

God is also manifested in the second Person of the Trinity—Jesus, the Son of God. Christ was revealed as the *Bar Nasa,* the Human One, the Son of Man, who will come at the End of Days (Dan 9:13, 7:13–14). Scripture reveals the second Person of the Trinity as Jesus Christ, who is "God the only Son, who is close to the Father's heart" (Jn 1:18). Jesus said, "The Father and I are one" (Jn 10:30). Jesus is the Messiah, the promised and anointed one who "came into the world to save sinners" (1 Tim 1:15).

The Holy Spirit is the third Person of the Trinity. In the Old Testament, the Holy Spirit is referred to as the "breath of God" or "wind of God" present in Creation (Gen 1:2, 2:7). The Holy Spirit is also referred to as the Spirit of God that brings wisdom and new life (Ezek 37:1–10; Wis 9:17). In the New Testament, the Holy Spirit is the Advocate who empowers, inspires, and forms the mission of the Apostles (Jn 14:16–17; 1 Jn 2:1).

The mystery of the Holy Trinity teaches us that while God is one, God is also a communion of love who does not live in isolation. Since human beings are made in the image and likeness of God, they are also meant to be in loving communion, not existing as isolated individuals. See also **God; Holy Spirit; Jesus Christ.**

TRUMPETS, FEAST OF: The most important new moon festival honored on the first day of the lunar month. The Feast of Trumpets was announced by the blowing of trumpets. The festival included a ritual sacrifice and a day of rest and feasting (Lev 23:23–25; Num 29:1–6).

TWELVE, THE: See **Apostle.**

TWELVE TRIBES: A confederation of twelve Hebrew tribes that traced their origin to the patriarch Jacob. The Pentateuch stories tell how God renewed with Jacob the promises of the covenant he had originally made with Abraham (Gen 28:10–17). Jacob then went on to have twelve sons by his two wives, Leah and Rachel, and their two maidservants, Zilpah and Bilhah. Leah bore six sons—Reuben, Simeon, Levi, Judah, Issachar, and Zebulun—and one daughter, Dinah. Leah's slave Zilpah bore Gad and Asher. Rachel, Jacob's beloved, gave birth to Joseph and Benjamin. Rachel's slave Bilhah mothered two more sons. Rachel named them Dan and Naphtali (Gen 35:22–26).

After Jacob's first eleven sons were born, God renamed Jacob Israel (Gen 32:28). Thus, the descendants of Jacob/Israel's sons became the Israelites, God's Chosen People. Their names came to symbolize the Twelve Tribes that settled in the Promised Land.

Things got a little more complicated later in the Bible. At the end of his life, Jacob blessed both of Joseph's sons—Ephraim and Manasseh—and gave these two grandsons shares in his inheritance (Gen 48:17–22). Thus, no tribe is named after Joseph; rather, two tribes are named after his sons (Num 1:32–34). However, the tribe of Levi, the Levites, became the priestly tribe and did not inherit any land (Josh 13:14). So although there were actually thirteen tribes of Israelite peoples, the symbolic number twelve was used to remember the actual number of Jacob's sons and the number of tribes that inherited the land.

Jesus chose twelve Apostles in honor of the tribes and as the symbol of the restoration of the people of God. See also **Benjamin; Covenant; Dan; Jacob; Joseph of Egypt; Judah, Judea; Laban; Naphtali; Numbers; Reuben.**

TYRE (tĭr): A Phoenician city south of Sidon. Tyre had an ancient reputation for commerce (Isa 23:8). Its merchants had legendary skill on the sea and built trade centers throughout the Mediterranean and Aegean coastal areas. Tyre was renowned for its purple dye, beautiful tints, weaving crafts, bronze artisans, and gold and silver. Solomon had extensive trade relations with King Hiram of Tyre in building the Temple, and craftsmen from Tyre assisted in building the Temple (1 Kings 5:1–12, 7:13–47).

U

UGARIT (oo′guh-rit): An ancient city that thrived as a trade center on the western Mediterranean coast of Syria (1450–1195 BC). The existence of Ugarit was known through Hittite and Egyptian sources, but its location was lost in ancient times as a result of a devastating earthquake. Early in the twentieth century, excavations unearthed the ruins of this ancient city. The discovery of Ugarit provided rich archeological finds that have profoundly affected our knowledge of the world of the Old Testament. The Ugaritic alphabet is related to Semitic, classical Hebrew, and Assyrian writing, but it is most similar to the Canaanite language. Among the finds were texts written on clay tablets that contained ancient Canaanite poetry and myths that sometimes had counterparts in the Old Testament. Thus, we know the authors of the Old Testament used well-known phrases, wisdom teachings, and stories from their culture but gave a unique twist under the inspiration of the Holy Spirit.

UNCLEAN SPIRIT: A term used almost exclusively in the Gospels to describe a malevolent being in the service of the devil and dedicated to destroy humans. The unclean spirit is typically thought of as a demon seeking to inhabit a human being and control the person's actions (Lk 11:24).

The evil nature of an unclean spirit was not intended by God but was the result of a fall from grace, a refusal to live as God intended. In reality, demons are powerless. The energy of demons dissipates like smoke in pure air as they recognize Jesus as the Lord. They are terrified of his name (Lk 4:33–36). See also **Demon; Exorcism.**

UNITED MONARCHY: The period when kings Saul, David, and Solomon ruled over all the Twelve Tribes of Israel and their lands. The united monarchy was seen as a golden age in salvation history. The tribes became unified under their king, who represented God, the ultimate King. The united monarchy had a national identity because of the teachings of the Law of Moses. It possessed the land of Canaan and began the process of creating a nation of justice.

Saul, the first king of the Israelites, reigned from 1020 to 1000 BC. He was a great military leader but not loyal to Yahweh. Because of Saul's lack of faith, the prophet Samuel anointed David as the future king, even before Saul had lost the throne.

David, the second and greatest king of Judah, reigned from 1000 to 961 BC. David was a warrior, statesman, and priest. David united all the tribes of Israel and submitted to the wisdom of the prophet Nathan. For the most part, David was loyal to Yahweh as a man of prayer and great faith. David and his house became the symbol of the eternal dynasty of the mission of the people of God.

Solomon, the third king of Judah and son of Bathsheba and David, reigned from 961 to 922 BC. Solomon was a statesman, wise politician, and man of ambition. He built the Temple of Jerusalem to honor his father and Yahweh but also built altars to foreign gods when it suited his aspirations of power. His reign ended with civil war and the end of the united monarchy. See also **King.**

UNLEAVENED BREAD: In preparation for the Festival of Passover, the Hebrew people removed all yeast and other leavening from their bread products as a remembrance of the hurried meal of flight their ancestors shared during their escape from Egypt (Ex 12:8, 15). When Jesus called his disciples to celebrate the Passover, he instituted the Eucharist, using unleavened bread (1 Cor 11:23–26). This is why we use unleavened bread for the Eucharist—in honor of the Passover. See also **Eucharist; Passover.**

UNLEAVENED BREAD, FEAST OF: See **Passover.**

UR (oor): The ancient home of the tribe of Abraham and one of earth's most ancient cities. Ur of the Chaldees was the ancient name for Babylon. The site of Ur of Mesopotamia was ten miles west of the Euphrates River and had been inhabited from 5600 BC. The patriarch Terah led his family—including his son, Abraham, and daughter-in-law, Sarah—from Ur to Haran (Gen 11:31).

URIAH: (yoo-ri´uh): His name meant "God is light." Uriah was one of King David's trusted soldiers. While Uriah was at war, David seduced Uriah's wife, Bathsheba. To cover his adultery, David had Uriah sent to the frontlines of the battle to be killed (2 Sam 11). See also **Bathsheba; David.**

URIM AND THUMMIM (yoor´im) (thum´im): Ritual objects used by the Israelite high priest for divination and discerning God's will (Num 27:21). The Urim and Thummim were breastplates connected to the ephod (Ex 28:30). The use of the Urim and Thummim seems to have died away after the time of Saul and David. See also **Ephod; High Priest.**

USURY (yoo´zhuh-ree): A crime against justice by extracting exorbitant interest on a debt. The idea of lending was acceptable in Jewish culture, but interest could be charged only to foreigners. Usury was condemned (Lev 25:35–37; Deut 23:19–23).

V

VASHTI (vash´ti): Her name meant "best." Vashti was the Queen of Persia and the wife of King Ahasuerus, known to history as Xerxes I (486–465 BC). On the Sabbath, after the seventh day of feasting and overindulgence with wine, King Ahasuerus had his eunuchs order the beautiful Queen Vashti to parade before the drunken horde at court. According to Jewish writings, Vashti was ordered to display herself naked. To her credit, Vashti refused to perform as a royal ornament (Esth 1:10–12). Her punishment was banishment. Esther replaced Vashti as queen (Esth 2:15–19). Esther, too, disobeyed the king's orders, but more cleverly. Her courage resulted in the protection of the Judean people from genocide. See also **Esther; Xerxes, Artaxerxes.**

VEIL: A covering of the head and face. Women of ancient Israel took the veil as a sign of marriage. During the time of the patriarchs, prostitutes wore veils as part of ritual garb or to hide their identity (Gen 38:14–15). Later, Jewish and early Christian women wore veils as a symbol of modesty and humility (Gen 24:65–67; 1 Cor 11:5–6).

VERONICA: Her name meant "true image." Veronica is identified in Tradition as the disciple who broke through the mob on the road to Calvary to wipe the face of Jesus with her veil, although Scriptures do not name her. Jesus gifted her with an image of his face on the blood-stained cloth. Tradition also suggests that she was the woman with a hemorrhage whom Jesus healed when she touched his robe (Mk 5:25–34). A relic treasured as Veronica's veil has long been venerated in Saint Peter's Basilica in Rome.

VESPASIAN (ves-pay´zhuhn): A Roman general in charge of putting down the Jewish uprising in Jerusalem. During Vespasian's siege of Jerusalem (AD 66–70), the Temple was destroyed. Vespasian was then called to be emperor and arrived in Rome in AD 70. The reign of Vespasian—the ninth Roman emperor—was marked by numerous attempts to restore Rome and the empire after Nero wreaked havoc. Vespasian died in AD 79, succeeded by his son Titus, who declared Vespasian a god.

VINE: A plant that spreads by way of tendrils attaching to objects and other plants. The use of the word *vine* in Scripture most often refers to the grapevine. From the beginning of life in the Holy Land, the fruit of the grapevine was celebrated as a symbol of prosperity and promise of the good life (Num 13:17–23). Grapes were eaten fresh, dried into raisins, or crushed and fermented to make wine.

Jesus offered the metaphor of himself as the vine and his disciples as its branches to show the intimate relationship between Christ and the Christian believer (Jn 15:1; Mt 21:33). Jesus is the vine that supports the continued life of the Church.

VIPER: A type of snake that lived in the Mediterranean area. Some vipers were harmless, but the bite of some vipers was deadly. When a viper bit Paul,

people thought it a miracle that he survived (Acts 28:3–6). In ancient times, the serpent was thought to be a god or have connections to religious powers. The viper became a symbol for indecency, betrayal, and the power of evil (Isa 59:5).

In the New Testament, the image of the serpent continued to function as a symbol of idolatry as well as social injustice. Matthew's Gospel depicted John the Baptist and Jesus calling the Pharisees and Sadducees a "brood of vipers" for their hypocrisy (Mt 3:7, 12:34). See also **Serpent.**

VIRGIN: In the Bible, a young woman of marriageable age who has never had sexual intercourse. The virgin remained under the protection of her father and brothers until she became married. The punishment for a young girl if she lost her virginity while in her father's care could be death by stoning—but by Mosaic Law, the loss had to be proven (Deut 22:13–21).

Virginity was valued in the Scripture as a sign of respect for the gift of sexuality. Another word to describe one's commitment to remaining a virgin is *celibacy.* Jesus used the analogy of eunuchs to praise those who accept virginity or celibacy for the sake of the Kingdom of God (Mt 19:10–12). Paul did the same thing (1 Cor 7:25–28).

VIRGIN BIRTH: The Gospels of Matthew and Luke revealed that Mary of Nazareth was the virgin who conceived and gave birth to the Christ child without having had sexual relations with a man (Lk 1:34–35). She offered herself as the Womb of God in whom the Word of God became flesh. She fulfilled the prophecy of Isaiah that spoke of a young virgin who would give birth to a son who would be called Emmanuel,

"God with us" (Isa 7:14; Mt 1:23; Lk 1:31–35).

The idea of a virgin birth announcing the dawn of a new age was already known in the ancient Middle East. A prophecy of a virgin birth from as early as 1400 BC was found in a Ugaritic text. The language is similar to Isaiah's prayer for the coming of Emmanuel (Isa 7:14).

VIRGIN MARY: See **Mary of Nazareth.**

VISION: A mystical revelation given visually to an individual or group of people. A vision is an experience that goes beyond the five senses by evoking the imagination and stirring strong emotions within the visionary. A vision offers a spiritual understanding of earthly events and heavenly things. Scriptural visions many times fall into types or into a blending of the types listed below.

- an image and experience of the presence of God (Ex 24:9–11; Rev 4:2–11)
- images of an early experience happening in the present or future (1 Kings 22:17; Amos 7:1–6)
- visions of words or symbols (Jer 1:11–14; Ezek 37:1–14)
- figurative images or allegorical visions (Zech 1:18–21; Dan 7—8; Rev 12—13)

See also **Prophet.**

VOW: An agreement or solemn promise made with God or made with God as witness (Gen 28:20–22; Num 21:2; 1 Sam 1:11); a sacramental commitment taken as an oath and covenant between members of the community and God. See also **Jephthah; Oath.**

VULGATE (vuhl´gayt): Saint Jerome's Latin translation of the Bible completed in the late fourth century AD.

W

WADI (wah´dee): A dried streambed. In the Middle East, streams often flow for only part of the year. The wadi functions as a ravine until the rainy season. The wadi can be used for travel, protection, or military campaigns. A wadi's sporadic pools provide a water supply and occasionally even fish. When the rains return, the wadi can quickly become a torrent of raging river water.

WAGES: In the time of Jesus, the minimum wage in Palestine for a day's work was one denarius. This was also the amount of the annual Temple tax. Judas was paid blood money—thirty pieces of silver, or 120 denarii—to betray Jesus (Mt 26:15). This was the same amount owed to the owner of a slave if one's ox killed the slave (Ex 21:32). See also **Money.**

WAILING WALL: The last standing ruin of the Third Temple of Jerusalem destroyed by Titus of Rome in AD 70. See also **Temple.**

WANDERING IN THE DESERT: After their Exodus from the slavery of Egypt, the Israelites spent a symbolic forty years wandering in the deserts of the Sinai Peninsula. When the Israelites first came to the Promised Land of Canaan, they sent in spies to see what they faced. The spies came back with reports of a land occupied by strong warriors, so the Israelites refused to enter the land (Num 13:25—14:4). As punishment for their lack of faith and courage, God decreed that the Israelites would have to wander the desert until the adult generation had died. Then God would lead their children to take possession of the land (Deut 1:34–40).

The desert wandering was a time of

cleansing, of leaving behind slavery and the ways of Egypt (Ex 32:41–34; Ps 106:19). It was a time in which the people received the Torah and learned true freedom by following the Law that fleshed out their Covenant relationship with God. See also **Exodus; Promised Land.**

WAR: Combat between two groups of people with the intent to destroy the other. Wars were often a part of the life of biblical people. Foot soldiers, horsemen, and charioteers battled with bow and arrows, spears, swords, and slings and stones. Wars were fought for political, religious, and economic reasons and usually ended when the defeated group surrendered its resources, land, and even people (2 Kings 8:12, 25:9–10). The reported death tolls were astronomical.

The ancient land of Palestine suffered more than its share of wars due to the geography of the land. Palestine connected the great kingdoms of northern Africa (Egypt) in the south to the great kingdoms of the Middle East and Europe in the north and west (Assyria, Babylon, Persia, Greece, Rome). Anyone wanting control of these important trade routes would need to control Palestine.

The Plain of Megiddo in northwestern Palestine was the epicenter of these trade routes and a strategic location to control. So many wars were fought there that in the Bible, the Plain of Megiddo is the symbolic site of Armageddon, the place where the final war between good and evil will be fought, where the forces of righteousness will ultimately overtake the forces of Satan (Rev 16:16). See also **Megiddo.**

WATCHMAN, WATCHTOWER: A watchtower is a platform for observing the movement of thieves, invading tribes, or enemy armies and for notifying the city and troops of imminent danger. Watchtowers were built in fields, outside and within cities, and as part of military fortresses (Judg 9:51; 2 Chr 26:9). Watchtowers were often built in two levels, the top level being the living quarters of the watchman and the lower level being storage for supplies or, as in the case of a winegrower, being used for production (Isa 5:2; Mk 12:1).

Watchmen—also called sentinels—were guardians stationed on a watchtower or sentries posted on a city or citadel's wall. Watchmen guarded fields from thieves who would steal the harvest. Watchmen guarded cities from outsiders, armies, or invading nomads (Ezek 33:2–6). The watchman became a symbol for those who provided warnings about danger to come, including prophets and God's angel guardians, who were the protectors of the new Jerusalem (Isa 62:6).

WATER: The essential liquid upon which all life is based. The main source of freshwater in Palestine was rain; few rivers or streams other than the Jordan River ran all year. People stored freshwater in cisterns and drew it from wells. The rules of hospitality required the sharing of a drink of water with strangers.

In the Bible, water was the source of blessings, nourishment, and cleansing (Ps 1:3; Mk 7:3). The lack of water was agony and the loss of God's blessing (Isa 3:1). Water in the Bible was a symbol of

God's power and compassion (Ex 7:15–19, 17:1–7). The Creator controlled the forces of nature, the power of the sea (Ex 14:26–31).

In the New Testament, water takes on new meaning because of its use in Baptism. Through immersion in water, we die to sin (Mt 3:6) and rise to new life in Christ (Jn 3:5). In the encounter with the Samaritan woman at the well, Jesus revealed himself as living water; those who drank from him would never be thirsty but would have eternal life (Jn 4:7–15).

WEANING: The end of nursing a child. A child stayed in the total care of the mother until weaned at about age two or three, after which time the child had more interaction in the community. A weaned child who gracefully played and enjoyed life was a symbol of peace and prosperity among the peoples (Isa 11:8).

WEDDING FEAST: In the Bible, a celebration that honored the binding together of two families, or houses, symbolized by the marriage of a man and woman. Vows of loyalty and care were exchanged by the fathers of the bride and groom as a sign of the union of the families.

The party that followed was a major social celebration that brought these families together as one. The festivities went on for a week or two (Tob 8:20). Men ate, drank, blessed, and joked with one another. Women cooked, served, and enjoyed the feasting and each other's company. In general, it was a time of great fun. Jesus performed his first public miracle at a wedding feast of his mother's family in Cana. The family had run out of wine. This was considered a shameful breach in hospitality. Jesus protected their honor by turning water into wine (Jn 2:1–11).

It is not surprising that Jesus offered the image of the wedding feast as a metaphor to understand the Kingdom of Heaven (Mt 22:1–14). His listeners would have understood the idea that in the Kingdom, different people would come together and celebrate life and communion with God and each other.

WEEKS, FEAST OF. See **Pentecost.**

WEIGHTS AND MEASURES: Literature from Mesopotamia and Egypt helps us understand values of the most common weights and measures used in the ancient world, although our understanding of their actual value remains an estimate. The Hebrew word *shekel* referred to the basic unit of measure. The shekel weighed about .3 ounces. A mina was a weight equivalent to 60 shekels, or a little more than one pound. A talent was a weight equivalent to 60 minas, or about 66 pounds. A balance with two pans suspended from a beam was used to measure weights. In the New Testament, there was a Roman unit of measure called the *litra*, sometimes translated as "pound." The pound of ointment used by the unknown woman who anointed Jesus is thought to have equaled 12 ounces (Jn 12:3).

Area measurements were less clear. A yoke referred to the amount of land yoked oxen could plow in a day. A furrow was less than an acre of land. A cubit was the length of the forearm of the average-size man, approximately 20 to 21 inches. A span was the distance from the fingertips to the wrist, or about 10 inches. A cubit could also be used as a measure of time as well as distance. A Roman mile equaled 1,000 double paces, or 5,000 feet. A homer was the amount of grain a donkey could carry, about 6 to 14 bushels. An ephah was the most common dry measure and equaled one-tenth of a homer. See also **Money.**

WELL: A deep hole dug to locate and access water. Wells and collection cisterns were the major sources of water in the Middle Eastern world. Discovering water in the arid land of Palestine was cause for celebration. The community's well was a gathering place (Jn 4:6–8). The task of securing and carrying water was woman's work (Gen 24:11).

WHEAT: A grass grain cultivated from ancient times from which was made bread. Wheat was a primary food source for Middle Eastern peoples. The people of Palestine cultivated wheat and other grain in fertile valleys. The exportation of grain was a thriving business. See also **Bread.**

WHEEL: The wheel was a significant invention that changed the status of humanity. When the wheel was created, humans accelerated their ability to transport themselves and their products. The wheel also represented speed. It was the basis for the chariot, the vehicle of honor and prestige used by kings, administrators, and warriors. Mystically, the wheel became a symbol for power and endless movement. The "wheel within a wheel" was a symbol of unimaginable transport and power (Ezek 1:16–28).

WHORE: A derogatory term used to describe someone willing to have promiscuous sex. The title *whore* was used to condemn sexual impurity, injustice, and idolatry. The prophets sometimes accused the nations of Israel or Judah of acting like whores when they embraced the practices of the foreign nations (Isa 1:21). The heathen practices of idolatry were referred to as "playing the whore," or taking on foreign gods as lovers or patrons (Hos 4:15; Jer 2:20). The image of the whore is most clearly seen in an oracle of Ezekiel in which two whoring sisters—Samaria as Oholah and Jerusalem as Oholibah—go after their lovers, Assyria and Babylon. God, the grieving Father, was outraged by their betrayal, adultery, and idolatry (Ezek 23).

Babylon came to symbolize the quintessential evil empire of the Great Whore, and her fall the apocalyptic image of God's judgment (Rev 14:8, 17:5). Rome was identified as the new Babylon in the Book of Revelation and also was identified as the Great Whore, a power that put itself before God and gained its wealth by injustice (Rev 17:18). See also **Babylon; Prostitute.**

WIDOW: A woman whose husband had died. A widow was a woman in grief expected to wear identifiable garments and a veil (Gen 38:14; Jdt 8:5). When a man died and left a widow, his brother was expected to marry the woman to perpetuate the dead man's name. This law was called the levirate and was sacred among the people of Israel (Deut 25:5–10). In many cases, however, a widow, particularly if she were advanced in years, did not remarry.

In ancient Middle Eastern societies, a woman depended on her father or husband to survive, so widows were in danger of going without food. The Law of Moses demanded compassion for widows and orphans (Ex 22:22; Deut 27:19). An Israelite was forbidden to hold the garment of a widow as collateral for a debt (Deut 24:17). Part of every harvest was to be left for widows, orphans, and foreigners to pick for food (Deut 24:19–21).

A widow represented the pious and the poor (Lk 2:37). Jesus held up the widow as a model of generosity (Mk 12:42–43), determination, and survival (Lk 18:3–5). The widow became a model of treasured dedication to faith (1 Tim 5:3–5).

WIFE: Ancient Hebrews considered the state of marriage as validated at Creation with Adam and Eve (Gen 2:24; Mt 19:4–6). However, how that was lived out evolved over time. In most biblical cultures, the wife was considered the property of her husband and subject to his will. At the time of the patriarchs and kings, a man of a large clan was legally free to have several wives, as well as concubines. A woman was permitted only one husband. The husband could divorce his wife, but she could not divorce him (Deut 22:13–21; Mt 19:3–9).

Scripture described the perfect wife as "more precious than jewels" (Prov 31:10). She was trustworthy and a hard worker in the crafts of wool and flax making. She got up before dawn, fixed food, and organized the workers. She had great business sense, purchased real estate, and planted vineyards. She was a weaver, a seamstress who cared for the poor and needy. She was wise and kind. She took excellent care of her house and was never idle. She was dearly loved by her children and husband (Prov 31:10–31).

The Scriptures used the symbol of the faithful wife's love for her husband as the model for God's expectation of Israel to honor the Covenant. The adulteress or whore symbolized the unfaithfulness of Israel and Judah (Jer 3:1–10; Hos 2:1–18). The New Testament imaged Jesus Christ as a wedding groom, heaven as the wedding banquet, and the Church as the bride of Christ (Eph 5:25–27; Rev 19:7–9). See also **Marriage.**

WILDERNESS: The barren, uninhabited territories in and near Palestine. The wilderness was a desolate, unpopulated area suitable only for pasturing herds. The wilderness was considered uncivilized and suspicious, a land of wandering nomads and wild beasts.

WINE: Fermented grape juice sometimes described as "the blood of grapes" (Deut 32:14; Sir 39:26). New or sweet wine was fermented in the current year. Sometimes, wine was mixed with water and spices to create a mild drink. A libation of wine was offered in sacrifice, and wine was served in festivals and feasts.

The Passover Seder used wine for ritual blessings. At the Last Supper, Jesus offered wine as a memorial of his sacrifice, the blood of the New Covenant "poured out for many for the forgiveness of sins" (Mt 26:28). Wine still is consecrated into the blood of Christ in the celebration of the Eucharist.

WISDOM: One of the gifts of the Holy Spirit. The Bible presents the wise person as one who seeks God and follows God's Law. Reverence for God is the beginning of wisdom (Prov 9:10). Wisdom is often spoken of in the feminine. Those who listen to her teachings find joy (Prov 3:13). Wisdom is more precious than silver, gold, and jewels (Prov 3:14–15). A fool despises her instruction (Prov 1:7).

In the Old Testament, wisdom is personified as a feminine aspect of God, spoken of as Lady Wisdom (Prov 1:1–36; Wis 6:12–25). She is the manifestation of the creative spirit of God called into being at the beginning. Lady Wisdom teaches skills for succeeding in life. She speaks to the inner soul, to the inmost heart. She teaches ethical behavior and is the source of the Torah. Jesus promised to fill his apostles with wisdom (Lk 21:15). See also **Wisdom Literature.**

WISDOM LITERATURE: A genre of ancient literature that extolled the virtue of wisdom and gave practical advice on what it meant to be wise. In the Old Testament, the books of Proverbs, Job, Ecclesiastes, Sirach, and the Wisdom of Solomon were wisdom literature. Sections of other books (Gen 37—50) and certain psalms (Ps 37) also had traits of wisdom literature. Typical themes in these books were the value of wisdom, self-control, patience, honesty, diligence, and respect for elders. A theme in several of the books was wisdom personified as a woman, Lady Wisdom (Prov 1:1–36; Wis 6:12–25).

Wisdom literature in the Bible had certain characteristics. There was little mention of Israelite history, the Law of Moses, or the Covenant. The emphasis was on what could be learned by experience and applied in daily life. The writing was often somewhat poetic; an idea was stated and then repeated in a slightly different way in the next line. See also **Wisdom.**

WISE MEN: See **Magi.**

WISE WOMAN: A female leader in her community, an elder of the clan who held the tribe's memories, stories, and wisdom teachings. The wise woman would be called on to settle disputes and remind the group of the old ways and their cultural values. The main tool of the wise woman was her ability to persuade and to use parable, simile, and allegory in her craft of storytelling.

Scripture recalled two examples in which the warrior Joab interacted with a wise woman: the wise woman of Tekoa, whom Joab sought to influence King David (2 Sam 14:2), and the wise woman of Abel, who during battle, engaged Joab in conversation so as to protect her people (2 Sam 20:15–22). The judge and prophet Deborah also functioned as a tribal wise woman, a mother in Israel who sat under her palm tree imparting wisdom (Judg 4:5). See also **Deborah; Joab.**

WITCH: The word *witch* is not a biblical word. It refers to the northern European nature religions, or wicca. Modern English versions of the Bible more correctly translate the word *witch* as "female sorcerer" (Ex 22:18). The biblical condemnation of witches is not against herbal medicinal practice but against idolatry, child sacrifice, and the dark arts of the sorcerer (Deut 18:10). See also **Sorcery.**

WOMAN: The role of women in the ancient world was essentially to support the life of the male: her father, brother, husband, sons, or slave master. Women had no legal status and were protected by their fathers, husbands, and masters. A girl's birth was considered a loss and was grieved (Sir 22:3). Many people believed that women needed to be watched and controlled, and her nature was deemed rebellious and lustful (Sir 26:10–12).

Fathers decided whom their daughters would marry. Virgins were most acceptable for marriage; widows, divorced women, or survivors of rape were not considered ritually pure enough to become wives of priests (Lev 21:14–15). Once married, a woman left the domain of her father and became the property of the new family, ruled by the eldest male, usually the father-in-law. A woman could not take a vow without her father's or husband's approval, and he could nullify her promise, be it to God or another person (Num 30:5–8).

Despite these limitations, women in the Bible often played important roles. They were matriarchs of whole races (Sarah), leaders (Miriam, Mary Magdalene), wise women (the woman from Tekoa), judges (Deborah), prophets (Isaiah's wife, Anna), evangelists (Priscilla, Phoebe), and great saints (Mary of Nazareth). Jesus elevated the status of women to that of disciple (Mk 14:6–9; Lk 8:1–3).

WOMAN OF THE ANOINTING:

All four Gospels have stories where Jesus is at supper, and a woman anoints him. In Luke, an unnamed woman anoints Jesus' feet with her tears and dries his feet with her hair (Lk 7:36–50). In Matthew (Mt 26:6–13) and Mark (Mk 14:3–9), the anointing is of Jesus' head with expensive oil. Only in the Gospel of John (Jn 12:1–8) is the woman given a name, Mary of Bethany. Scholars are unsure if this is a story of one single event or if several women anointed Jesus at different times. In Luke, it is clearly a story about forgiveness and the lack of hospitality of the Jewish leaders. In Matthew, Mark, and John it is a story about recognizing Jesus' imminent sacrifice and death.

It was a common practice in the culture of the Middle East to offer hospitality and honor through foot washing and anointing. The woman took an alabaster jar filled with perfumed oil and expensive nard and poured the rich essence on Jesus' head. Her action suggested the practice of anointing someone as a king, prophet, or messiah. In the Gospels of Matthew and Mark, Jesus and the woman was criticized by bystanders for her interaction. Jesus defended the woman's actions, saying, "Wherever the good news is proclaimed in the whole world, what she has done will be told in remembrance of her" (Mt 26:13).

WORD OF GOD: God's word is the power through which God created all that is (Ps 33:6). The Bible is called the word of God because it has the power to create new life within the soul, to renew spirits, to teach, and to give hope (2 Tim 3:14–16). The Revelation contained in the Bible is inspired by the Holy Spirit to be without error in teaching the religious truth people need for salvation.

Jesus is also called the Word of God—the *Logos* in Greek (Jn 1:1; Rev 19:13). This title describes the divine nature of Christ: "the Word was with God, and the Word was God" (Jn 1:1). See also **Bible.**

WORKS OF MERCY: Two traditional lists of seven ways in which human beings are called to reach out to others in material and spiritual need. The works of mercy are works of love and justice. They include loving God by loving the neighbor. The seven corporal—or material—works of mercy are derived from Matthew 25:31–46: feeding the hungry, giving drink to the thirsty, sheltering the homeless, clothing the naked, caring for the sick, helping those in prison. To this list is added the work of burying the dead (Tob 1:17).

WORLD: In the Old Testament, *world* referred to God's creation of earth and the entire universe. The essence of the world was goodness, and when in covenant relationship with God, it was full of the presence of God. When sin entered the world, woundedness appeared in various ways. It was symbolized as chaos, destruction, flood, and warfare. The Old Testament held out the hope that God would ultimately triumph over sin and heal the wounded world.

In the New Testament, *world* was often used as an image of evil power that stood in contrast to the call of Christ (Mt 4:8; Mk 4:19). The wealth and power of the world were seen as temptations against goodness (Lk 9:25). The world was a rival kingdom (Jn 17:16), and the godly person was a light in its darkness (Mt 5:14). God so loved the world that he gave Jesus, who rather than condemn the world, offered salvation and eternal life (Jn 3:16–17).

WORSHIP: To adore and honor God. Worship is reserved for God alone (Ex 20:5). In the Old Testament, worship was usually accomplished by the sacrifice of produce and animals. Priests who were descended from the tribe of Levi led worship. After Solomon built the Temple in Jerusalem, it became the primary place for Israelite worship. However, as the leaders and the people fell into idolatry and injustice, the prophets warned against meaningless worship (Mic 6:6–8).

After the return from the Babylonian Captivity (586–539 BC), worship was also done in synagogues, communal meeting places where people outside of Jerusalem gathered on the Sabbath. Sabbath worship in the synagogue did not involve animal sacrifice. It involved singing psalms, reading the Scriptures, and listening to a rabbi explain the meaning of the Scriptures.

In the New Testament, Jesus continued to worship in the synagogues and Temple according to the custom of his Jewish ancestors. So did the early Christians who were also Jews. The early Christians, though, also celebrated the Eucharist on the Lord's Day (Sunday) in memory of Jesus' death and Resurrection. Eventually, Christians were expelled from worship in the synagogues and Temple, and the Eucharist became the primary worship of the Church. See also **Eucharist; Psalms; Synagogue; Temple.**

WRATH OF GOD: The anger of the gods of the Middle East was understood as without motive, irrational, and merely a whim against humanity. This was not so with Yahweh. God's nature was steadfast love (Ps 33:5). In the Hebrew culture, the concept of wrath of God was not connected to anger as we think of it, but rather to justice. Wrath of God was understood in the Hebrew Scriptures as the logical outcome of one's free-will decision. God's wrath and punishment were not a divine whim, but rather necessary discipline and a response to evil and injustice (Isa 13:11). The breaking of the Covenant Law caused chaos and put into action unavoidable consequences based on cause and effect (Deut 28:58–59).

However, the mercy of Yahweh was infinite and outweighed Yahweh's just wrath. "Return, faithless Israel, / says the LORD. / I will not look on you in anger, for I am merciful, / says the LORD; / I will not be angry forever" (Jer 3:12).

X

XERXES, ARTAXERXES (zuhrk´seez) (ahr´tuh-zuhrk´seez): The name of one or more kings from a dynasty in Persia. Xerxes I ruled the Babylonian Empire from 486 to 465 BC. Ezra called him the king of kings (Ezra 7:12), using the name Artaxerxes. Ahasuerus is the Persian form of this name, used in the Book of Esther. Darius the Persian (Neh 12:22) was probably Darius II or Xerxes II, son and successor of Xerxes I. See also **Ahasuerus; Esther; Vashti.**

Y

YAHWEH (yah´weh): The personal and unutterable name of the Holy One. Yahweh was the name revealed to Moses within the burning bush in the theophany on Mount Sinai. The name means "I AM WHO I AM" (Ex 3:1, 14). Yahweh is the English pronunciation of the consonants YHWH, which seems to be some form of the Hebrew verb "to be." Yahweh is used more than 6,000 times in the Old Testament.

Out of reverence, the Israelites did not pronounce the name of God. They substituted the word LORD for Yahweh. So in English translations of the Bible, when you see the word LORD—with small capitals—it is filling in for Yahweh. See also **Adonai; God; I AM.**

YAHWIST (yah´wist): A particular school of writing woven throughout the Pentateuch, attributed to the Yahwist authors or Yahwist school. This is the oldest literary source in the Pentateuch. It is sometimes called the "J" Tradition because the scholars who first noticed this were German, and in German, Yahweh is spelled *Jahweh*. This "J" Tradition was probably written by unknown scribes from Judah who in 950 BC wrote sections of the books of Genesis through Numbers.

Looking closely at these writings, one sees a pattern in style, language, and theology. God to the Yahwist had human, or anthropomorphic, qualities. This God walked in the Garden (Gen 3:8), sculpted humanity with divine hands (Gen 2:7), planted groves of trees (Gen 2:8), and grieved at the human beings who were lost among the trees or idols.

YESHUA (yeh´shoo-uh): A Hebrew name translated as "Joshua" or "Jesus." Yeshua means "God saves." In Greek, *Yeshua* became *Iesous*. When the Greek was translated into Latin and English, the name *Iesous* became "Jesus."

YOKE: A wooden or iron frame connected by a crossbeam (Jer 27:2). In farming cultures, this frame helped the animals work together and protected them from going astray or failing their task. A yoke could symbolically refer to a heavy load, a burden, or the conditions of servitude (1 Kings 12:1–12). It could also refer to assistance and guidance.

Jesus said, "Take my yoke upon you, and learn from me; for I am gentle and humble in heart, and you will find rest for your souls. For my yoke is easy, and my burden is light" (Mt 11:29–30).

YOM KIPPUR (yom´kip´uhr): See **Atonement.**

Z

ZACCHAEUS (zah-kee´uhs): His name meant "pure one." In the Gospel of Luke, the story of the tax collector Zacchaeus showed how Jesus saw into the heart of a person. Zacchaeus was an unlikely person to be called as disciple. He was a superintendent of customs, a chief tax gatherer in Jericho. Jericho at the time produced and exported a great deal of balsam (an expensive spice). This rich trade in Jericho had made Zacchaeus a wealthy man.

Because Zacchaeus was short, he climbed a sycamore tree so he could see and hear Jesus as he passed through Jericho. Jesus looked up, saw Zacchaeus, called him by name, and said he'd like to stay in Zacchaeus's house. The crowd began to complain because Jesus had chosen as host someone they thought of as a sinner. Zacchaeus listened to the accusations and repented on the spot. "Half of my possessions, Lord, I will give to the poor; and if I have defrauded anyone of anything, I will pay back four times as much" (Lk 19:8). Jesus defended Zacchaeus to the crowd and proclaimed him "a son of Abraham" (Lk 19:1).

ZADOK (zay´dok): His name meant "the righteous." Zadok was a descendant of Aaron, a priest in the court of David. Just before David's death, Zadok and the prophet Nathan supported Solomon as the new king (1 Kings 1:32–40). Zadok's descendants became a line of priests in the Temple of Jerusalem. After the Babylonian Captivity (587–538 BC), descendants of Zadok helped with the rebuilding of the Temple in Jerusalem (Neh 3:4).

ZEAL: A virtue of passion. Zeal suggests excitement, commitment, and enthusiasm for a concern, such as a consuming love for God (Ps 69:9). God has zeal for humanity (Isa 26:11). The emotion of zeal can lead one to respond to injustice (1 Macc 2:24–26) and hypocrisy (Jn 2:14–17).

Scripture cautions that zeal can be misplaced (Prov 19:2) or misdirected (Rom 10:2). Saint Paul admitted he was wrongly zealous in his dedication to the Torah and in his persecution of Christians (Gal 1:13–14).

ZEALOT (zel´uht): A member of a loose group of people who banded together during the time of Christ to resist the Roman occupation. The Apostle Simon the Zealot was a member of this group (Lk 6:15; Acts 1:13).

ZEBEDEE (zeb´uh-dee): A fisherman and the father of the Apostles James and John (Mt 4:21–22). Zebedee's wife, Salome, was one of the holy women who stood watch at the Crucifixion (Mk 15:40; Mt 27:56). She also was present after the Resurrection of Jesus on Easter.

ZECHARIAH (zek´-uh-ri´uh): His name meant "Yahweh remembers." Several men in the Bible are called Zechariah. One was a king of Israel who ruled for only six months (2 Kings 14:29—15:12). The most significant Zechariah was the writing prophet who returned with the exiles of Babylon and worked for the rebuilding of the Temple (Ezra 5:1).

Zechariah the prophet returned to Judah with the second group of exiles to rebuild Jerusalem. He was a contemporary of the prophet Haggai. Zechariah wrote about the nation's history, and his visions warned the present generation of the pitfalls of the past and offered hope for the future. He called for a return to "kindness and mercy" and care for the "widow, the orphan, the alien, or the poor" (Zech 7:9–10). Zechariah had a famous prophecy treasured by Christians as a foreshadowing of the coming of the Christ, the Prince of Peace (Zech 9:9–10).

In the New Testament, Zechariah was the father of John the Baptist. He was a priest in the Temple in Jerusalem. Zechariah was sacrificing incense in the sanctuary when the archangel Gabriel appeared before him and told him that his barren wife would have a child. Zechariah doubted the words of the angel and so was made mute until the child's birth (Luke 1:5–25).

ZEDEKIAH (zed´uh-ki´uh): This last king of Judah (597–587 BC) was also known as Mattaniah. He reigned for eleven years in name only as a puppet leader for Babylon in the last years of the occupation of Jerusalem. When Zedekiah decided to rebel against the Babylonians, Nebuchadnezzar ruthlessly put down the rebellion by destroying Jerusalem, leveling Solomon's Temple, and taking the bulk of the survivors back to Babylon as slaves. Nebuchadnezzar tortured and murdered the royal family, put out Zedekiah's eyes, and took him in chains to Babylon, where he died (2 Kings 24:17—25:7).

ZEPHANIAH (zef´uh-ni´uh): The name of several Old Testament men. The best-known Zephaniah was the writing prophet of Jerusalem who prophesied during the reign of King Josiah in the early sixth century BC. In the short collection of his prophecies, Zephaniah warned the people of Judah that their idolatry and sin would be punished. His book ended with a hopeful song of joy, reminding the people that God's punishment was to teach them, not destroy them.

ZERUBBABEL (zuh-ruhb´uh-buhl): A member of the House of David who became governor of Judah and leader of the exiles freed from Babylon by Cyrus of Persia. Zerubbabel led 42,360 people home to Jerusalem (Ezra 2:64) and began rebuilding the Second Temple (Ezra 3:2–8). He was remembered in the genealogy of Jesus recorded in Matthew's Gospel (Mt 1:12). See also **Babylonian Captivity; Ezra.**

ZEUS (zoos): The father of the Greek gods enthroned on legendary Mount Olympus. Zeus was the sky god, the deity of thunderbolts. When Barnabas evangelized in Lystra, the people thought he was Zeus in human form (Acts 14:12). See also **Jupiter.**

ZIGGURAT (zig´oo-rat): A Mesopotamian temple built as a high place for a god. Ziggurats were temples with a sanctuary on the ground level and a stairway that permitted the devotees to climb to the top, where the god was thought to dwell. Some scholars suggest that ziggurats functioned as astrological observation towers from which constellations were observed. The ziggurat may have been the basis for the tower of Babel story. The ziggurat built for Marduk in Babylon was named the Foundation of Heaven and Earth. See also **Babel, Tower of.**

ZILPAH (zil´puh): Her name meant "drooping." Zilpah was the slave girl whom Laban gave to his eldest daughter, Leah, when she married Jacob (Gen 29:24). When Leah stopped bearing children, she gave Zilpah to Jacob as a concubine (Gen 30:9). Zilpah gave birth to Gad and Asher, who became patriarchs of two of the Twelve Tribes of Israel (Gen 30:9–13). See also **Jacob; Leah; Rachel.**

ZION, MOUNT (zi´uhn): The hill on which the citadel of David and the city of Jerusalem stood. On Zion, David built his palace and Solomon built the Temple of Jerusalem and the city that came to represent the people and faith of Israel (Psalm 87:2, 149:2). In the Scriptures, the use of the phrase "virgin Zion" represented the ideal, pure relationship between the people of Israel and God (2 Kings 19:21; Lam 2:13–22). During the Babylonian Captivity (586–539 BC), the prophets promised a time when God would make his home again in Zion (Zech 2:10–11). In the Book of Revelation, Jesus Christ, the Lamb of God, appeared on Mount Zion (Rev 14:1).

ZIPPORAH (zi-por´uh): Her name meant "bird." Zipporah was one of seven daughters of the priest of Midian known as Reuel, or Jethro. Her mother is not known. She met Moses after he fled from Egypt. Her father was so pleased with Moses that he gave him Zipporah in marriage (Ex 2:21). She and Moses had two sons, Gershom (Ex 2:22) and Eliezer (Ex 18:4). When Moses returned to Egypt to lead the Israelites to freedom, he took Zipporah and his sons with him. Before they reached Mount Sinai, Moses sent Zipporah and the boys back to her father, Jethro. After this, she disappeared from the story of the Exodus (Ex 18:2–6).

ACKNOWLEDGMENTS

The scriptural quotations contained herein are from the New Revised Standard Version of the Bible, Catholic Edition. Copyright © 1993 and 1989 by the Division of Christian Education of the National Council of the Churches of Christ in the United States of America. All rights reserved.

The biblical word pronunciations contained herein are adapted from *The Harper-Collins Bible Pronunciation Guide,* edited by William O. Walker Jr. (New York: HarperSanFrancisco, 1994). Copyright © 1989 by the Society of Biblical Literature. Reprinted by permission of HarperCollins Publishers.

Maps.com grants no license or rights, expressly or otherwise, beyond the rights of Saint Mary's Press. Maps.com revised the maps in the full-color insert following page 94. Contact *www.maps.com* for all your mapping needs.

The quotation on page 101 is from the *Sacramentary,* English translation prepared by the International Commission on English in the Liturgy (New York: Catholic Book Publishing Company, 1985), page 563. Illustrations and arrangement copyright © 1985–1974 by Catholic Book Publishing Company, New York.

During this book's preparation, all citations, facts, figures, names, addresses, telephone numbers, Internet URLs, and other pieces of information cited within were verified for accuracy. The authors and Saint Mary's Press staff have made every attempt to reference current and valid sources, but we cannot guarantee the content of any source, and we are not responsible for any changes that may have occurred since our verification. If you find an error in, or have a question or concern about, any of the information or sources listed within, please contact Saint Mary's Press.